Maturity
in the Religious Life

Maturity in the Religious Life

by John J. Evoy, s.j.
and Van F. Christoph, s.j.

SHEED AND WARD : NEW YORK

© Sheed and Ward, Inc., 1965

Library of Congress Catalog Card Number 65-12203

IMPRIMI POTEST
    JOHN J. KELLEY, S.J.
    PRAEP. PROV. OREGON

NIHIL OBSTAT
    RT. REV. MSGR. JOHN J. COLEMAN, J.C.D.
    VICAR GENERAL, DIOCESE OF SPOKANE

IMPRIMATUR
    ✠ BERNARD J. TOPEL, D.D., PH.D.
    BISHOP OF SPOKANE

Manufactured in the United States of America

Foreword

One can only greet with joy every effort to examine the religious life in all its human dimensions. It is in this line that the work of Fathers John J. Evoy, S.J., and Van F. Christoph, S.J., proceeds. Already in a previous work [*Personality Development in the Religious Life*] they studied the development of personality within the framework of the religious life. Continuing in the same direction, the present book is a dynamic and vivid study that examines in detail maturity in the religious life. The problem is an important one: the more fully adult the religious will be, the more capable she will be of assuming the apostolic responsibilities which the Church wishes to entrust to her more completely. Human development will be an invaluable instrument for apostolic development and for the strengthening of vocations. The pages of this book are of great value: they will help religious to live their magnificent vocation with full understanding and clear-sighted generosity.

✝ *L. J. Card. Suenens*

LÉON-JOSEPH CARDINAL SUENENS

ACKNOWLEDGEMENTS

Religious communities of both men and women owe an enduring debt of gratitude to the forthright manner in which Cardinal Suenens has encouraged them to achieve the "aggiornamento" in religious life comparable to the updating of the Church in other spheres. *The Nun in the World* has been an inspiration to religious all over the world and has encouraged us in our work. For his generous encouragement we express our deepest gratitude.

Eleswhere in this volume we express our great debt to the many, many Sisters who have been the inspiration for this book and our best teachers regarding so much of its content.

Specifically we salute a small group of Sisters who have spent themselves over long hours in offering expert criticism, making valuable suggestions, typing and editing the manuscript. To them our debt is incalculable.

To the Administration of Gonzaga University for granting us the opportunity to give these talks to Sisters and Priests across the country, and for generously arranging a sabbatical semester leave for one of the authors to work on this book, our sincere thanks.

To the Administration of Loyola Academy, in Wilmette, Illinois, a Jesuit High School, for being most gracious hosts to Father Evoy, S.J., during his semester writing effort, our deepest gratitude.

To Father Charles Keenan, S.J., of Gonzaga University for his tireless attention to the final editing of the manuscript, our genuine appreciation.

To all the others who in so many different ways have contributed to this work, we say "Thank you and God bless you."

Gonzaga University   JOHN J. EVOY, s.j.
October 3, 1964   VAN F. CHRISTOPH, s.j.

Preface

As in their other book, *Personality Development in the Religious Life,* the authors again retain their unusual style, sometimes called the "interruptive technique." A few words should be given in explanation of this unusual type of presentation. The printed form retains the actual pattern of delivery employed by the two authors in their talks. While they were delivering them, both priests studied the audience in an effort to see how clearly the speaker was conveying his thought. If at any time, the one not speaking felt that he should interrupt the speaker to clarify, exemplify, question, or take issue, he felt completely free to do so. It was consistently reported by the listeners that this give-and-take, alternating type of presentation made prolonged, close attention easier and enhanced the impact of the thoughts of each speaker.

The substance of this book is largely taken from the manuscripts of Institutes given to groups of religious women in different parts of the United States during the Summer and Fall of 1963. These Institutes in Applied Psychology were concerned with considerations of maturity as befitting the life of religious. The authors have also given a good number of Institutes to groups of priests, particularly priests who are religious. These

Institutes to men, for the most part however, have not been recorded. It is, nevertheless, the judgment of the authors that many of the applications made to religious women in these pages also could readily be made to religious men.

The most generous and widespread reception given the authors' other book, as well as the embarrassingly enthusiastic comments on their talks on Maturity, have been most encouraging in motivating them to prepare the present volume.

The authors appreciate that without their own academic preparation for this field of work, they would never have undertaken these lectures. They wish, however, to acknowledge immediately that, had they been confined to such knowledge, they would have approached the work lacking the information and understanding requisite to it. Their debt to all the women who have trusted the authors with revelations, personal and sacred, can never be fully repaid. It is their hope that these pages may tend to balance the scales of their indebtedness by bringing to religious and others understanding that will benefit them in some small measure.

Never for a moment have the authors doubted that they have received more than they have given. While they have indeed been enriched by what they have so generously received, they have also been most gratified at the warm reception accorded their comments, written as well as spoken. To all of those who have given such heartening response, they wish to express their sincerest gratitude.

Contents

Contents

Maturity
in the Religious Life

1 *Exploring Maturity*

Father Evoy: Sisters, you are participating in the revolution taking place in the Catholic Church today. It seems to me that the Sisters of the world, at long last, are coming into their own. As Cardinal Suenens points out in his book, *The Nun in the World,* it was not too many years ago that a girl standing on the threshold of a religious vocation had to make a choice as to whether she was to engage in Catholic Action or go into the convent. Today such a choice appears to make very little sense.

That she would have to think of giving up Catholic Action in order to enter an active religious order, in fact, now appears unthinkable. Yet, it seems to be correct to say that up until recent times Sisters have not expected or have not been given enough freedom of apostolic action in the Church nor have they received the recognition in the Church that they deserve. But that is all changing and *this is your day.*

In speaking on the subject of maturity, I invariably find myself somewhat embarrassed and a little self-conscious. It almost seems brash to speak about maturity, since to do so is implicitly to assume that the speaker is himself quite mature. My only consolation in the matter is the comforting reflection that Father Christoph at his age should be still more embarrassed!

I should like to begin our treatment of maturity with the following consideration. You have all watched an apple maturing. In the growth of such a thing as an apple you recognize a built-in, biological dedication to become that which it should become—this mature thing according to its species, which happens to be a ripe apple. In order to attain this end product of growth, all that needs to be done is to keep harmful things away from the apple. This may call for spraying and other attentions to keep harmful agents from it, but if an apple is kept from such deleterious elements, it will by its self-directing mechanism strive toward becoming a ripe apple. Moreover, this apple possesses a characteristic self-correcting tendency so that when it tends off course it automatically works its way back toward maturity.

The same things are not equally true of a human being. If you were to take a person and merely protect her from all damaging influences, she would not move with any automatic, built-in, biological dedication toward becoming a mature person. Her dedication, far from being biological in nature, is rather both psychological and moral. Both her impelling motivation and the correction of her growth errors must be real achievements in terms of her own prudential judgment, and should she be a religious, also of her religious obedience.

It is very difficult to make a comparison between a human being and such a thing as an apple, especially in terms of growth considerations. A human being in order to mature must not only be free of the harmful, as is true of the apple, but must also positively accomplish in terms of her own proper human nature, which completely outdistances any parallel in the apple.

While the apple, left completely to itself, moves irrevocably toward its own maturity, a human being cannot really come to maturity all by herself. To do so, she needs others, and principally other human persons.

For the apple simply *to be,* is to be maturity-bound. Is this also true of a human being? If this human being were *to be* her fullest, then she would indeed be headed toward maturity. But for her fully *to be* necessarily implies relationship to other persons. She cannot *really be,* all by herself. In fact, if you were to place a human being as an infant on an island someplace all by herself, even though you were to arrange for the mechanical provision of all her necessities of life, I am certain that this individual would not develop as a complete, wholesome, well-rounded human being.

Father Christoph: The thesis is that many of our traits are social, and that many of our needs can be satisfied only by association with others. I would like to make that even stronger. So many of our traits are social precisely because our very *being* is social. These traits are but expressions of that which we are. We *are* social.

Hence I cannot mature in isolation. As a matter of fact, one of the founders of American sociology made a remark that has since caused much consternation. He said, "A human being is not born social; he is not born with complete human nature; but he becomes social and fully human through association." His remark certainly makes sense in that it focuses our attention on the necessity of social experience. For man matures only when he meets the challenge of life, by coming into contact with other people. Man is not oriented, merely by his own nature, toward maturity in every respect. Other people bring growth to us emotionally, socially, intellectually, and I think, morally and spiritually.

So supposing—just for an example—I am by myself and have never been thwarted, challenged or frustrated while growing up. I am now thirty years of age, and something comes into my life that prevents me from attaining a desired goal. What is my reaction? It would be only by accident that my reaction would be mature, because I have no previous experience with this type of situation. I have not before been faced with a challenge and hence I do not know how to meet it. That is why we said we grow in maturity, because a person with ten experiences in handling one emotion is more mature than the individual who handles that emotion for the first time.

As children we accept practically anything that is told us. We do not have the maturity to compare or challenge, to go back upon our own experiences, to put this new knowledge in its proper category—to build upon it. There is a certain type of maturity that is the result of experience, so that we grow toward more and more and more maturity. We do not get this way automatically. We have to achieve it through experience, through action, through communication—in general, through our social experiences.

Father Evoy: This means principally through our experiences with other people. Perhaps we have been guilty of over-simplification when we have talked in Aristotelian terms of the perception of other *things*, as though such perceptions were of the same experiential cloth as our perception of other *persons*. In a word, we seem to have assumed that our awareness of another person is pretty much the same kind of experience as our awareness of a non-personal thing. Yet when we check our own experience, you and I know that such is not the case. For whatever the formal, academic paraphernalia under which we study these two classes of perception, experience says there is a great difference. You know that when you are one of three people present in a room and one of the other two leaves, there is a world of difference in the experience of the two of you who are left there.

Being confronted with and by another human being is psychologically a unique experience. It is not so much a question of your merely seeing or perceiving this person, as of your being over against another person and becoming aware of this other human with your entire being. I am fully aware that this experiencing another person goes begging for adequate expression; I do not particularly like the term "awareness" to characterize the experience, for in a sense I know this other person with my whole self. It is an experience which can never be reduced satisfactorily to a simple statement. It is indeed an experience, which of its very nature can either enrich or impoverish me in a way that never could find adequate expression in mere words.

This recognition that we sorely need other persons is, I feel, something which must permeate any discussion of maturity. This is particularly true of any treatment of maturity in religious life, because while it is almost taken for granted that there is present a closeness, a "togetherness" of an intimate nature in family life, the same is not necessarily presumed to be true of religious life.

Father Christoph: There is a cynical and cryptic description of religious life which goes like this: They enter religious life without knowing each other; they live together without loving each other; and they die without regretting each other.

Now this is admittedly a cynical comment, but the disconcerting thing about it is that sometimes it is true. That is the horrible part.

Father Evoy: As a matter of fact, there are things that happen between human beings in religious communities that make one wonder if there is not some real foundation to it. But why are we talking about this business of maturity to a group of religious women? First of all, I would say that to be aware of what makes us more complete persons is a distinct gain for us. To the extent that it is possible for us to know what we ought to be striving toward, such knowledge is to our advantage. We are therein enriched, because by the nature of our make-up as human beings we are in particular need of sighting what the philosophers call a "final end." We need some kind of a recognized goal toward which we can strive before we can say that we are progressing. Progress necessarily implies advance toward a *goal*. So it is to our benefit to have some clarification of our very objectives.

Such knowledge should also give us a better understanding of other human beings—the members of our community and the other people with whom we come in contact. Moreover, such clarification of goals can furnish us with some kind of a yardstick with which to measure the maturity of any given individual, according to his or her age and circumstances.

There is a related consideration here. I should like simply to mention it and then go on. It is that there are immaturities in certain individuals which these persons cannot overcome without a special kind of help. This normally would mean professional assistance. Such a recognition should make for a more genuine and sympathetic understanding, so that we could be able to accept such a person and say, "Here and now, perhaps, she cannot without professional help go beyond her present point." We would at least feel for her rather than yield to the temptation to sit in judgment on her.

Father Christoph: The goal of maturity for anyone is to be an adult, socially well-adjusted, capable of meeting and solving the ordinary problems of life in a reasonably acceptable manner. We are complimented by a reputation for being mature in our judgments, for being considered mature in our thinking and actions; and the reason for this, is that people think that religious do things with deliberation, with due consideration of means and ends. They give us a vast amount of credit for being mature beyond the average person. Why then should we choose this topic? The fact of the matter is that so many religious are immature. It seems to be an occupational hazard of religious life to be arrested at certain immature levels. I say an occupational hazard, because in religious life there are certain aspects of our dependence that tend, in a way, to prevent us from becoming mature. Yet these things are not necessarily characteristic of religious life. In the past they have sometimes been regarded as intrinsic to the very nature of religious life, but spiritual writers today and practically everyone who has given any consideration to the vows of religion have emphasized the fact that when it comes to obedience and the ancilliary virtues associated with obedience, there is still room for the individual to be a self-determining person and not dependent in a way that negates her personality. There is a special need to insist upon maturity on the part of religious men and women because it actually is so easy for religious to be content with immaturity.

By definition, man is a self-directing being. He is able to choose intelligently his goals and also the proper means to achieve them. But there are individuals who have found it difficult to cope with life, and in order to maintain the minimum social adjustment, they want to be in an atmosphere where things are done for them. They are dependent and need to be directed. Only in this way are they able to adjust to life. Some religious fall into a kind of immaturity which bears a resemblance to the individuals whom we have just described—who do not want to take responsibility. Because of this, it is important that we study the areas in which we, as religious, develop a very great deal of maturity and also understand the limitations of independence.

Father Evoy: It is well to keep in mind that when we are dealing with the human personality, we are dealing with something that has far more facets than the most valuable diamond. Because we are treating of the complexities of something so exceedingly rich, it would be quite arbitrary to stake out exact sections of personal maturity and then proceed to treat each independently of the others, even avoiding all leakage to others, as though these different areas of a human person were sealed off in airtight compartments. They are not.

Hence, in the order to be followed throughout this presentation, we will not always draw sharp distinctions among spiritual, emotional, moral, physiological and various other aspects of personal growth, because to make such distinctions would at times do violence to the reality of the integral person.

Father Christoph: When we are talking about maturity we are talking about a completely developed individual, not merely physically, because that is presumed, but emotionally, intellectually, spiritually, and morally. What do we mean by a mature individual? A mature individual is one in whom these characteristics are developed to an extent that is regarded as normal for an adult. As an aside, I might just mention that the dictionary tells us that "maturity implies the full development of the natural faculties, a completeness of growth."

Father Evoy: It is very important here, I feel, to clarify one notion. When Father Christoph uses the term "adult," he is by no means talking about something static, as though a person would grow to a certain stage and then stay right there at his "adult" level.

Maturity is a relative term. I daresay that most of you here who are in your late twenties regard yourselves as adults. Yet those of you who can look back upon thirty-five years of age feel that in many ways, you were not nearly as mature in your twenties as you are now. Those of you who can look back on forty-five, feel that same way about your thirties.

In this connection it was interesting to note during the 1960 presidential campaign what people were saying about the candidates. Many held that at least one of the two individuals was too young. I believe he was forty-two, while the other man was forty-six. Even at forty-two, the younger of them was long since past his physical prime; and past the peak of some, at least, of his intellectual operations. His speed of memorizing, for instance, was probably on the decline. It could be further assumed that some of his other intellectual operations were decreasing in their effective functioning.

But the people across the country were not talking about these things. What they were saying in effect was that a man of only forty-odd years of age might not yet have the requisite maturity of judgment and of outlook, simply because he was not yet "old enough." They were pointing out, whether or not they realized it, that maturity is a continuing thing; that it is always relative. It is not static; it is dynamic. As human beings grow older, they *should* continue to mature in important capacities. Theoretically, at least, as long as an individual's powers are intact, he should become more mature the longer he lives. There are many people who have a great deal of respect for what they call the "wisdom of the aged." But then Father Christoph would be more familiar with that than I. You can see why, at times, I have some slight misgivings in regard to my challenging of Father Christoph's opinions.

Father Christoph: Father Evoy mentioned that this concept of maturity is relative. There is a point I should make when we are talking about a socially well-adjusted individual. Maturity, outside of physical maturity, is always relative to the society to which a person belongs. I can readily conceive of a primitive society, the members of which, acccording to our standards, would be socially arrested at an immature level.

Our culture demands an appreciation of man and his environment, and so the aspect of maturity that we are emphasizing is the social—although the components of it will be intellectual, spiritual, moral, and emotional. Social maturity is a going-on process, which means that we should, as we grow older, become more mature. This occurs by reason of the development of the different facets of our personality, which, as Father Evoy mentioned, merge into one because each of us is a unity. By new experiences, by new adjustments, the results of new contacts and social environment, we have constant occasion to re-examine practically all the aspects of our development.

Now it should be noted that we do not always mature in every area at an even pace. A person may be a very capable individual, we will say, intellectually, even emotionally, but he seems to have no prudence. A person might be very spiritual, but have a very poorly developed self-critical capacity. So development or maturity is not a kind of built-in mechanism that guarantees that after a certain age, or after certain studies, we will "act our age." There is no guarantee that when we reach the age of twenty-one we are going to have so much maturity with respect to intellectual development; or that at the age of thirty we will have this much maturity; at the age of fifty, this much maturity. The things we have to work with, our own capacities, the things that we have to work against, the environment in which we work, the people with whom we work, and our appreciation of these factors —these are the things that determine to what extent we will be mature individuals.

We recognize the fact that man has a nature which physically matures. You cannot stop the passage of time, and normally this brings on physical maturity. But there are many factors in religious life which seem to prevent the development of those qualities which we regard as natural and which we expect to find in a normal, socially adjusted adult. Outside of the cloister, one must very frequently fend for oneself even at an early age. In our society, a girl is much more protected and for a longer period of years than the boy. So the maturation of a girl, even in the world, especially in terms of her emancipation and everything that goes along with it, is somewhat delayed.

In religion this can be a pattern that persists throughout the life of a religious, even though she be sixty, seventy, or eighty years of age. Hence there is a peculiar need to understand the characteristics of maturity in general, especially those facets of maturity which a religious is supposed to develop, despite the fact that she has a vow of obedience and is expected to submit to the regulations of Superiors and others in those areas in which they have authority.

Because there is a natural desire to be independent and to be someone in one's own right, there are apparently occasions for conflict. That is why we think it so important to address ourselves to religious men and women in the matter of maturity.

I would like to add that if Father Evoy or I seem deficient in not giving an adequate definition of what we mean by the mature individual, it is because it is so difficult to define the normal, and maturity presupposes *normality*.

When we begin to analyze more fully the implications of maturity we have to break things down into categories, and Father Evoy constantly warns of the peril of dividing things up lest we lose sight of the fact that man is an individual whom we cannot really dissect so as to put one part over here and one part over there. Though we are composite beings, and though our emotions, for instance, are highly complex, nevertheless we always operate as a unit, as a complete whole. Our behavior is molar, if you want to use a technical expression.

There is another point which we should make before continuing and it is this: the expression "grace builds on nature," with which you are so familiar, should not be interpreted as meaning something superimposed on nature but rather that we are, as it were, emulsified. We are homogenized. I think you catch what I mean. Grace permeates the whole being. For the sake of our psychological understanding we here prescind from grace. But we are always supposing grace in human development.

Father Evoy: So it is that immaturity can coexist in a religious with the presence of grace. On this point of persisting immaturity there is something peculiar about us as religious. Religious life, it may be said, entails a *recapitulation* of our entire life. Before one enters the community she advances up to a certain point in terms of maturity; she enters religious life, and then and there in a very real sense she goes back and starts her life over again. Let us see if we can make this a little clearer. We are maintaining that, in the matter of maturity there are some considerations which are proper to religious life and only to religious life.

When we reflect on the individual history of a human being we see a pretty clear-cut pattern of development. The little child who begins life as utterly helpless soon begins to assert himself and to stress his own willfulness as he moves up past his second birthday. There is no longer any question about this baby's possessing a mind and will of his own. Rather than giving any evidence of his need for other persons, the two-year-old is only too often demanding of their services as if he were perfectly entitled to them. He gives us the impression that he feels important enough, by himself, to manage things nicely, thank you; and so we are not surprised at his repeated manifestations of independence and his strivings for independence. In common parlance, this little child is already beginning "to throw his weight around." A little later he will manifest a tendency to identify with his parents in an identification which is an acceptance of some surrendering dependence on the will of his parents.

In a very real sense it seems that this child's own personal importance and worth are then felt by him to be dependent on the love and acceptance of his parents. Now I feel certain that it is no news to you that in the eyes of a small child his parents take on the dimensions of giants.

The child gives evidences of this identification with these giants and also of the resulting feeling of his importance in many different ways. For instance, later on, one youngster will say to another, "My dad can lick your dad. I am more important than you." His importance as a human being, in other words, is largely measured by him in terms of the stature of the father he worships. Now as we continue to observe this youngster we see that, starting somewhere around about nine years of age, he begins to show the beginnings of efforts toward emancipation. He is starting his own break for freedom—for independence.

Among some of the earliest manifestations of this revolt is the fact that it is common to find parents being concerned about a youngster at this age on the score that the child does not hear well. According to the medical records, I believe, the years ten to twelve constitute the healthiest, most disease-free period in the life of an individual. Yet it is at this particular time that there is the highest incidence of youngsters brought to medical centers and physicians on the parental complaint of defective hearing.

You are by no means surprised to learn that the parents normally find no hearing deficiency whatever in their children. This appears to be simply a covert expression of the youngster's declaration of independence. It is the beginning of negative behavior at this stage of his life. Look at this pattern of behavior for a moment. A child's characteristic reaction is not to come when called, not to obey, not to respond, in fact, not even to hear when called by the parent.

As we observe the youngster at this same period we note his growing tendency to pester adults with such as the following, "I can do it myself; let me do it; let me . . ." He is increasingly insistent on standing on his own two feet. He is saying in effect, "I am no longer going to lean on you, my parents, as my principal source for being somebody. I am beginning to move toward becoming 'me'." (Perhaps I should here say "I," but "me" does seem so much clearer.)

To be an individual in one's own right means, above all, to do one's own thinking, and one's own deciding. In fact, the individual who does his own thinking and his own deciding is ordinarily considered to be mature for his age. The person who, regardless of his chronological age, does not do so, is not regarded as mature.

Father Christoph: Of course, it depends upon the nature of the thinking and the nature of the deciding, because there are many people physically mature who do some thinking and some deciding, but their thinking is singularly immature, and their decisions very obviously reflect this. So the caliber of these operations is an important index to one's maturity.

Father Evoy: This brings us again to the concept of recapitulation in religious life. Say, for example, that a girl of sixteen, seventeen, eighteen or older is about to enter religious life. At this stage of her existence, there is a certain amount of thinking and a certain amount of deciding that she has been doing for herself. True, these may have been of light caliber compared with those of adults, but still they were hers.

Now she comes into religious life and, in a sense very really relevant to what we have been speaking of, she starts her life all over again.

Once again there seems to be a period in her life that parallels the self-assertiveness and the self-sufficiency that were hers as a very small child. Now, as a young religious, she is resolved to become a saint by generosity and sheer will power. She is willing to concede that it may take even several months to get there, but no matter, one way or the other this she will do. As she looks at the older members of the religious community, particularly her Mistress of Novices, she feels that they are a sort of giants in the religious life. She would find it difficult to settle completely for the fact that they are mere humans.

Somehow or other she senses that her Mistress is indeed her religious institute incorporated into one person, and walking about in that person. Little by little she begins to identify, to throw in, so to speak, with the members of her religious community who are looked up to as those "big persons," and particularly with her Mistress. Then quite aside from any awareness that she is doing so, she slips into a pattern of thinking which is reflected in her thinking and saying, to almost everything, "Yes, Sister," and "No, Sister."

Years later, as she looks back over her religious life from her present vantage point, she sees that she unwittingly let some of these people, and especially her Mistress, do much of her thinking and deciding for her in religious life. Particularly in regard to such matters as what a religious person in her community should be, what her community really stands for, and what are the genuine earmarks of sanctity for one of her Sisters—in all of these and other related areas she now sees that her Mistress furnished her with her yardsticks. She tended not to question the correctness of her Mistress' judgments nor the correctness of her decisions.

At this point I would like to interject my own thoughts here. We should remember that these things are quite foreign to the beginner in religion. Most of us enter communities with which we have had some contact. Indeed, very few enter communities with which they have had no personal contact. So we do know something about the community we enter. In fact, we sometimes feel that we know quite a bit about the community; but then we enter and find it a good deal different from the ideas we had formed from our experiences with the Sisters. We had found them free up to a point; they were cordial; they were gracious; they talked and communicated rather freely with us and encouraged us. Then, when we entered religious life and saw the institute and received a rigorous interpretation in an atmosphere that is up to a point threatening to the individual, this whole thing became very different from the world we left, and quite *unlike what we expected*. We are once again beginning our life, and just as an infant is in a sense bewildered by the world into which she comes, so too is the young girl bewildered by the religious world which she enters.

Father Christoph: Remember now, you have a vibrant young girl, anywhere from seventeen on. She has a reasonable amount of health to carry on the work of the institute. She has proved herself in many respects, because the religious community is not a haven for the inept or those who "could not make it otherwise." She most probably had dates; she has had some academic achievements; she may have had athletic achievements; and she has cultivated a certain amount of independence. She has been doing things more or less on her own, depending upon the stratum of society from which she came. She has had more or less latitude in expressing herself and doing as she pleased. Now she comes to a religious community where her activities are completely regulated and supervised. This is all bewildering to her. It is such a different kind of life; it calls for a reversal of behavior.

When she goes into the community for the first time as a postulant the patterns of behavior of her companions are very different from that of the world from which she just came. She notices that in each of these postulants and in each of these novices there is—I hate to use the word—a certain kind of "regimentation." The "regimentation" is not only in thinking and deciding but also in acting. Perhaps it is noticed first in acting because one can accept the external discipline of the religious community long before she can internalize it. It is a matter of "Here I am, this is what they are doing; I will do it. Later I will find out why they are acting the way they are. Then I will think the thing out for myself."

But it seems that there is a certain diminution of one's person. This individual who has been so free in the expression of her own individuality, her own personality, now finds that she is living in an atmosphere of restraint. The point that we want to make is that there is a change in the attitude of the individual. She comes with all the good will in the world. . . .

Father Evoy: These young individuals are striving, at least, though not entirely without mistakes, to stand on their own feet in terms of doing some of their own thinking and own deciding. True, there are times when because of the unaccustomed nature of these experiences, they find it difficult to keep them within the framework of their religious life. It would be unreasonable on our part, I think, to expect youngsters not to make mistakes in their strivings for adulthood. This seems to be just what these young people are actually doing. So rather than attempting to view such behavior in terms of bad will or rebellion unsuited to religious life we should see it as evidence of healthy growing pains.

In and of itself, regardless of the number of mistakes made, any such attempt at self-actualization is in a wholesome direction, because a religious is going to be her best *as a religious* only when she is really her best *as a person*. We need to remind ourselves of this frequently, because one thing we cannot afford in religious life is "avoidable" immaturity in the members of the community.

Father Christoph: Certainly the young Sister should be allowed the opportunity to express her thoughts modestly, with a certain amount of deference to the experience and learning of others. To dismiss her suggestions, etc., because she is only young in religion or because she does not have a Ph.D. is a little short of ridiculous. How much more difficult for those who enter religion after having been successful business women, teachers, and the like? We admire their humility in accepting direction, but at the same time we have to recognize the fact that they may have ideas too.

In this particular area, I think, juniors or novices should be allowed fuller expression of their ideas to see what they are thinking. I would rather correct the thinking of an individual in the novitiate than to try to correct her thinking fifty years later.

2 *Compensatory Reactions*

Father Christoph: I would like to discuss another aspect of the mature personality: the area of frustration tolerance. You know, nothing that is man-made is 100% perfect, and no man is 100% perfect, because he is limited by nature. So it is intrinsic to human life that there should be situations that frustrate us. Small children have little need for frustration tolerance. As we grow older and as we become adult, however, we realize that we cannot have everything our way, and it is the characteristic of the mature individual to accept frustrations as part of life in practically every area of our activities. But we are not surprised when we find people who do not always manifest what we would regard as adult behavior with regard to frustrating situations. To be able to conduct one's self and to have enough self-discipline not to be crushed, and not to give up, and not to think the world is collapsing, simply because the things wanted are not accomplished—this is an achievement to which we should all aspire.

Father Evoy: First, I should like to say something about what frustration itself is. Frustration is *not* a characteristic of the environment. Let me exemplify immediately what I mean. Let us say that we drop two men from an airplane into the frozen mountain country. We are practicing cold weather survival. Both of these men have been trained to exist in the frozen wilds with the minimum equipment required to sustain their lives for several days in such an inclement atmosphere. Two days after the drop, we send rescue parties into these rugged mountain areas where we dropped the two men. Some ten days later they find one of them "holed-up" in an improvised lean-to surrounded by several feet of snow. When they reach him, he is pacing nervously back and forth with a most frustrating case of "cabin fever." He blurts out, "Thank God, you have found me. If I had had to remain here another day by myself, I think I would have lost my mind."

Two days later, several miles away, they come upon another improvised lean-to. A butchered deer is hanging from a tree near the entrance. Within the lean-to, the second individual is ensconced in an improvised rocking chair, calmly smoking his pipe. Things are neat and orderly inside where a cheerful fire is burning. His first remarks to the rescue party are, "Go away. For years I have been looking for a little peace and quiet. I have at long last found them. I never had it so good. Come back in a month."

Now it becomes clear from our example that the intense experience of frustration which we termed "cabin fever" is not a property of the physical situation itself, but rather of the person's reaction to the situation. It is not something outside the person; it is the person's reaction *to* something.

In order to make a point here, I would like to ask Father Christoph something I have never asked him before: "Father, what is the best way for a person to avoid *all* frustrations throughout life?"

Father Christoph: Well, I do not know how I could live and completely avoid frustrations . . .

Father Evoy: Precisely. There is no way. You cannot avoid all frustrations. Why? Because even though frustration is not a property of an outside situation, still we are human, and frustration has its origin in a particular type of human experience. Our frustrations arise from the fact that we are being blocked from getting what we want or from the fact that we must accept what we do not want. At least some of this type of experience is unavoidable. Sisters, non-human things can be frustrating but not nearly so much as people can be. "People frustrations" keep getting in our way. You remember the old saying when you were youngsters that went this way: "Sticks and stones may break my bones, but names and faces never hurt me." Clearly, this saying is a fallacy foisted on the youngsters of the human race. The fact is that sticks and stones are relatively easy to take; it is people who can hurt. As a matter of fact, it is largely what happens to us in terms of other people that can be so frustratingly hurtful. Since people have this ability to be able to call forth frustrating reactions from us, we can say that frustration is inevitable in the life of everyone. It is human to be frustrated, at least occasionally.

If we should ever find a religious who had never experienced frustration, I think we would say, "I wonder what is the matter with her? There must be something the matter." She would be that different. Now let us look at the origin of such experiences of frustration. Specifically, from what do your frustrations arise? Before we talk about those that come from you because you are religious, we ought to look at those that arise in you because you are human beings.

Father Christoph: As Father Evoy said, frustrations are inevitable because a person wants certain things and cannot have them, and does not want other things and gets them. You want Sister to like you. She does not. This is frustrating. You lean over backwards trying to get her to like you. Despite all your efforts, she still does not like you—this is very frustrating. Again, you want this special project of yours to go well, and you know that it is *not* going well. This is frustrating. You do not want certain things to happen—at least not at this particular time—and you are almost certain they are going to take place in spite of anything you can do about it. This is frustrating. It is even frustrating if the weather turns hot and you do not want hot weather.

Father Evoy: As we go through life we find that from time to time there are situations arising that are frustrating, and these include "thing frustrations" as well as "people frustrations." Take a typical kind of "thing frustration," which will immediately strike a chord in your experience. You are in a room, your left elbow on a book to hold down a page, and scotch tape ready on your right thumb. You had not noticed that the window was open. All of a sudden the wind comes up. Papers are being blown all over the room. Just then the telephone begins to ring and someone else knocks at the door. Close to your boiling point, you feel like throwing the whole thing over and just walking out of there. This kind of happening checks readily with your experience. So you understand immediately the statement that life furnishes an abundance of "thing frustrations" precisely because we are human beings.

Father Christoph: And there is a sex difference in frustration. More women are frustrated because they are women than men are frustrated because they are men. In several surveys taken to see how dissatisfied men and women were with being the sexes they were, it was found that about three or four times as many women were annoyed because they were women, than men were annoyed because they were men. So there may be frustrations that arise from the fact that you are a woman.

Here is a fourteen-year-old girl and she wants to be tackle on the Chicago Bears' football team. She will never make it. Physically there are frustrations that arise from your size and strength. If you weigh only ninety-eight pounds, you can hardly expect to lift a two-hundred-pound weight.

Father Evoy: Sisters, because you are women you can be hurt, and hurt even more intensely than can men. It seems that this is true, at least in part, because of the delicate sensitivity and acute perceptiveness which are yours as women. Even men who are highly educated, probably because they have no experiential appreciation of the kind of emotional suffering possible to a woman, can both by omission and commission, cause her hurts of the deepest nature, without even being aware that anything of such a nature has taken place. In a word, since you are women, you can be frustrated and hurt as only a woman can.

Father Christoph: There are frustrations that arise from one's life as a religious woman. Father Evoy and I are religious men, so we feel we can speak very freely here. Frankly, Sisters, I may come into religion as an educated person and find some things there that tend "to drive me crazy." Some of these things may be in the rules and customs, and as I intelligently evaluate my community, I might find it, in my judgment, far from being adapted to the needs of our day. I might be of the opinion that we are carrying on, under the guise of "the spirit of our community," antiquated methods of doing things, and even of looking at things. I find particular community problems that are not being dealt with judiciously. I may recognize what appears to me a clear-cut lack of wisdom in authority as it is expressed in Superior-Subject relationships. When I meet these things, the experience can be extremely frustrating.

Again, I assume that a Superior in a religious community should be a natural leader. I simply take that for granted; and the first point to note here is that if I allow the fact that the Superior is really *not* a natural leader to frustrate me, am I not being somewhat unrealistic by assuming that she *should* be, and am I not also leaving myself open to a great deal of frustration? I wonder to begin with, how many religious people are natural leaders? I wonder on reflection what percentage of people, in or out of religion, are natural leaders? That raises a very interesting problem. A community, say with about five or six hundred people, and say fifty or sixty houses . . . Do you expect to find many individuals from that number who will be the type of leaders that you would actually desire—the ideal type of leader? I think it is asking too much.

Father Evoy: Later on when we are treating obedience, we will point out that imperfection is an inevitable aspect of the operation of obedience in the authority-obedience relationship. Suffice it to say at the moment, that there are a number of things at times expected under the guise of obedience and religious discipline, which of their very nature tend to be frustrating. Incidentally, living day in and day out exclusively with a group of religious, with very little provision for privacy or sanctuary outside of the chapel (and even that at times does not guarantee privacy from the others) can be a prolonged, frustrating experience. Sisters, just as married life contains within itself potentially frustrating situations of which the religious woman knows little, so also there are possible frustrating situations in the convent of which people outside simply are not aware.

Consequently any adequate treatment of maturity in religious life which fails to take account of frustration tolerance is simply unrealistic. Moreover, it seems to me that there is precious little point in stressing to religious women the importance of the development of frustration tolerance without indicating at least some typical frustrating situations and revealing what the mature reactions on the part of the religious should be to such situations. Given the fact that frustration is an ingredient of living in religious life, what are some of the more adult ways of dealing with it?

Father Christoph: Self-discipline demands that we be able to master our frustrations. Our reactions to situations that frustrate us should be spiritually, morally, emotionally, and socially acceptable. They should be on an adult level. When the frustrations are occasioned by, say, physical objects outside of us, we can sometimes do something about them. The first thing that an adult does is to reassess the problem—a small child does not. A small child fails in trying to move a heavy chair. He is frustrated. He may scream and cry because he cannot move the chair, and it may not occur to him to get others to help him move it. He simply is unable to do what he wants right now and he cannot accept this fact.

When we assess a problem that is demanding a solution and when it cannot be solved right here and now, we reassess the problem and try some other techniques to achieve our goal. *If* we cannot get the goal or achieve it through some other method, we again examine the situation to see if there is any possible error in our perception of the problem. Then either we have to give up since we cannot solve the problem, or we choose some other goal as a substitution. This is, in general, how we handle our physical problems—the things that arise from non-human agents. In the case of human agents it is different.

Father Evoy: Many of you are very familiar with the hypothesis that frustration leads to aggression. This point is something we should never overlook in the matter of dealing maturely with our frustrations. You should be mindful that when you are frustrated, you would like to have something you could throw or kick. You find in you the tendency to hurt, smash, or damage. As a religious, you may walk with perfect external self-control into your room, close the door, and then proceed to beat the living daylights out of your pillow. Regardless of what you do, at least the tendency to some such kind of aggression is there. You may cry yourself to sleep and this crying might be one of anger, or hurt, or more likely both.

Father Christoph: I may live in a world of my own, with a tendency to think that my world is the only world that exists. It is very easy for me to think that *everything* should revolve about me. I am the sun. I am interested in my department; I am interested very much in the achievement of my students, and it is easy for me to divorce myself from the general welfare of the whole student body and of the whole faculty.

What is important for me is not necessarily important for everyone else, and so when someone says, "You can't do this," or "You can't do that,"—my reaction is to be hurt. I feel like saying, "Wait a minute, you don't understand." I may do my best to make my needs known and even to stress them, and if my Superiors insist, then I simply have to yield. Certainly it is not any indication of maturity for an individual to equivalently stamp and say, "I'm not going to play any more. I'm going to take my toys and go home."

Father Evoy: Let us assume, in order to carry through on this example, that Father Christoph, living in his own little world, feels that he should now have five more teachers in his department. He goes to the proper person in administration and makes his request for the five additional teachers. He is turned down. Father's point is that his reaction should not be an adult temper tantrum, but rather that he should approach it much more maturely. How? First of all, he might reassess his needs. For instance, he could reflect that it was his judgment that he does need five new teachers, but that is also conceivable he *could* be wrong about this. Moreover, he can give credit to the administration for at least good will, because as far as they see his need, they say that he does *not* need these five teachers. Finally, he can reflect at this point that here is an area where compromise would make a good deal of sense. If they will not permit him to acquire five more teachers, has he asked for three, or has he asked for a number of part-time teachers? Such would be a much more adult reaction to this problem, which of its very nature frustrates him.

Father Christoph: We said that our reactions to a frustrating situation should be emotionally acceptable, as well. They should be on an adult level. For instance, you ask for permission for something and Sister Superior says, "No, you may not do that." Well,

if you get down on the floor and begin to pound your fists and
scream and yell, it is pretty obvious that this type of reaction is
not consonant with any type of adult maturity. But we can do
practically the same thing by going to our room, slamming the
door, pounding our fist on the table, throwing down a book, and
no one may know this but ourselves. But this is *not* a mature way
to react to a frustrating situation. Nothing is helped by such
behavior, and if we realize that frustrations are a part of every
one's life, then the earlier we begin to learn how to react to
frustrations, the better.

The big keys to proper reactions to frustrations are self-discipline and the Ignatian principle of indifference. These two virtues, that of self-discipline, which is the control of your reactions
to the extent that you rarely let any of your emotions get out of
hand—anger, fear, love, or whatever it is—and the virtue of indifference give us the keys to the proper way to handle all our
frustrations.

So frustration tolerance means the capacity which an individual has to experience blocking and yet not to be broken
by the blocking. Religious life certainly has a goodly number of
opportunities calling for tremendous frustration tolerance.

There are unquestionably very good ideas of yours which are
put in the "round file"—the waste paper basket—and given no
further consideration. This is most irritating. After all, how
many times can one take "No" for an answer? How many times
can you have your ideas disregarded? I do not know, but I admire the individual who keeps coming back and I am a little
upset by the individual who gives up. All I know is that to give
up at the first obstacle is most characteristically immature.

Father Evoy: Father, I think you are a little hard on some of the
persons who give up after only once. We should recognize, I
think, that at times it would be very understandable if after only
one experience a person simply said, "That's it. If they want me,
they know where I live. Let them come and get me." I say it is

understandable, because "people-hurts" can be so deep. I can understand that a person would be cut down so badly in one experience that it would be almost super-heroic for her to come back the second time. I would agree with Father that she would be a bigger person if she could rise above this and come back again. Nevertheless, I would be very sympathetic toward her because she was really crushed. After only a single devastating experience, she could feel that she was a shell, that she had been emptied.

Father Christoph: Yes, I would agree. We could easily give you an example. You do a terrific job on some public relations deal. It may be a play, it may be a bazaar; whatever it is, it was excellent publicity, and besides more money was made by this event this time than any time in the previous history of the place. *No one* gives you a "pat on the back." This is the kind of "people-hurt" about which Father Evoy was talking and as a result of which you say, "Never again will I extend myself. This finishes it for me."

You know that as religious we do not do things primarily for Superiors, we do not do things primarily for our fellow religious, we do them primarily for God. But if Superiors or those with whom we live do not show any appreciation or gratitude or do not give us any kind of recognition, our personal morale is not only threatened, it may be destroyed. Under these circumstances it is very hard to measure up to the expectations of religious life. Surely we always have the spiritual motivation, but there is nothing like recognition by human agents to let us know we are doing a good job. We do not do our work in order to be complimented or appreciated, but the absence of these acts of recognition destroys enthusiasm to do and accomplish.

Father Evoy: Unhealthy reaction patterns to frustrations are found all too commonly in religion, and frequently enough they are not recognized as such. To unmask them for what they are is

to deprive them of the further opportunity of masquerading as
something else. In this undertaking of "unmasking" it will help
to return to the reflection that frustration seems to be closely
associated with the tendency to anger, to break and injure. This
would appear to be especially true where the frustration originates in "people frustrations" rather than in "thing frustrations."

Let us look at some of the more common, less mature patterns
of reaction in religious life. For example, Sister A either over-
hears or directly receives a wounding remark from Sister B. The
remark does not seem to have much impact on Sister A at the
time, but she has no sooner retired for her night's rest than up
looms that remark. In the matter of a few minutes she is upset
with a highly frustrating experience in which she finds herself
getting more and more angry at Sister B and even conjuring up
devious ways of getting even with her or of hurting her in return.
Men normally stand aghast at the ability of women regarding
"infighting." One woman, if you will excuse the remark, can
really "do a job" on another in a way that would never occur to
a man.

Father Christoph: This particular individual allows herself to be
upset—she cannot sleep all night long. What kind of behavior do
we call that? Is that an adjustive mechanism? It is supposed to be
adjustive because she is reacting to something that has frustrated
her; but she is not adjusting at all. She is being eaten up with
anger, with this aggressive hostility, and she is very unhappy with
herself. In the morning things are not any different, except that
she is more tired and perhaps very much less able to do her work.
So although this commonly happens, it is not an adult's way of
reacting to a frustrating situation.

Father Evoy: I should like to suggest but one mature way of
handling this. It takes a great deal of courage even to contemplate employing this approach but in the experience of many

individuals it has been found to be strikingly successful. Framing the suggestion in reference to our example, Sister A would approach Sister B as calmly as possible and say to her, "Sister, you hurt me very deeply when you made that remark." Often it proves to have been, at least in large part, a misunderstanding. As a result of this type of dealing with it, the hurtful interpretation of the remark tends to be dissipated and so the frustration at least thins out, if it does not disappear entirely.

On the other hand, it is easy to let frustration build up inside one and then explode into the first justifiable outlet that one finds. To take but one instance, such might be the explanation for what occurs when a Sister goes to one in authority, only to find that this person in authority manifests unmistakable impatience and irritability with her. Frequently in such a case the one who has just exploded fails to see that this irritation is being taken out on the wrong person.

Father Christoph: You know, we are always protecting or salvaging our ego. We never want to be wrong and we never want to be unfair. We feel a need to justify our conduct, and, you know, we can usually find some justification for it. One of the needs we have is that our conduct be always correct, and when we take out our frustrations on individuals in patterns which we would resent in others, we must always find some justification. Hence the alibi and like devices.

Father Evoy: This is precisely why it is so difficult to spot this type of reaction and why vigilance is called for lest we do considerable damage to someone without ever appreciating what is happening. This thing can be very subtle, but nevertheless, lethal. For example, a Sister has experienced a real frustration in dealing with someone in authority. Shortly afterward, seething inside, she walks into her classroom. Before the day is over she says, with real feeling, "The whole class will stay here in this classroom until I tell you you may go home. You are going to work and work."

The youngsters are startled. They look at her in open disbelief. In justification, she tells herself, "They have really asked for this. They have been particularly difficult and dull today. They are not even trying. What they need is to be shaken up good, and punishment such as this is the way to get the best results out of them for *their* own good."

By no means is this the most destructive form that the aggressive urge can take without even being recognized. Let me take an instance which comes much closer to what I have in mind. After Sister has been hurt very severely by this person in authority, she goes over to the resident students' quarters in her school and singles out this one child who for one reason or another annoys her, and then proceeds to give herself the adequate justification for what she is about to do. She tells herself that unless one is really honest with the children, it is horribly unfair to them. The important thing, she reiterates to herself, is to be at all times completely and openly honest with them. Thus she has laid the justifying foundation. Then, with considerable feeling, she addresses this one little girl, "Look, dear, we must make one thing clear which you simply have to face. You wouldn't be here as a resident student to begin with, unless your father and mother did not want you. We might say that they do not want you at home, but it would be more honest and more correct just to say that *they do not want you.* I am being fully honest with you. Do you understand?" So Sister thus justified could crush that child as you would crush a grape between your fingers, and never really recognize what she had done.

Looked at from an objective point of view, this would be a monstrous thing to do to a small child, but the Sister who did this probably covered the whole thing over so well that she failed to see any fault whatever in her action. She was just being strictly honest! So you see that the first protection against this disastrous type of thing is the seeing of her experience as it is and for what it is. Were she to be fully aware that she is upset and experiencing feelings of hostility, she could at least be on guard against taking it out on the wrong person, and then salving over all personal culpability for so doing.

You see, when you are really frustrated, especially by a person, there are many well concealed ways of hitting back. The hitting back can assume many justifiable forms. You might say, for instance, "I'll show them. They will be penalized and suffer because I am no longer going to put forth spontaneously anything that might help them in any way."

This same end can be accomplished in fantasy, by means of taking a bath of self-pity, so to speak. She can spend hours imagining herself killed or terribly maimed. The whole flavor of it will invariably be, "They will be sorry, then and only then will they appreciate me and be fully cognizant of their loss. Then they will *really* feel it."

She might take it out of the realm of fantasy but accomplish the same goal of making them sorry in still another way. It can be done by taking grave and unnecessary risks while morbidly contemplating the consequences. For instance, it could be accomplished by walking along precarious places as she tells herself that if she should be blown over the edge or if she should slip and fall over it—then they would really miss her. She might even find herself being notably careless in driving the car while entertaining the same thoughts that if she should be accidentally killed how terrible would be the loss which would be theirs. Then, she could tell herself, they would fully realize at last, but too late, the great contribution she could have made had they not treated her so shabbily.

Father Christoph: This "They're going to miss me when I'm gone," happens to be narcissistic thinking. We begin to think in fantasy all kinds of things that we could have contributed to the community, but now we cannot because this disaster is going to occur. In the area of fantasy we can tell ourselves, "I am going to

jump out the window, then they will really miss me." I am not
going to jump out the window, of course, but I would *like* to,
and the enjoyment of the contemplation of the effect of such a
thing is hardly a mature reaction to frustration.

Father Evoy: My preoccupation is with the feeling that it would
serve them right. I really feel like doing some of those things.
Now, maturity of reaction enters at the point of coping with this
frustration. What do I do about it? I can return, as we mentioned, to my room and say, "That does it!" I can slam something down, and then maturity begins to assert itself. I can say to
myself, "Oh, well! I can't go back to infancy—true, this just
about killed me, but I will go back again. I shall have to expose
myself even though I could get hurt again, because I am *not*
going to retreat. I could not face myself in the mirror if I did. In
my eyes to retreat would be cowardly, even though I feel I could
somehow justify it. In fact I believe I could make a strong case
for such a withdrawal, but on reflection, I cannot let myself be
that immature."

Father Christoph: An all too common way of reacting to frustration is one of rather complete retreat. After a hurt, I go to my
room and I say, "That does it." Not only do I withdraw physically but I withdraw emotionally and psychologically from the
world that surrounds me. Too many people who are hurt practice this form of retreat, because it seems to be a guarantee
against further hurt. If I can maintain this type of retreat, no one
can hurt me.

Father Evoy: This takes many guises. For instance, after you
have been hurt you resolve once and for all that *no one* will ever
get close to you again. You swear it to yourself. Never will you
permit it. You are sure that you must keep yourself safe after so
severe a hurt. Look at the forms such isolation can take: you are
walking down the corridor and you see someone coming who

might try to chat with you, so immediately you go into an act. You stop, look thoughtfully at your watch, or check a note with genuine concentration, hesitate, and then turn and walk rapidly the other way as if you had forgotten something important. This keeps you safely away from the individual. Or you may choose just to keep walking right on past this individual and turn on the old stand-offish protective smile. As you keep going you are carrying out your resolve that no one is ever going to engage you in anything that is personal or serious, or get close to you, no matter how close the person is physically—you simply will not have it.

If you happen to be caught with one other person in a situation from which you cannot readily extricate yourself, you become politely formal. You say, "Yes." "Yes, indeed." Between the two of you, you construct a wall of ice higher than your heads which this other person will never get through—you will see to that. In a way this metaphor of "ice," would seem to be a very apt one because it expresses something of the cold that you experience. If and when you are not receptive of the warmth of another human being, you are cold. Sisters, Our Lord, as Man, is possessed of a personal, human warmth but ordinarily does not communicate any of that comforting warmth tangibly to you this side of the grave.

Father Christoph: You have said, "I can't afford to let anyone hurt me anymore. So I must withdraw psychologically even when I cannot withdraw physically." Most people who withdraw psychologically create physical isolation. Do you know what I mean? If you are not communicative, if you are not going to be more generous in speaking to and about others, and if you are not going to give anything of yourself to others in the recreation room, for example, you finally find you are sitting down reading a magazine by yourself. No one will talk to you, so your psychological withdrawal creates physical isolation.

What is the next thing? You then deliberately find some excuse for not attending recreation because no one talks to you anyway. Yet the whole source of the difficulty originally arose within you because of this withdrawal technique, to protect your ego.

Father Evoy: Father Christoph said that one deliberately finds some reason for not attending recreation. How will this reason do? The reason you cannot get close to these Sisters is, let us face it, that they are very dangerous persons. Take this particular individual, Sister B, for example. She can annihilate a person without even really trying. You do not know why she personally dislikes you, but she does, and because she dislikes you and is lethal, you do not think even God would ask you to expose yourself to her. It sounds pretty good, does it not?

You understand that you spontaneously try to square with yourself what you are doing. You must not see it as in any way improper or unjustifiable. Hence without even realizing it you might find yourself projecting into another person characteristics which would justify your treating her as you do. What are some of these? Well, first of all, there is the point that she does not like you. Again, there is the fact that she has a tongue on which you could sharpen one of the finest edged razors ever honed. You give this person full credit for the ability to be able to cut a person into small ribbons. While you are crediting her with these characteristics, you might never even suspect that you simply *have* to see her as inimical to you and as very dangerous to you, in order to justify your treatment of her.

So much, Sisters, for our treatment of frustration tolerance. From these remarks I think that it becomes unmistakably clear that the first line of defense against immature reactions to frustration is the recognition of the frustration itself together with its concomitant feelings and inclinations. From that starting point, one can at least begin to strive to cope with a given experience of frustration in as mature a pattern as possible.

3 *Confrontation of Self*

Father Evoy: When we recall Socrates' insistence on knowing one's self and both Kierkegaard's and Shakespeare's emphasizing "to thine own self be true," we wonder if they were speaking of the same thing. We have no way of knowing whether or not these men were thinking precisely in terms of maturity, but it does seem that they were talking about maturity. Implicitly, I believe, they were saying that the ability of an individual to recognize *real* feelings in himself is indeed a characteristic of an adult.

The mature religious woman says to herself: "Be real." By this she means that she dares to face her own experiences, whatever they are. At times this is far from an easy thing. Let us say a Sister is afraid to walk into a classroom or afraid of a teaching situation. It is almost unbelievable in how many ways she can mask such experience from herself. She may simply not see that she is afraid or that she experiences fear with regard to something. What she needs to know is that it is a mark of maturity for her to look at her experience and to say to herself, "I am afraid of this situation."

It is of the utmost importance to stress the point that to recognize one's real feelings is a characteristic of maturity. One can find so many "good" reasons for not recognizing such feelings.

For example, there is an individual who irks you. You do not like her. Now you might say to yourself, "I am a religious and religious charity demands that I love her, therefore I must *like* her." This is self-deception. You *do not* like her. You should admit this at least to yourself. This is being mature, because it is confronting an aspect of the real. We are emphasizing the importance of facing such areas of reality, because there are so many ways in which one can turn away from them. Often, for instance, you cannot afford to see them. It may be that you cannot bring yourself to see that you do not like her. As a matter of fact, it might be that your real feeling is the fear she does not like you. This is even more painful. In this latter case, if you can look fully at the feeling you have that she "does not like me," it is going to hurt; but in so doing you are being true to yourself. To do so is mature. It is in fact much more mature than to say to yourself: "That is just a temptation. It is just my unfounded suspicion or feeling that she does not like me." This is an attempt to explain out of existence a real feeling. It might be that the reason you could not admit even to yourself the feeling that she "does not like me," is that, were you to do so, you are afraid you might become angry, and you could never dare to become angry. You just could not afford to experience anger for the reason that you are not sure you could control the anger if you ever gave way to it.

What I am saying is, I think, somewhat familiar to you. You are aware that there are individuals who can never even pretend to such feelings. They can never act the role of having any negative emotions, because they fear that in such an event an emotional conflagration might sweep them away. Let me exemplify this. I could never, for example, go into a class and pretend that I was angry at the class, because were I to do so I would indeed become angry, and this might be catastrophic. My fear is that I might be carried to such an extreme that I could actually be tempted to kill someone.

Again, I might happen to resent very much the way I am being treated in the community, or the fact that I have been left out of something important or somehow or other passed over. I resent this very much. In such a situation I am acting maturely when I can say to myself, "I really feel hurt and I also feel very strong resentment." When and *if* I become really aware of my feelings of hurt and resentment, then, and only then, can I begin to handle them, to work with them and to cope with them as becomes an adult.

If I will not let myself see such experiences, I simply push them away down inside me, where they seethe. I push them emotionally to the back of the stove, where they continue to simmer. When I employ the term "simmering" I mean slowly boiling, but boiling, nevertheless. Should you have a vessel boiling, even though slowly, and leave no outlet whatever for the steam, what would you expect to happen? Would you not look for an explosion? There is something of a parallel here. Psychologically, the individual who pushes these feelings down where she does not look at them still has them there on the back of her emotional stove, cooking away very slowly. Emotionally she is on the verge of an explosion. She really does not know whether or not she is going to burst.

Often enough it is more difficult to confront negative feelings and emotions than positive ones, but nevertheless, the latter can be a source of real difficulty. To exemplify, it might be that I happen to like Father Christoph. Actually, reluctant as I am to admit it in his presence, I do. Now it might be that I am afraid to admit that feeling even to myself. To the extent that this would be true, I would be immature. But as I just finished saying, greater difficulty yet is to be found in coping with negative feelings. It would be rather surprising if, at least at some time or other, Father Christoph would not start to get on my nerves, just as I would expect, I hope only occasionally, to get on his nerves. To the extent that I face the fact that at least occasionally he can get on my nerves, and moreover, the additional fact that I occasionally must irk him, I am being mature. The failure to see . . .

Father Christoph: Father Evoy made some remark about my reaction to his behavior. Well, I was frustrated because I wanted
the microphone awhile ago and he refused to yield it to me. In
this recognition, I bear out the importance of what Father
stressed—of knowing one's real experience. It is mature to be
able to say to oneself, "I am selfish; I am fearful; I am envious; I
have the reactions that anybody would have to this or that situation. I bubble over with satisfaction at success; I am downcast at
failure." But some of these are socially approved emotional reactions and some are not.

When they are not socially approved, they have a tendency to
go underground, or to use Father Evoy's figure, we put them on
the back of the stove and let them simmer. Sometimes this activity is automatic and we are not aware that it is happening; we
are not even aware that these are socially and sometimes religiously disapproved reactions and since they have been sup-
pressed we do not have to cope with them.

Father Evoy mentioned that an individual could not afford to
get angry because his anger tended to get out of bounds. It might
be that a religious could not afford to get angry because it is not
becoming for a religious to become angry—to show anger. To
deny certain experiences because it is unbecoming to have certain emotions is not healthy. Now, for instance, I could understand a religious woman being attracted to someone of the opposite sex, and it might be so unbecoming from her point of view to
have this attraction that she could not admit it. To admit it,
might objectively seem to her to be a repudiation of her goal, of
the kind of life that she wants to live. But if she puts it in the
proper perspective, there is nothing abnormal about this experience. There are socially and there are morally and religiously
accepted ways of reacting to this particular experience. But to
deny it would not be being one's self, and would not be reality.
So name the emotion. We have it. We should at least attempt to
recognize it in ourselves for what it is and not be ashamed to look
at ourselves and see that it exists. As Father Evoy said, you do not

always have to admit these things to others, but you *have* to admit them to yourself, otherwise you are deceiving yourself.

Father Evoy: At times it takes tremendous personal courage to look at certain feelings. For instance, take this thing that Father Christoph just talked about. Say I have been a Sister in religion for twenty years and I have become aware suddenly that I find this particular individual highly attractive personally. It could be that this attraction would be threatening to me, because I am far from sure I could handle the situation. To admit the experience that this individual, Mr. X, or Sister Y, is very attractive to me as a person, might be so threatening that I could not bring myself to look at it. Why? Because to get close to him or her, to go out to this person, is to leave myself open to be hurt. The boy selling newspapers down on the corner, who makes an insulting remark when I pass by, cannot *really* hurt me. The only individual who can painfully hurt me is the one I *let* hurt me, and the only person I let hurt me is the person I let close to me.

There is, if I may use the term, a certain "gun-shyness" in many religious, in the sense that they can never permit themselves to get personally and warmly close to anyone. Because they are afraid they could not manage the experience, they prefer to be alone and safe rather than to be in an exposed and dangerous position. Because as soon as someone gets close to such a one, she is, in effect, dropping her guard. She is showing the other person more of her—of the real her; and if this person should disapprove of what is shown, it would have a most painful impact on the religious.

Father Christoph: We have to face these realities. Then, of course, when we face these realities, it means that we are taking a stand, and we have to take a stand that is socially, morally and religiously acceptable. So, somewhere along the line we have to be realistic as far as our emotional experiences are concerned.

Father Evoy: I should like to say one additional thing about the recognition of feelings. The mature viewing of an adult's own feelings has a twofold aspect, which, I think, is very important. It demands that the mature person be able to be both participant and spectator with regard to the same experience. For example, I am threatened by a given situation, or I am terribly disappointed by someone. Now my seeing either one of these says first of all an awareness that I am really *feeling* this thing. This means the viewing of it as a *participant,* which as we have said, is a very definite characteristic of the mature person.

But maturity calls also for a further ability with regard to this experience. I refer to my being able, as it were, to step aside, and look at this same experience objectively and almost impersonally. I accept the fact that this has happened and so I feel hurt; but I also stand back and endeavor to regard it as another person might view it, who would not be personally and emotionally involved in it. I strive to view it from this other vantage point.

A little child, for instance, going into a dentist's office, is so completely engrossed in his fear that he can in no way stand aside and view his fear. I, as an adult, on the other hand, can walk into the dentist's office, and say to myself, "I am afraid of what he is going to do to me. I am perspiring; I am also shivering." At the same time, I can try, at least, to view this visit to the dentist as an investment which I have to make, since to neglect the care of my teeth now will be costly later. Thus I can face my fear, and still tell myself that I must go to this man—even while afraid. This ability of a person to be able to look past the feelings in an emotional experience and examine it rather objectively, is very much a characteristic of maturity.

Father Christoph: In fact, to so act demands great maturity at times. Remember we said sometime back that maturity admits of degrees. Well, it takes a great deal of maturity to be able to study one's emotions objectively.

Let us suppose now that I feel that a certain Sister is very upset with me. My emotions reflect this. I am unhappy that this Sister does not accept me. But then as a mature individual I begin to study myself a little and to study the situation. First of all, does she have to accept me in this unique friendship relationship? No, because we only have a *few* friends. But I *want* her friendship. Does she not have a right to have her own friends? Does she *have* to be my friend? Friendship expresses individuality. Now if I can look at it objectively, then I might say, "Maybe she doesn't like me." That is no reflection upon her, nor, necessarily, any reflection upon me. I like to think that people who do not care for me, do not care for me simply because they do not like my kind of individuality, rather than what I am, say, or do.

Father Evoy said to go out and look at yourself objectively. I question the capacity of an individual to get outside of himself and look at himself perfectly objectively. You know why? Because one is always trying to protect his ego even when he is trying to be most candid, most sincere, and most objective. I feel that all along the line, I am still trying to protect me. I am certain that I am not always able to be anywhere near one hundred percent objective. But at least it is a sign of maturity to recognize this, and also to attempt, as far as possible, to look at one's self objectively.

Let us take a Superior-Sister situation. The Superior, from her point of view, sees that particular object as concave. The Subject, from her point of view, sees the same figure as convex. Why do you not give the Superior credit for her point of view? Why do you not give the Subject credit for her point of view? If you are perfectly objective, you say, "It is both concave and convex." Then you are being wholly objective. This viewpoint is difficult to attain. My point of view is the product of many factors—my temperament, my background—cultural, religious, spiritual, social, etc., and all these are reflected in my point of view. I see the object as convex because my point of view psychologically allows me to see it only in that manner. Since perception is functionally selective, it becomes extremely difficult to appreciate and, sometimes, even to see another's point of view. This is an extremely important observation and even the mere recognition of it points to considerable maturity. People are not necessarily stubborn or willfully obtuse. They simply are unable to get outside of themselves and view a total situation with passionless objectivity. Yet if we are going to be objective, that is what we have to try to do. We have to try to get outside of ourselves and to see how much of this is objectively true, is the real, and how much is the imagined, how much is the result of attitudes, etc. Practically every experience that is mine has an emotional overtone. The mature individual is able to peel off the emotional coverings or eliminate these emotional overtones, and get down to the real thing. That is certainly the epitome of objectivity.

Father Evoy: Some of the existentialist psychologists have pointed out repeatedly that an individual is simply not going to see clearly an experience that requires some action on his part until such time as he is ready to take that action. This normally has reference to some commitment on his part. This point has an important bearing upon what we have just been treating, namely, the seeing of experiences both subjectively and objectively as they are, or as Father Christoph says, both from the concave and from the convex side. To the extent that I can objectify my viewing of an experience, I find that I am less helpless in dealing with it. I may see, for example, that I am deathly afraid of failure, or even of making a mistake. I may know that I am frozen into inactivity by this fear. Yet, to the extent that I am able to view it objectively, I recognize that this tends to shackle my abilities, and so I have at least a starting point from which to work towards freedom.

Granted that I feel that a decision to undertake a specific course of action is just about impossible for me because I cannot afford to fail, I nevertheless try to face this fact as clearly as possible. From this vantage point, since I cannot afford to fail, I appreciate my very strong tendency to go to another individual and say to this one: "What should I do? How should I act here?" In so doing, I am seeking advice. I want this person to make the decision for me. Once the other individual tells me what to do, I am safe. For should his advice prove wrong, it is not *my* mistake; it is *his*. I only hope that in such circumstances I can face the fact that this was a decision which rightly should have been made by me, and I have not made it. I hope that I am able to face the fact that it was my obligation to have made it, even though I was most uncertain in the matter. I have avoided making it by having another make it for me. Yet, in this type of situation it is possible to look squarely at the fact that I am very much afraid, and accordingly want someone else to make the decision for me, and still not surrender to this urge. I can say to myself: "I am afraid; I am terrified at the thought of failure; but I am a human being, hence I simply must be responsible for myself; I cannot turn over my personal responsibility completely to anyone else." Despite the fear, I can make the decision myself. This is a great stride toward maturity.

Father Christoph: But even at that, it is a sign of some maturity to recognize the fact that you go hat-in-hand to somebody else to have him solve your problems. It is the beginning of the type of insight that will bring about greater maturity. From that point, you hope to work your way, as far as possible, face fear, and make your own decisions, even though your decisions may be made in an atmosphere of fear. If I did not feel envy, jealousy, and hatred and everything else, I would not be human. It is the height of immaturity to pretend that one does not have these emotions.

The Latin playwright, Terence, could, with reason, boastfully write: *"Nil humanum a me alienum puto"*—"Nothing human is foreign to me." He is saying, in effect, that one need not apologize for experiencing a human emotion. Neither the religious habit nor the vows of religion ought to make us less human. Nothing human is foreign to me—even when I am a religious.

We have all these human emotions. That is what Father means
when he emphasizes being *real*. Do not deceive yourself. You
love; you are angered; you fear; you hate; you take pleasure in;
you have aversions. You would not be human if you did not have
these things.

Father Evoy: Father and I are human, too. But there is one
thing, by reason of which, you differ from us. You are not
only human—you are also women, and we are men. Because you
are women, you have certain things which are proper to you as
women. You will never be otherwise. Because you are women,
you want to be wanted by someone who *counts* in your life. For
the rest of your life this will be true. To the extent that you
might say, "I do not see any such need in me for this type of
being wanted," I think, Sisters, you are not being *fully* real. You
are women and you are also human beings and because you are
human beings, you need the companionship, you need someone
to turn to, someone to go to, someone with whom to share. You
are not sufficient in yourselves, and you should not fool yourselves by saying, "That is not being real."

The all-important thing that you must do is recognize this in
yourself. First, as a human being, you do indeed *need* to be
needed. You need to love and be loved. Father Christoph is fond
of repeating, "God, as we experience Him, doesn't have skin."
Because you are human you have in you a need, a longing for
someone who does have skin. This, incidentally, is one reason
why God became Man. But for the most part here and now, you
still do not have evidence of Our Lord's skin. Yet you have in
you the need to be needed, to be wanted, to be loved and to love.
Moreover, as I just indicated, these needs should have in you the
particular characteristics which are a woman's.

Precisely, Sisters, because you are women, your need is to give
yourself, to give yourself to the person loved, and to give yourself
in every way that is an adequate and becoming expression of
your love. This is part and parcel of your womanly nature. And
because it is, maturity says that at times you must go back and

reassess the commitment to religious life of the woman that you are.

For instance, you should again recognize that this need to be appreciated, to be needed in a warm, personal relationship with someone else, to be loved and to love, might have been realized for you in marriage. What you gave up was not something that is somehow or other unbecoming or improper, but was one possible fulfillment of all these needs. You gave up marriage gladly and willingly as something that was good, not as something bad.

Father Christoph: Let us emphasize this: in the married state, the presumption is that if anyone asks you to marry him, he wants you. And even if he did not need you, you would be needed and wanted by your offspring. If you did not have the love of your husband, you would at least have the love of and for your children. So there is no question that in the natural order, the way in which woman seeks self-fulfillment is through marriage. In religious life you have these same wants and needs but not the natural outlet. Nature abhors a vacuum, and this is true even in the religious life. You do not have the outlets that the married woman has; therefore in whom do you find that you are wanted, that you can love and be loved? God expects us—you and me—to get to Him through our fellow men. Therefore there is a place for friendship and for an attitude toward another individual that will satisfy these needs and still be very spiritually acceptable. Father Evoy and I listened to a young priest recently say that Sisters go to Holy Communion and that it is pretty much a matter of a "God and me" relationship. They are just so united to God that there is no union among them—there is no love. Sisters, I think that this is a by-product of religious discipline that was not intended, but nevertheless is real, the result of a pattern of training which said, "Just look at God. Just look at God. Find all of your affection, find an outlet for all your affections, for all of your interests, in Almighty God. If no one wants you, don't worry; God wants you."

Father Evoy: But you want to be wanted, and you need to be wanted. You want to be needed, and you need to be needed. You need to love and be loved in return. God gave you your neighbor so that you might find much of this type of fulfillment.

The individual person who does not love is not *really* a complete being. In the context of Father Christoph's remark, I think I could say that the individual religious who loves no other human being, but only God, is not functioning as a complete human being. I am aware that this is a pretty strong statement in this connection. I recall the remark of an admittedly cynical individual who said of religious women, "I wonder what community life would really be like if religious women *really* loved each other?" Since, Sisters, we have given up this tremendously beautiful thing which marriage can be, what are we going to do with our love now that we are in religious life?

Father Christoph: I do not know whether it would pay to try to define love. I can define it philosophically, but that would be very cold and very sterile. It would not convey the full meaning and notion of love as we experience it. I suppose that when we define love philosophically we prescind from the affective aspect of it. Love is the union of wills. I want what you want; you want what I want; I want your good; you want my good. That is what love is.

This is the intellectual dimension of love, and love is an emotion, so it has a sensible counterpart. Since it does have this sensible counterpart, I am aware of a movement in my sensibilities directing me toward the individual whom I love. Therefore, I want to be near; I want to be with; I want to hear the individual's voice; I want the touch of a hand; and such things.

First of all, the word "love" has at times an unfortunate connotation. We tend, when we hear it, to think of a romantic relationship. But what word can you use? If "love" sounds like something romantic, "charity" sounds like a dole. We run out of words. As we mentioned earlier, religious are sometimes inclined to think that there is something wrong with them religiously and spiritually if they are attracted to anyone. Such a notion is, of course, certainly the negation of a very basic and fundamental trait in man. I say to the one experiencing this emotion: "No, there is nothing wrong with you; you are perfectly human."

The object of your love must be someone toward whom you may direct it. I do not mean that you should direct it in a general way to all mankind, but in a specific way, because one cannot have many close friends. I may have a thousand acquaintances and I may call them friends, but among these there will be a very, very few who will know me very well, simply because to know me very well would suppose a great deal of communication. I cannot communicate thus to a great number of people. So my constellation of intimate friends is going to be limited to one, two, three, four, maybe five, but scarcely more. The point is that there is this inter-communication, and that when I love I want to be near the individual; I want to share with the individual. All of these things ought to be permissible to religious. We are not to be less human because we are religious. We are to be more human in a divinized manner. So I do not completely substitute the love of God, who is a Pure Spirit, nor even the love of Jesus Christ, who is God Incarnate, for my desire for friendship. I direct my love toward individuals.

Father Evoy: Father Christoph has just said that love in man has affective aspects. After he finished giving a definition of love which was philosophical, he implied that there were affective elements present as well. Love in an angel would fulfill Father Christoph's definition of the "union of wills," but it would certainly not be distinctive of human love.

Martin Buber, the existentialist philosopher at the Hebrew University in Jerusalem, points out clearly that there is no human love which does not have feelings associated with it. It is true that human love is not constituted by nor identified with human feelings, but at the same time, human love is *always* associated with feelings. The feelings are there, even though they are not to be identified with the love. A love which had no feeling whatever as a companion experience, would be suspect as not being a really human love. While the feeling itself is not the love, there is no human love unaccompanied by feelings proper to the particular relationship which we call human love.

Buber brings this out very well with an example. He says that Our Lord's love for Lazarus was genuine; His love for Mary, the sister of Lazarus was genuine; but he adds that it is simply unthinkable that His feelings toward the one would have been identical with His feelings toward the other. Does this make sense?

I think Father Christoph would be willing to go along with me on the position that any human love which is completely devoid of feelings is highly suspect of not being love at all. This pure union of will to will, with no feeings whatever associated with it, is something which seems beyond the nature of a human being. Moreover, it is almost unbecoming a human being, because God made us this combination we ordinarily describe as body and soul.

Someone has defined a man as an emotional being. Incidentally, in passing, this is not a bad definition. Anytime that man *really* cares, there is emotion present, because emotion is, in a sense, the perfect marriage of the spiritual and the bodily.

Let me see if I can attempt some clarification of the possible outlets of your needs for human love. We mentioned your need to be needed by the *right* person. I am talking now in terms of a warm person-to-person relationship. This exposition must, of course, take cognizance of the strong inclination in you as women to give yourselves, not just for the sake of giving yourselves, but rather as the most perfect expression of your love for another person.

As Father Christoph said, you cannot exist in the spiritual igloo in which God and you alone are, and in which there is no one else. Most unfortunately, many of us religious, both men and

women, have been taught that a religious not only can but
should avoid human love and friendship. As we already mentioned, Our Lord, as far as tangible evidence to you goes, does
not have skin. This in no way discounts the importance of the
central, all-important fact of your life that He is real and that He
is much more humanly understandable because He is not just a
spirit, but a Man like unto you. He is a Divine Person, but He
happens also to be a Man. It might be helpful here, to state in
briefest fashion that a man is a person who has his own body and
soul. Christ is a Divine *Person,* Who has His own Body and
Soul, and is therefore a Man.

A human being is capable of dedicating himself in love to
another person. Accordingly, as a religious, you can dedicate
your life, perhaps more easily to the Second Person of the Blessed
Trinity because He is a Man, and as such is more meaningful
within the framework of your own human experience. That in a
woman which says, "I must be needed," can also find outlet
there, although the tangible evidence that Our Lord really needs
her is something that cannot with certainty be anticipated this
side of the grave. The part of a woman which manifests itself in
her need for a warm, affectionate love must be ordered to another human being of whom she does have tangible evidence.
God made us social beings.

A woman religious should clearly face the presence within her
of certain strong inclinations which flow from her womanly nature. Because she is a woman she would like to be held in the
arms of a man she loves. She would also like to hold in her arms
an infant of her own. She lives in full awareness that she has
freely renounced these very satisfying experiences for a life of
love which has different expressions of being loved and of loving.

In my judgment, we really have not made much progress in
unfolding the full meaning of the statement, "Man is by nature
social." If you take a phenomenon such as hypnosis and observe
in it what one person can do to another, you have but an example of what we are pointing out. We are not concerned here

about hypnosis in itself, but simply recognizing it as one instance of what one human being can do to another human being. It certainly is a striking demonstration of the impact of one person on another. It is safe to predict, I think, that no machine is ever going to be able to do that kind of thing to a human being.

Precisely as human beings, we cannot fulfill the need in us to love and be loved in a personal, warm relationship with another person *solely* in and by our relationship to God. We simply cannot just go to God and leave people behind. We need people.

Father Christoph: So we are to understand and love our neighbor as Christ intends that we should. It is a kind of an anomaly that we should have to talk in this fashion. There should be love and affection in religious life of a kind which carries out the first and second commandments—to love God and your neighbor as yourself. If you detect a certain emphasis on this point, it is because both of us feel that love has been so misunderstood and misconstrued, especially in religious life, and the proof of it is the real, crushing loneliness of so many religious.

Father Evoy: Would you want to say that again, Father? When Father mentioned the loneliness of many religious, I could not help but think that people outside might be shocked if they really knew how terribly lonely some, and not a few, religious are. How terribly lonely they really are. They have built themselves a small, compartmentalized area of life in the protection of which they keep people at a safe distance and somehow or other continue to exist. Such existing is not *really* living.

It is noteworthy that so often it comes as an almost complete surprise to religious themselves to realize that they really have not loved people. They have used the word. They have said repeatedly that they loved others. They did not see the contradiction of such declarations with the fact that they did not even try to trust others, did not get close to others, did not go out to others, did not really feel for others. They had been misled into thinking that because they used all the right words, they really loved others.

To begin with, it is simply unthinkable that religious should live together and not love each other. It is unthinkable. Can you imagine a family all living together day and night, breathing down each other's necks—and you know only too well to what I am referring—who would not love each other? And I mean *really* love each other. How seldom does ill will explain such absence of love? Fear, I think, is the culprit here. Let us see if we can throw more light on this. Some of this fear, it would seem, has unfortunately been instilled into us by the teaching that so many of us received in regard to what is called particular friendships or "P.F.'s." One result of such teaching is fear in one of its most hurtful aspects, I feel, as far as religious are concerned. I say this because there are many religious who, apparently as a result of such teaching, are "gun-shy" about relating personally to other people. They are afraid to let anybody close, and they are afraid to do so on the score that somehow or other this is dangerous to chastity and dangerous to purity.

What a horrible, almost monstrous attitude to implant in the mind of a human being! What a frightening thing to leave her feeling that to love another individual is of its very nature somehow or other tied up with impurity. It is difficult to think of anything more calculated to destroy a human being. Yet I am afraid that this is the kind of thing that has been taught to many of us. It surely never occurred to these teachers that this was telling them it is wrong to do that which Our Lord commanded them to do. Sisters, one of the most regrettable things in our whole religious life is that so many have been afraid to love each other. We have been afraid of love. We have been afraid of affection.

You see, because you are human beings and also women, your love for other persons, as we mentioned earlier, is going to be associated with feelings which are proper to you. Your love *must* be associated with such feelings. Because you are mature persons, you must stay on top of the expressions of this love, in the sense that they are not in childish fashion let run away with you or let run rampant. You are as calmly as possible in control. Any unbecoming expression is simply not permitted. For example, you do not walk down the sidewalk with another Sister, looking like two ten year old girls with arms wrapped around one another's waist, because you are too mature for that kind of thing. After all, it would be unacceptable to you as adults, not even to mention the objections to such behavior arising from your rule. It would not be done first of all, because it would be in poor taste. You understand?

Sisters, your affections should never descend to mere sentimentality, but you should never be afraid to love. Accordingly, a religious woman should feel free to love and moreover to give love an expression which is proper to a woman, rather than that which would be more proper to a man. This is something which you should never fear. In the last analysis, no matter how your rule is worded, I believe, if it is correctly interpreted, it would never say that you should not love each other. Is that right?

If such is the case, then the rule would never say that you should forego the appropriate and becoming expressions of your love for each other, because the two are inseparable in a human being.

Note that I say the appropriate and becoming expressions of it. According to your rule and your customs there are expressions of affection more appropriate to certain occasions than to others. So, for example, when you are going away, or when you are arriving home there are expressions which would be considered "right and becoming" which at other times would perhaps not be wholly appropriate.

In the matter of this "P.F." we mentioned, it would be far healthier to be vigilant for sins committed against charity rather than against chastity. To exemplify, were Father Christoph to be quite monopolized externally, or even mentally, by some other religious, and thus be taken away from the rest of us by that other religious, I think the following reflection would be called for: "I joined a religious family. I did not enter to become a recluse or a hermit. Since I joined a family, I have a right to a reasonable amount of Father Christoph's attention and time and there is a corresponding obligation on Father's part to acknowledge my right to a sensible amount of his time, attention and love. If someone else is taking him completely, or almost so, away from me and the others in our religious family, then that someone else or Father, or perhaps both, are failing, at least materially, in charity." Father Chistoph belongs to our family, and you do not take a member of the family away without any regard or consideration for the other members of the family. To do so is out of kilter. Clearly, then, in this matter, there are some dangers to charity.

Father Christoph: What are some of these dangers? Well, for one, exclusiveness. I want to be with this individual all the time. This exclusiveness usually implies jealousy. I am very annoyed if I see this particular Sister with anyone else. It bothers me no end if I feel she is even interested in someone else. "She should be interested only in me." That exclusiveness is a very great defect against charity. I do not want to share her. In religion, the others have as much call upon her socially as I have.

Again, there may be clandestine meetings in times of silence. You know if I have to be with this particular individual it suggests, at least, a kind of abnormal dependence, particularly if I have to be with this individual practically all the time. Here I have already spent recreation with this Sister and I go to my room for awhile and then I have to be with her for another hour or two. Does not this suggest that something may be getting out of hand? Again, if when I am trying to study or prepare class, or trying to pray, the image of this individual habitually obtrudes itself upon my imagination, this is out of line. It suggests again that the relationship with her is liable to be getting out of bounds. These are things which should be watched and which must be guarded against.

Father Evoy: Given the fact that as a religious you would not be afraid to love and to express this love in appropriate fashion, is it possible that this thing might tend to get out of bounds in terms of that which might run counter to purity? It is possible, surely. You are still a member of the human race. Now it is perfectly true that ever since the fall of man there have been difficulties associated with loving one another, and there is no reason why we should expect all such difficulties to be completely absent from religious life. You are women. Because you are women, if you are not occasionally attracted to an engaging man, you had better take another look at yourself and see if you are not reacting unwholesomely like some kind of a robot. In being fully real you can afford to recognize that you are being attracted to this particular individual who happens to be a man. You look at it calmly. There is no panic. You simply adjust to it by taking it in stride within the framework of your religious life.

Because in a woman affection can at times be so completely separated from the sexual drive and sexual pleasure, there are experiences of an affectionate nature between women that are highly pleasurable, and satisfying, which might have expressions ranging from talking together in real confidence without touching each other to the sensible giving and receiving of affection through embracing and kissing. None of these need involve the qualitatively distinct pleasure which is termed "sexual." Experience has shown, however, that such affectionate relationships can, even quite unexpectedly, be joined to that which is unquestionably sexual. Because a Sister is a woman and reacts as a woman, her temptations with regard to another person might persist so that she would be moist for hours or days on end with little or no moral imputability. She can experience something of a vicious circle here, since, as a woman, her spontaneously erotic imaginations can both cause in her arousal feelings and as a result of the impact of these feelings, her imagination can persist and acquire an almost unbelievable intensity and clarity that tend to monopolize her entire attention and also reinforce further the strong feelings and inclinations associated with sexual arousal. You might be surprised, and almost invariably it does take one by surprise, to find yourself experiencing feelings and emotions associated with your love for another Sister which you would expect to feel toward a man who was attractive to you. It is quite possible. Again, if it should happen, there is no call for panic.

Though surprised that the feelings and the inclinations associated with this love or attraction are those which you would expect to feel toward a man rather than a woman, this is nevertheless the actual experience. An immature reaction to such an experience is to be terrified, to throw up one's arms, to regard the one having the experience as bad, as terrible, and that sort of thing. The mature reaction is more along the following lines. In the face of such an experience one simply says to herself, "Let's see, this is something I want to do something about, because the first corrective for anything in my love tending out of bounds is my very love itself for this person."

Sisters, when St. Augustine said, "Love, and then do what you will," he knew exactly what he was saying. If I love an individual, I could never in any serious way really damage that person. I simply could not.

Now you understand that when I use the term "damage," I am not talking about a passing, painful experience which is in no way destructive to the person. Let me exemplify this. Assume that you are a very close personal friend of Father Christoph. The doctor comes to you and says, "Look, Sister, Father Christoph will not take this medicine, and unless he takes it, his life will be endangered. True, the medicine is very bitter and nauseating but it will save his life." Would you not out of your love for Father, persuade him to take it? Would you not do so even after you realized the passing pain it was going to cause him?

Your answer is clear. This type of pain, a passing thing, at times must be allowed to happen to individuals you love.

But you could not think of doing something to an individual that would make him less a person. If you really love someone, it is simply unthinkable that you would destroy that person. You could never do anything to make a particular person less a person as long as you loved that person. It is true, and should be noted here, that you could thus damage someone if you were just "in love" with that person. This in no way contradicts what I have just said. While both loving a person and being "in love" with this individual may exist together, they need not do so. Being "in love" with a person in and of itself does not exclude self-seeking on the part of the one who is "in love." But, as Father Christoph said earlier, to *love* someone always means regard for the good of the one loved.

What if a religious were to find that such an affectionate relationship had become damaging to another person? What should she do? First of all, not only would she want to change it because it is displeasing to God to carry this on deliberately once it has started, but she would want a corrective because she really loves this person. It is because she loves her that she could not thus hurt her. What should she do in order to correct? It depends. Very often it is extremely difficult to work it out all by one's self. She is so close to it and so involved in it that it is exceedingly difficult to achieve a vantage point from which to get the whole thing in proper focus. Perhaps the one person that she might be able to talk to about it might also be the one person that she could not afford to talk with because this individual is too involved.

The goal is somehow or other to keep it under control. How would you go about this? If there is a priest available to whom you might talk, you are fortunate. By this is meant that if you know of an accessible priest who, in your judgment, would *understand*, you are indeed fortunate. You sense immediately that because you are a woman it is going to be difficult to talk to *any* priest. How do you go about telling a priest who is a man, that this thing tends out of bounds in terms of purity? If he understands, you do not have to enter into any detail whatever. You sense that he understands perfectly. If he does not understand, you feel that you cannot really make it clear to him. You know that if you could talk to an intelligent, sympathetic woman rather than to a man she would understand because she is a woman. Spontaneously, you sense that there are a number of things that a man does not ordinarily understand but which are perfectly clear to a woman.

For instance, a man does not naturally tend strongly toward affection as affection. I mentioned before that a woman can separate affection and passion. A woman, even a married woman, can want affection and nothing else but affection even from her husband here and now. At this moment this is all she wants. She is hungry for affection. She is not now interested in nor inclined toward the physical aspect of the marriage relationship. Some men are aware that a woman can be looking just for affection though they really do not understand it on the basis of their own experience. Moreover, some men may even have developed the requisite control to be able to hold this relationship at the level of affection, and abundantly give affection. In such a man this kind of control would normally be indicative of very great consideration for the woman. Now remember, even this well-controlled man does not really understand how this woman, who he knows can at other times be just as passionate as he, at this particular time wants solely affection with no relationship to the physical whatever.

Often enough the woman who starts this quest for affection may find, to her great surprise, that passionate desire begins to assert itself in her. But she can correctly say to herself, "I did not start out with anything physical in my mind. I started out seeking affection only."

A religious woman could say the same thing and also be surprised by the fact that what started out as affection alone suddenly begins to express itself at the level of the passionate. If she thinks that a priest would not understand that the problem developed while she was seeking affection and affection only, can she talk to him about it? Maybe! She may be brave enough to try. Here I would like to remark, Sisters, that many priests will understand something about it and some will comprehend it very clearly.

If you could talk to a priest who would understand, you have already begun the corrective pattern. But what if you cannot talk to a priest? Then you are fortunate if you have a Superior to whom you feel free to talk about something like this. You sense immediately that all you would need would be to have a Superior say, "Oh, no! Not that!" That would be your crusher. Almost as bad would be some frightened panicky reaction on the part of a Superior. You must be able to speak to her as a person. Perhaps you can; maybe you cannot. If you can, and you find that she is understanding, you are most fortunate. I think you should know, Sisters, that it is by no means uncommon for a religious woman to feel, "There is no woman I know to whom I could completely confide everything." If you are fortunate enough to find someone you feel you can trust, then your working this thing through with someone else is less hard than handling it all by yourself. At any rate, it is good to find out that this kind of problem is something that in one way or another you can take in stride, no matter how rough the going. Moreover, it becomes something which, after you have experienced it, in God's good Providence, will enable you to be more receptive and understanding of someone else who may come to you later, with heart breaking, frightened to death by a similar problem. Perhaps by reason of having had this experience you will then have a real feeling for this other individual who is hurting, who is in need of help from someone who can understand. At any rate you can say to yourself, "Thank God, I do understand."

If you personally feel that you cannot talk to your own Superior about this kind of problem, may you go to someone else?

May you approach another religious? It goes without saying that you would not talk to a group of people about this. You should consider yourself fortunate, I think, if you can find one religious with whom you feel you could speak about this problem. She would have to be in your eyes mentally and emotionally mature, completely trustworthy and one with whom you feel comfortable. It may be that you could not talk to anyone there on the scene because to reveal it would mean necessarily identifying the other person. Unless the other person were to give you full permission to do so, you do not have the right to divulge the identity of that other person. This would be true, even though the relationship had not yet gone out of bounds. If you can find *one* person to whom you can speak about it, I think you will find that just the fact you can tell someone about it, and that there is someone who is listening and trying to understand, will be very helpful.

Sisters, there are some things that we cannot look at clearly until we can communicate them to another person. Here is one more evidence of the fact that man is by nature social. To be able to speak frankly about a troublesome matter to someone is often the beginning of the end of the problem. But what if you are unable to talk to anyone? Then you simply do what you can. This would mean working out whatever precautions you would think wise and taking whatever measures you would judge necessary to put this relationship back into the proper focus. It will be once again in focus when it fits properly with your love for her and your love for God. Between these two loves there can actually be no conflict. When it gets out of bounds with this other individual, you soon see that it is also out of bounds with God. Your love for another human being can never take you away from your love for God. Should it seem to do so, you misunderstand one of the two loves, because God made this individual and wants you to love her within your love for Him.

There are individuals whose particular cross is a heavy one. They keep getting hurt, in the sense that as soon as they get really close to someone they find the tendency of the relationship

is, in one way or other, to get out of bounds. There are such
individuals. Is it to be expected that none of them whatever
would be found in religious life? Such an assumption would be
most unrealistic.

There are many crosses which a religious might have. It might
be one's cross to have to recognize the fact, gathered from experience that her affections spontaneously tend out of bounds almost
immediately as soon as she gets close to someone. If that happens
to be her cross, her coping with it may be found in this, that she
remains calmly aware that she cannot get as close to another
individual, whether man or woman, as someone else can, because
for her this thing tends to be more difficult to control. Accordingly, she sometimes has to retrench a bit, so as to stay a little
further away from a given person in order to maintain the relationship well within the bounds of her love for this other person.

Father Christoph: Most young women enter religious life right
after high school, and very frequently they have not experienced
very great affectional attitudes toward others, apart from their
parents or brothers or sisters. Affectional relationships toward
others after being in religion for a time come sometimes as
somewhat of a surprise. Religious are embarrassed and ashamed
because they feel such an attraction. Now it is normal, as adults,
to feel attraction to the opposite sex and not terribly uncommon,
especially in the absence of the opposite sex, to feel attraction to
someone of the same sex. All I am saying here is what Father
Evoy said a moment ago—religious should not become panic-
stricken under such circumstances.

If you find that in this area you are extremely human, well
then, accept yourself. This is the mature way of beginning to face
your problem. You do not run to cover or deny the fact. You are
not frightened by it. Granted that you did not know that this
would happen to you, yet this is not inhuman. You are not less
good or less holy because you experience it. What will you **do**

with it? Your ability to handle these things is an index of your maturity.

We expect fifteen, or sixteen, or seventeen year-olds to fall in love romantically. We expect them to have crushes and infatuations. When we are in religion for some time, we forget this is still a distinct possibility. Now the way to handle this, of course, is to say, "Look, I am a human being; this is something that I have given up." Did it ever occur to you that, at least in part, the greatness of our vocation consists in this, that we gave up something that was good in itself? If the second vow involved giving up nothing, there would not be any heroicity in it. All we have to do is to keep these relationships within bounds. Father Evoy said, and I agree whole-heartedly with his remark, that you do not want to hurt in any way the individual toward whom you feel this attraction and, therefore, you will master this emotion.

Now how do you keep this thing within bounds? When do you have to worry about it? It can tend out of bounds in terms of your second vow or it can tend to get out of bounds on another score. For instance, as I mentioned, if this person occupies your mind during your meditation, if you are jealous of the attention that is paid her, if you want to occupy her time exclusively, and if you have clandestine meetings, especially after the great silence, then you have reason to suspect that this thing is getting out of bounds. It needs some attention right away.

This in no way belies the fact that you are entitled to one or two individuals to whom you can unburden yourself completely— one to whom you think you can open yourself completely, and one or two who think they can open themselves to you. If your affectional relationships with your fellow religious were right, I think you would not go around dried up affectionately. You would not be going around depriving yourselves of something that is part and parcel of our nature as human beings.

We can be defined as "loving beings," and to deny us the right to love, is to deny us something essentially human. I can say this is essentially human, but not exclusively human, and my love of God need never suffer by reason of my genuine, human love for my fellow man.

Father Evoy: There is a danger present where an individual never learns to love others. Without love you shrivel as persons. As Father Christoph said earlier, you must love someone "with skin." You must, to be mature persons, love other human beings, and the expressions of your love for other human beings should be directed first of all to your own Sisters in religion. I would go further and state, that unless a woman in religion loves someone who is very human, and through her loves her God, she has not arrived at that which she should be. She has not come, in other words, to the maturity that should be hers in life. Someone has well said, "More lessons can be deeply learned through real love than any other way."

Father Christoph: I do not think that we ought to be surprised that we have these emotions and drives, or that once in a while these may tend to get out of line. But the realization that we have *not* lost our vocation or have *not* even offended against chastity, is something that ought to give us assurance. There would be something wrong with us if we did not have these reactions to some member of the opposite sex. And I think that this is one of the reasons why, when we make the vow of chastity, it is so great in the eyes of Almighty God. We are giving up something that is natural. We are giving up something that is good in itself and, as a matter of fact, we are giving up something that is a strong drive in us. If we did not give up something that was good, something that was a strong drive in us, what would be the particular merit of the vow of chastity? It would have no more value than my giving up candy for Lent or something like that. So because we are giving up something that is very deep-seated in us, and very strong in us, we should not be surprised if once in a while these drives have a tendency to get out of hand. As adults we should recognize this, but we should also know how to handle it.

I would not, as we have pointed out repeatedly, give the impression that community life is not a beautiful thing, and a source of happiness, but I must also remind you that, as Jerome, I believe it was, put it, a monastery without charity is hell on earth. Sometimes, there is not that type of charity that we would expect to find in a religious community. While I would not go so far as to say that a specific community is "hell on earth," it is purgatory, anyway, and *that* should not be. And it is this way because religious are afraid of love and afraid to love.

Father Evoy: What of the Sister we already mentioned who finds time and time again, as she gets close to any individual who is appealing to her, that in one way or the other, this thing tends immediately to get out of bounds? It might be that she finds her attention monopolized by this person, or that the physical asserts itself, or that feelings of jealousy and possessiveness begin to dominate the picture, or some combination of these. She may have found that she simply cannot get really close to anyone without becoming involved in some unwholesome way. If this should be the case, then for the immediate foreseeable future at least, this, as we said, is her cross.

Now, some individuals have as a cross defective arches, or bad feet or something else. This person's cross is *not* going to prevent her from loving individuals, but it *is* going to mean that she must remain at a distance by no means required, for instance, of her next-door-neighbor. Her love itself is not to be limited, but she does not have the freedom which another possesses in the matter of the expression of her love. Again we point out that it is a person's love itself for another that dictates these restrictions on the expressions of love and affection which are fitting in a given situation.

Now, it might be that the individual who is particularly allergic to getting psychologically and physically close to anyone might find a certain occasion most painful. She might handle this problem of the proximity of such a person either very lightly, on-the-run, as it were, or else somehow or other devise a plan that will excuse her from the situation. This latter course would enable her, without attracting undue attention, to absent herself from that to which she is allergic. Should this be the course she chooses, then she calmly seeks to work out a pattern of interpersonal relationships which is characterized by caution that others do not need. In certain of these relationships, out of her love for the other person, a distance would have to be maintained by her, which for some other person would not be in order at all.

It might be that a Sister would find that as soon as she gets really close to a man who is, in her eyes, admirable, she spontaneously and quite involuntarily finds herself getting emotionally involved. This could very well be. Here again, in this type of situation, the stride in which she takes this whole thing, could be notably different from the stride of a Sister who does not have this particular kind of problem. More specifically, she might well find that she is unable to remain physically close to anyone of these appealing individuals for any length of time. She might also repeatedly have to turn away mentally from the image of this particular individual.

Should this be her cross, she faces it and she deals with it. Accordingly she says to herself realistically that for the predictable future she will somewhat calmly be vigilant and careful about either physical or mental proximity to certain individuals, simply because of her particular tendency to rush into emotional involvement. There is here certainly no grounds for panic of any kind whatever. She faces it and copes with it as an adult. If and when she judges she needs help, such as someone else to talk with in order to be able to handle it better, she looks about for such help.

The person who has been hungry for affection all through her life, or even at one early period of it, is especially a candidate for this type of cross. All of a sudden she finds someone at long last whom she can trust and to whom she can get close enough to give and receive affection. As we mentioned in our other book, *Personality Development in the Religious Life,* this individual very likely still has the hunger for the *type* or *kind* of expression proper to the age at which she was starved for affection.

The expressions of affection appropriate to an adult are not those appropriate to an eight-year-old. We readily appreciate the tendencies of an eight-year-old to monopolize her mother's attention. While this does not surprise us in a child, it *does* surprise us when we discover it in a person in her twenties, thirties, or forties. Yet, an older person can have these same inclinations, because the hungers for affection which she had as a young child were never really satisfied and so they are still with her. Indeed, they may even prove embarrassing to her. On the other hand, she might not recognize them as being unreasonable, and therefore would not see why she should not be able to monopolize almost all the time of another person.

You will probably remember Karen Horney's well-known remark when speaking of such a person's attitude. She said, "Her need is your obligation." Unfortunately, this is the basis upon which some people even in religion actually function. This is the type of person who would feel, if not actually say, "What do you mean you haven't time for me? Didn't you hear what I said? *I need you.*" On such an individual all the reasoning in the world will have absolutely *no* impact. Her position is air-tight. *She needs you.* Do not try to tell her anything else should interfere with that all-important fact.

Her inclinations may have a strong tendency to get out of bounds in the sense that her demands become unreasonable, burdensome, and a real imposition. As Father Christoph mentioned, even when such a one is not physically present with the person she feels she needs, she is mentally preoccupied with her while she is doing her work, and while she is supposed to be praying, making spiritual reading, or other things. All these point out the tendency of this relationship to get out of bounds.

Father Christoph: I should like to interject something at this point. I think it important. It has reference to what Father Evoy has been saying. Father has talked about these strong inclinations and tendencies. These are not a proof that a person does not have a vocation, that a person does not love God as she ought, or that there is something suspect in her affectional life. But we have these strong drives, and they serve to remind us of the beauty of our vocation, especially with regard to the second vow. They say clearly that we *do* give up something that was really worth while. And I emphasize again that if it costs nothing to serve God, then our service of God is not worth much. I think you ought to emphasize this when you talk about the second vow. We gave up something that was good and beautiful but we still have these fundamental basic drives in the sensible order. It is more understandable, I think, in view of this fact, why we need the affection of those about us, or at least of a few. I would like to add something to Father's remarks about those who go overboard.

Here is a religious who up to the present has never found affection and now, for the first time in her life, she finds acceptance. This might have a peculiar reaction in her which she immediately holds suspect because it never was experienced by her before, and she becomes frightened because this is something so different. It has some affectional dimensions. Instead of looking at this from an adult standpoint and saying, "This is perfectly all right; there is nothing unholy or the least bit unbecoming about it," she pushes everyone aside again and reverts back to that particular attitude that enveloped her life in her younger years. No one has accepted her like this and she is afraid of it.

Father Evoy: I am in full agreement with Father Christoph that it needs to be stressed and repeated that the presence of these experiences is not a sign that a religious does not have a vocation. In fact, we need to reflect on the fact that such tendencies and drives, even when very strong, in and of themselves are neither moral nor immoral. By themselves they cannot make us unworthy or unfit for religious life. Only our own voluntary actions could do that. Now I want to introduce another note here.

I once asked Father Christoph a question on the spur of the moment. I said, "Can you love someone and not like that person?" I asked him because I am far from sure that I know the answer to that question. Father indicated that he did not know the complete answer. The bearing of this on the present subject matter is the fact that when we enter religion we do not choose those who are already there nor those who come in with us, nor those that come in later.

The people who come into religion are very much human beings. Because they are, you look about you and find among them that you like this particular individual. I mean that you find her company pleasant. You are inclined toward her. It feels good to be with her and near her. It is nice to have her around.

There are others among them who do not particularly impress you one way or the other. Naturally speaking, you do not really care whether this individual is present or not. She does not have any notable impact on you one way or the other. Then again, among them you may find a particular individual you do not like. You do not know just exactly why you do not like her. What is that little jingle? "I do not like thee, Doctor Fell; the reason why, I cannot tell. But this I know, and know full well, I do not like thee, Doctor Fell." Many times we just could not say why we do not like an individual, but nonetheless we know that we do not like her and would rather not be with her. Being with her is uncomfortable.

Does your effort to love someone act as a huge eraser that wipes out the whole dimension of liking and disliking? We would be very surprised if it did. You begin to wonder what, then, can be accomplished by trying to love an individual you dislike? Later on we will develop the area of how a person goes about the business of getting to love someone. At that time, we will also indirectly throw some light on the connection between liking and loving someone. For the present, I would like to look briefly at the connection between loving and acting, at the tie-in between our loving a person and our behavior toward that person.

Father Christoph has, on occasion, startled people by telling about a group of Sisters in a small religious community who went to Communion very fervently each morning and then did not talk to each other the rest of the day. I think perhaps even worse, in a sense, is the community where everyone receives fervently in the morning and are all at least tacitly in perfect agreement on one point—that they will not talk during the course of the day to this *one* particular Sister. This kind of thing, I think is more likely to occur among religious women than among religious men. I do not think it is at all necessary to remind you that this pattern of behavior can destroy the person who is the victim.

Father Christoph: I see this kind of damage all the more clearly against the background of a remark one of the Sisters made to me today. She said that when a religious woman enters a community she gives up so much, she is even giving up herself and if we do not make some room for, or give occasions for satisfactory human-personal inter-relationships of an affectional nature with her companions, we are just taking away things, leaving no substitutes in their places, and creating an unnatural and wholly undesirable vacuum.

Father Evoy: In a way, her remark strikes me as strange. She said that she gives up herself. Is this "giving up herself" different from "giving herself"? Is not that what everyone does in every act of real love? So this giving of self is done in every properly motivated religious life. Unless ultimately the motivation of a religious is an act of love, her motivation is *not* what it should be.

I would infer she meant that when she entered religion she gave up those particular expressions of love and those relationships which she rightly might have had in the world. She was, however, pointing out that she did not give up all human love or all human affection. Hence she feels that when she finds herself wholly bereft of close human companionship and friendship, she has been deceived. She did not contract for a complete renunciation of all human love. She still needs people and knows that she should never have to give up them and their love. Our Lord reassures her that she is correct in this position.

4 *Religious to Others*

Father Christoph: We are now moving into the very important area of inter-personal relationships on the adult level. First of all, I should like to make a few general remarks about maturity in relationships to others. A well-known psychiatrist, Doctor Strecker, has said that there are four characteristics of maturity, and while this may be an over-simplification, nevertheless, if you have these you have a good purchase on maturity. The first one is that you learn how to compromise. It is quite obvious that you cannot compromise in matters of principle. But is it not a sign of immaturity, is it not childish if you *have* to have your own way— if it must be your way or no way? In anything less than principles, sometimes you must compromise if you wish to achieve harmony.

It should be understood that one cannot always have her own way. So it is the part of adults to recognize the fact that in inter-personal relationships there is need, at times, to compromise. So you give in. But you say, "I'm tired of giving in. Let someone else give in once." What difference does it make if she had her way yesterday? What difference does it make if you are going more than fifty per cent of the way?

When we plan to do *only* our share, invariably we fall short of it. If we are willing to go the whole way, perhaps we will go fifty per cent of the way. So in all our dealings with others, we can become very self-centered—not only self-centered, but even selfish. "Me first. No one thinks of me—I'd better think of myself." So my own interests, my own concerns, my own pleasures, my own satisfaction, assume monumental proportions and I am out to get "what I'm entitled to." It does not even occur to me that other people, too, have rights.

We may be indifferent to the justifiable claims other people have against us. The recognition that when we compromise we are showing tremendous wisdom should encourage us to compromise, because it takes a big person to see one of his schemes or one of his pet ideas or projects shelved for something else.

Another element is cooperation—a readiness to work with others. By definition, society is made up of individuals cooperating to achieve a common goal. Sometimes in conferences with the Sisters, in retreats and the like, I get the impression that in some communities "cooperation" is only a word and not a fact. There is a fear of giving up or compromising, and so in people's effort to maintain their own rights and maintain control over what they think they have a right to control, there is a lack of cooperation.

Sisters, the most important thing for us is the success of God's church on earth, and insofar as it affects you, it is the success of the projects of your institutes. Therefore, we must submerge our own individual likes and dislikes in the interest of the common good. You cannot achieve the common good without the cooperation of everyone in the group. The selfish desire to see that your own interests triumph may encourage you not to cooperate with others. The little portion of your own work that looms up as more important to you than your institute—maybe it is the department that you head—the jealous desire to see it surpass another religious community's department or public institution, may *look* all-important to you. As a result you are going to have what you need, regardless of how it harms the rest of the community. This is unreasonable individualism, and an undesirable trait in religious life. Cooperation builds, and the reason that we form religious institutes is the obvious fact that ten people together can do more, not only than ten people singly, but maybe more than a hundred or a thousand singly. But to do this we *have to* work together.

The third characteristic that Doctor Strecker mentions, "to contribute," is certainly a desirable characteristic in an adult. Indeed, a part of the longing to be needed is satisfied when one is able to contribute.

A fourth trait, "the ability to accept responsibility," is certainly one of the major indices of a mature person. Once one goes through the adolescent "rights" stage, the recognition that responsibility is a correlative of being on one's own becomes manifest.

Father Evoy: What I would like to develop here ties in very closely with what Father Christoph has been saying. It is that in religion we must, from the very beginning, develop a sensitivity to other persons. We must be most perceptive of other people, so that we become "people conscious" in every way. In this context we think immediately of the divine precept which says that our approach to God should be together with other people.

Father Christoph: This turns the spotlight on the development of a social consciousness that we are working together, that we are in this together, that, for example, I cannot get very far without you—I need you. I have to be conscious that you are beside me and helping me, even if I am physically alone. Father Evoy is saying, in effect, that we can never exercise too much sensitivity to the reality that *we are one.* What needs to be stressed greatly is the over-all delicate sensitivity that we should have to people.

Hence it is necessary to cultivate a Christlike sensitivity to others. This should be the general orientation toward everyone. This sensitivity is characterized by a recognition, first, of the fact that others are persons. You know it is easy enough for us to wrap ourselves in our dignity and to conduct ourselves in an unbecoming way in dealing with inferiors—those who are entrusted to us, whether they be college girls, high school girls, or boys and girls on grade school level—by being bossy, condescending, aloof, demanding, needlessly severe, and at times, boorish. We must never forget that they are human beings. They are persons; they likewise are made to the image and likeness of God. Sometimes this image is frightfully obscured, but if we knew their backgrounds, if we knew how they struggle to be as good as they are, maybe we would be a little more sympathetic toward them and less condemnatory.

We can do a tremendous amount of good or harm simply on the basis of our attitude toward these individuals. Are we sympathetic? Are we understanding? Are we ready to forgive? Are we careful of condemning? Do we engage in double talk? Are we unjust and unfair? Are we so wedded to our own opinions that we reject the justifiable inquiries of the students relative to what is done? Do we lie? My dear Sisters, one of the things I have heard most often condemned in religious women is that they do not tell the truth.

Self-justification is ingrained in all of us. We want to be right. We do not like to be found wrong in the decisions we make. Sometimes we may act immaturely; we act in haste, for example. Then we justify our action, and to do this, we sometimes do some little violence to the truth. I think that the fathers and the mothers, the boys and girls, the Catholic and non-Catholic world, will excuse practically anything in a religious—they will excuse the worst kinds of faults; but one of the things they will not excuse or tolerate in religious men or women, is not telling the truth.

This is something I want you to think about seriously, because through your religious training and your knowledge of moral theology, you may sometimes be able to justify some of the things you do—but if you cannot justify them before the people who are concerned, you create a problem. Most people have a very high regard for honesty. We have to be sensitive to the sensibilities and sensitivities of other people. What hurts me, hurts other people. I must be very careful that I give no unnecessary hurt to anyone. You will recall that Cardinal Newman's definition of a gentlemen is "one who gives hurt to no one."

That is the type of sensitivity we mean. The things that hurt us, hurt other people; so to "bawl out" youngsters, humiliate them in front of the class, is to hurt them. What do we gain by it? You know, in self-justification, that we always do it for their own good; but I wonder how many times we are actually achieving emotional release because we need it.

This sensitivity means kindness and consideration for people with whom you come in contact. We can hurt without meaning to hurt. Once a man in his twenties came to me. He was no longer practicing his religion. He had gone to a Catholic grade school—and when I asked him what happened, he told me when he was in the fifth grade, he had brothers and sisters above and below him in school, and his family was very poor. He went on to tell that at Christmas time the weather was very bad. The youngsters were sick and the children did not have the clothing to go to school. One of the Sisters in the school said to the others, "Let us take up a collection and buy this family what they need." Now, I cannot think of a gesture more kind on the part of this particular Sister.

But when the children came back to school after getting all these nice things at Christmas time, the Sister in the fifth grade made the boy get up in the front of the class and thank the members of his class for their kindness. Surely this Sister lacked an appreciation of the sensitivity of other people. I suppose she thought she was teaching gratitude, but she succeeded only in scarring him by a needless and ill-considered humiliation.

Father Evoy: The example Father just gave rather amazed me. I do not believe I have ever heard him say that before, and it sounded as if he had been listening to the narration I had heard. The story given me is different only in that the Sister took up this collection for the family, and announced in the class in which the youngster was, that, "Because they are poor, we are going to take up this collection for these children." Then she named them. It is very understandable that this person has never gone back to Church, even as an adult.

Father Christoph: People can be and are deeply hurt. It is very easy for us in religion to become self-centered, although our whole training is designed to make us other-regarding. We may become very zealous and concerned about ourselves, our rights, and the like, insofar as we retain rights in religious life. It is interesting to observe to what extent we can transfer some of our interests from one area to another.

A leading psychologist in this country points out that some of the natural desires for possessions manifest themselves in religion in the desire, say, to retain things that are permitted. This psychologist gives a whole list of possibilities with which the vow of poverty may be concerned—pointing out the way the human mind is able to get around things. The point I want to make is that we in religion become deeply concerned about our rights and our own egos, and sometimes forget that other people, too, have egos and rights. There is a lack, very frequently, of sensitivity to others, to the rights of others, to the needs of others. I think that this can be exemplified in a number of ways. We can make one individual the butt of all kinds of jokes. We are insensitive to the feelings of others when we are harsh in our judgment; when, on the pretext of being outspoken, we say cruel things.

Father Evoy: It is much easier to give charity than to accept it, for it takes a good deal more virtue for us to accept something from another than it does to give something to someone.

Father Christoph: Ronald Knox, speaking on a B.B.C. broadcast about the Golden Rule, said there are very few people who cannot fulfill the first part of the Golden Rule. But the second part, "as you would have others do unto you," brings out that there are many people who are unwilling to have things done unto them. Perhaps it is because they are afraid they are going to be beholden to another. Knox said we have the example of Christ, Who was administered to by the holy women; Who had Joseph and Mary to take care of Him while He was a Child; Who was carried across the Sea of Galilee by the fishermen; Who accepted the ministrations of friends and dined with other people as their Guest. It is a sign of sensitivity and graciousness to allow others to help you.

Sensitivity means, therefore, that we do not refuse the little acts of charity, the kindnesses that people, even though they are embarrassing at times, wish to do for us. When people with good intentions offer things, it is a sign of maturity, or urbanity, and of Christian charity to allow them these acts. For years I thought it was the mark of the mature individual to do everything for himself, not realizing that people would like to do acts of charity for another. I remember a man saying in this connection, "I feel sorry for people who have nothing to give, because they are being denied one of the greatest satisfactions of being a Christian. People want to give."

It may be that the giving takes the form of only a kind word, and if we brush this off because we think our vanity is being fed—we can give real hurt. Jesus Christ did not object, I am sure, to St. Joseph's words of commendation when He turned out a good rung for a chair or something like that. Can you imagine Christ saying, "Oh, it's nothing"?

If it is good—admit it. When people compliment us, it is part of humility and charity to *accept* the compliment. We have to be sensitive enough to realize that we hurt them when we do not allow them the privilege of thus giving us something. This is but another way in which we can lose touch with people.

Father Evoy: As apostolic religious, if we should lose touch with people, we lose a great deal. There is the real danger that we can lose sympathy for people. There is a very solid reason why a religious can readily fall out of sympathy with people in their problems, trials and tribulations. Let us be concrete about this. As a religious, you go to bed at this particular time and you get up at this other particular time and you know that unless something very unusual happens you will have a full night's sleep. No one is going to disturb you until you get up. You may, therefore, not be particularly appreciative of a youngster who leaves home upset and comes into your class by no means the cheerful, bright youngster you would like to see there. It is easy for you to become insensitive to the fact that the undisturbed sleep of your night's rest may not have been true of hers. You may not even have a suspicion that the mother has fed the baby every two and one-half hours during the night. Each feeding of the baby required a half-hour; it took the mother a good half-hour to get to sleep again. She had probably one hour's sleep when the baby awakened her again with his crying. Again the heating of the bottle and another half-hour in feeding the baby; another attempt to get to sleep, less than an hour's sleep and again another feeding. This was the picture when none of the children was ill.

In the morning the mother dragged herself into the kitchen and with nerves on edge screamed at the child now in your class. We do not even mention what has happened when she has had a fight with her husband or has been otherwise particularly upset. At any rate, the little child arrives at school all disturbed, and here you are expecting her to be bright and cheerful. Are you in the real order? Do you wonder about it when you find yourself thinking, "This is a naughty child. This child needs to be disciplined"?

Sisters, if we love people, we want to understand them. Really to know them we have to know them in the world in which they are. Until I do know them and appreciate how they live and what some of their problems are, it is difficult really to feel for them. They have all kinds of problems, you see. But we are not really apostolic if we are withdrawing from these people. We are not mature if we are hiding within the sanctuary of our own little religious castle, psychologically drawing up the bridge across the moat so as to keep the world and its problems out and confine ourselves to those who are taking refuge with us within the walls.

No matter where you live, Sisters, if you happen to be in a place where there is no contact with people outside, you can be as isolated for all practical purposes as if you were living in an Indian wigwam out in the wilderness.

Father Christoph: Why did God give you your neighbor in the first place, anyway? He gave him to you not to withdraw from him, but to love him. Just as there are still filial love, maternal love, marital love, there is the love of God and there is a different dimension of God's love—love for your neighbor.

Father Evoy: The real welfare of others should be of great importance to you. While charity begins at home, it certainly must not remain confined there. Charity rightly understood is love. Mature love seeks knowledge of the one loved. This knowledge of those religious persons whom you are supposed to love does not always seem to be there. Father Christoph and I have stated repeatedly that religious suffer so often because they are afraid to love. We have said that there need be no limit on your love for other human beings, and moreover that your vow of chastity, which has infrequently been offered as the reason for not loving others, is itself the very thing which *frees* you to love others.

Because your life is lived under a vow of chastity, you do not have the natural obligation of devoting a major portion of your time and attention to members of your immediate family. It is because you do not have a husband and children of your own, to whom you would have to devote yourself, that you are freed to spend yourself for the individuals with whom you come in contact within the framework of your religious life. In my judgment, some of the hesitancy of religious really to love others originates in a lack of clear understanding of human love. By and large, for instance, people do not draw a clear line between one's love for a person and the expressions of that love.

A little reflection shows us that a woman's expressions of love for her husband are quite different from those for her children, and yet one love is just as genuine as the other. In each case, her love selflessly seeks the good of the other, and through her love she gives herself to the other in the way that is most suitable to the particular relationship. We remind you again that it is of the utmost importance that, as religious women, you realize that the expressions of your love for any individual are going to be the expressions flowing from a woman's nature. This is what we meant when earlier we said that the expressions to which you will be inclined are going to be quite different from those natural to a man.

By nature, a woman hungers for love; hungers to give herself to one or more persons. For her, love means a *giving of herself* and a receiving of the other's love. Just as she gives herself in love, so she also desires to receive not just *things* from the other, but to receive the other *person* in love. With a man, there is the urge to express his love by taking, by protecting, and by guarding, rather than primarily by giving, even though his love requires the exclusion, as far as possible, of self-seeking motivation.

Jean Guitton, among others, agrees that perhaps no married love can be wholly free of self-seeking and perhaps even selfishness. So the aspect of giving of self seems more characteristic of the woman's love, and even though the man's love need be no less altruistic and considerate than hers, it does not seem to have as its principal inclination that of giving self. It is nature that has equipped the woman to give her own life to others. The tendency to give herself and receive the loved one physically is but one manifestation of a woman's need for love. She may give herself in many other ways, and she cannot really love and not give herself.

She may have a strong tendency to do things for another and

she may give herself in and through what she does for another. A
woman who loves, often finds herself impelled to give to the one
loved some personal thing—something, for instance, that would
be worn on the person of the loved one; or she would like to take
care of something belonging in some way to the person of the one
loved.

It is very clear to a woman why she might want to do the
personal laundry or care for the personal attire of one whom she
loved, whereas a man, for the most part, would not as readily
understand this. Neither would many men comprehend a woman's natural inclination to treasure over the years some personal
gift from the one she loves, irrespective of its monetary or other
practical value. This thing which she treasures somehow retains
for her the person of the one loved, in a way that would be
bewildering to most men.

Sisters, I believe that a man's need for love is no less than a
woman's; but his need to love and be loved exists in a dynamic
pattern notably different from hers. For instance, a woman could
experience a strong urgency to seek recognition and prestige for
herself, as well as for her religious community. But for a woman
to know she is loved, wanted and needed by the person that
really counts in her life—this is the thing of real moment. This is
it! These other things are secondary. If she feels that she is not so
loved, all the prestige in the world, all the publicity and recognition, will not fill the resulting vacuum experienced in her life.
Clearly, no woman wants to be loved because she is needed. She
does want to be needed because she is loved.

Now, we treat of another facet in our discussion. As we said, it
seems that a woman's expression of her love is always some kind
of a giving of herself. Besides, human love tends to find tangible
expressions, and since you are women, the expressions of every
genuine love incline toward those proper to a woman's nature.
As we mentioned, the one thing that might demand that a curb
be put on a given expression of your love, and especially of your
being "in love" with someone, would be the *love itself* for that

person. There can be considerable difficulty for both men and women because each does not clearly understand the expressions proper to the love of the other. For this reason, at times, the limitations imposed socially on the expressions of a woman's love strike her as most unreasonable. In the case of the man, such limitations seem in order, since he is fully aware of the impact on him of certain expressions of a woman's love for him. A man knows that affection is inflammatory. By and large, more control is required in his affectionate relationships. A woman would be surprised were she to find that her expressions of love tended to run away with her. This can happen to her, but it is ordinarily not expected. For a man, usually there is not this element of surprise, because he is aware of the involuntary out-of-bounds tendency characterizing expressions of his love. For him, control is clearly called for, but it is a control not of his love, but of a given expression that his love would tend to take. Of course it is his love itself that is dictating this control of its expression.

To be perfectly candid about this, more than one woman, including religious, has actually seen no reason at all why she should not put her arms around a person whom she loves. If she even suspected that this might be troublesome to the man or woman concerned, she simply would not do it. In general, both the giving and the receiving of expressions of affection are somewhat more passion-linked in a man than in a woman.

If a woman were to see that she was hurting or even troubling another individual by her expressions of affection, she would then and there have all that would be needed as a deterrent, all that would be needed in order for her to refrain. Just as soon as the delicately perceptive woman sees that a given expression of her love is becoming problematical for another person, out of her very love for that person she immediately curbs the distressing expression.

Father Christoph: For instance, I love this person so much that I do not want to do anything in any way that would diminish this person before God or man, and therefore this means for me self-control, self-discipline. It means respect and esteem for the dignity and moral integrity of the other. Is that not what you are saying?

Father Evoy: Emphatically. Sisters, so often a woman does not understand how a man reacts. The corollary of this, unfortunately, is that neither does a man understand how a woman reacts, and hence he can so easily misinterpret her expressions of love and affection. This would be especially true when he does not know her well. He might assume that she reacts on the whole as a man reacts. A woman is capable of passion just as is a man, and even of intense passionate reaction; but a woman is also capable, with no great need for controlling herself, of unalloyed affection and nothing else at a particular time. This is something which is foreign to a man, in whom affection is much more closely associated with sexual expression than in a woman. In a given man there might be sufficient control over the various fitting expressions of affection, but such would not necessarily be presumed, whereas such a presumption could normally be made in the case of a woman.

In many religious communities of women throughout this country there exists the highly commendable practice of bringing in an experienced physician, who in a series of talks explains to the young religious women the facts of life. Moreover, often in this country, seniors in high school receive some enlightenment in this area in a course on marriage. These are fine, and yet even with these helps there are any number of problems along these lines that do not arise until considerably later in the life of an individual. There are troublesome facets of loving another person which probably will not confront a religious until she is in her twenties or thirties or even forties. Incidentally, this is also to some extent true of religious men.

When a woman enters religion she willingly gives up marriage and everything that marriage could mean. She freely renounces this kind of intimate, personal relationship with another human being, as well as the tremendous human experience of bearing and rearing children of her own.

Yet, for the most part her renunciation was the renunciation of a straw man and straw children. The man she gave up was not this particular attractive man whom she later encounters, and the children she gave up were not her own offspring. This is why Father Christoph and I have insisted that here, as in other areas, she should fully face her experience as it is. This includes her awareness that perhaps for the first time she has the realization of what a tremendous human adventure is this relationship to husband and children. Accordingly, for a religious there is a need for recommitments to her vocation in view of these newly arising aspects, not really seen or appreciated by her earlier.

If religious would do this, I think a number of torturing experiences that sometimes occur later on could be prevented. The turning away from such realizations is invariably unhealthy if such is the characteristic way of dealing with them. Obviously, I am making a distinction here between the understanding which might carry with it involuntary feelings and tendencies of a sexual nature, and any activity that would be the voluntary carrying out or promotion of these tendencies and feelings. Accordingly, I am in no sense saying that the individual ought to go ahead and follow through on the inclinations unavoidably associated with what is presented mentally.

Let me exemplify this distinction in another kind of experience. Say I am angry with someone. I do not have to go ahead and actualize my urge to say something sharp to this person or to strike him, but I am insisting that I should recognize that I am in reality angry. In addition, I feel the anger flowing through me, now. Just as to feed deliberately that anger once I have clearly looked at it would be immature, so there are areas such as those concerning my second vow where, after having calmly viewed the full implications of my renunciation, I deliberately and calmly turn away because these do not belong in my state of life. This would be no more unhealthy for a religious woman than it would be unhealthy for a married woman to recognize clearly that someone other than her husband was indisputably attractive to her, and then calmly say, "Fine. Now I'll try to put these thoughts aside because they do not fit into the framework of my married life." This is simply wisdom.

Father Christoph: Father Evoy has been talking about the affectional dimensions of love, and he mentioned there is a difference between the male and the female, which is pretty obvious, but which, I think, is not adequately appreciated. Father remarked that there could be certain manifestations of affection which for a woman would be purely legitimate and have no sexual connotation. That is true, I think, but we have to recognize the fact that men do not always understand this. Indeed, if a Sister wanted to show only affection to an individual, with no sexual component whatever, and so put her arms around him, he might suspect that she was interested in him physically and sensually and was looking for a response of some sort. He might think that she was unhappy in her vocation and that he could pursue this thing further and then he could put his arms around her. He would most probably misinterpret her action.

Father Evoy: That is a good point. In our culture we do not ordinarily do these things. Not that this is merely a cultural overlay, but in our culture we normally do such things as shake hands with people by way of a friendly gesture, and a man and a woman who are friends do not ordinarily put their arms around each other, or at least remain in each other's arms. It is one of those things that simply are not generally done in our culture, and especially in religion. Aside from members of their immediate family, religious do not put their arms around members of the opposite sex.

Now while there might be some difficulty with regard to a woman's putting her arms around another woman, at least there is not present in the other person this basic need for the understanding of the sex differences, both psychological and physiological. The embracing of another woman does not really parallel the difficulty of the man endeavoring to understand a woman and of the woman endeavoring to understand a man. Yet, despite these real sex differences there are also similarities. By way of an illustration, it is unrealistic for us to suppose that complete control over the display of affection is present not only in every man but also in every woman. On one score or another, we all, both men and women, need some restrictions on some of the expressions of our affection and love. Let me exemplify this. If a Sister taking care of old people in a hospital were to put her arms around the male patients and kiss them goodnight, this would be regarded as an unusual way of saying "Good night."

Moreover, because of the sex differences involved, the realistic supposition is that this would prove somewhat troublesome to some of the men, and it could very easily be misunderstood by them, even though it would not bother the Sister herself a bit. The same would hold true for a Sister who would put her arms around a boy in her class, especially if that boy were close to adolescence or were already in it. He would have real difficulty in grasping the meaning of such behavior and it might very well trouble him. In fact, he might somehow feel that this particular Sister was teasing, or was endeavoring in some way or other to awaken some kind of response.

Yes, awaken a kind of response that would not be intended by her at all. So we return to the point that it is love itself which must dictate any needed restrictions on the various expressions of love. There is not *any* question whatever of inhibiting or suppressing love itself.

A good lay nurse in the world, I believe, would not embrace her male patients in the evening, at least on the score that it would be forbidden by her code of ethics. As far as any physiological impact such an embrace would have on her, it could be that it would be negligible. But the recognition is there in the code of ethics that there could be ethical implications were she to practice it. In fact, the ethical implications would most likely come from consideration of the effects on the man rather than on herself, but they would be there, nevertheless.

This nurse would therefore have the same attitude as a Sister of genuine love for the patient, but she would direct her love into acceptable channels. So, as a religious, your love for other people postulates a sensitivity toward them. Accordingly, from the very beginning of religious life you should be very concerned about others, and I do not mean about them just in as far as they are children of God, but also precisely in as far as they are persons. You should be concerned lest they be hurt, and really feel for them when they are hurting; you should be vigilant for their welfare; you should be solicitous about their needs. You should care because you love them. You should be concerned about each and every one of those you know.

Sisters, in this matter of really loving others, I think there is a danger that we can move into words, words, words, while concealing behind them our lack of true interest in other people. There is also a danger, and it is a horrible one, that our charity has about it the mark of condescension. It is unfortunate that the word charity today should have the connotation of something condescending or patronizing.

Surely the concept of genuine charity, which embraces doing to others and also being done to by others, is something to which we ought fully to subscribe. There should never be any condescension in human relationships. To condescend means to look down upon. Charity should never be that. It should be a relationship of a *person* to a *person*.

There is an additional consideration here, particularly relevant to a woman, in terms both of her loving and being loved. The love for another person, whether proceeding from a woman or being received by a woman, should be strong and stable enough to weather changes and variations in mood, temperament and disposition. As a woman's bodily chemistry changes, so frequently her feelings are altered. Today she is feeling wonderful, positively radiating, and is very easy to like and befriend. Now, there is no problem in realizing that you love her. But what about next week? Then, you find that you cannot stand her. Maybe she cannot stand you, and perhaps she cannot stand herself. Why? Because of the baffling, bewildering impact of the change of her bodily chemistry on her feelings and her emotions.

If your love for her is a genuine love, then it is a love of the whole person and not just of something about her. It is not a matter of loving her when and because she is cheerful and pleasant company. Since you are a human being, when you genuinely love someone you are to some extent emotionally involved with that person. If you are not, you can begin to suspect the genuineness of your love. But, because of this involvement, your emotional reaction may be very notably affected by the change you see in her emotionally; and this, therefore, is something regarding which you must be on your guard. You love her as she is, for better or for worse, no matter what. You hope that she will be her best in every way, but you realistically recognize that you have no guarantee whatever that she will be, and that it would be preposterous to expect her not to have her emotional ups and downs.

Father Christoph: The sensible dimension of human relationship is human love. If I am a human being, I love; and I cannot exclude the sensible dimension if it be real love.

In your dealings with others it is not necessarily true that your friendship is going to destroy their respect for you; that what you are doing for them, or your interest in them is going to create the wrong kind of affectional relationship. In one area of relationships we do have a special kind of problem. Social workers are always cautioned not to become emotionally involved with the individuals with whom they work, since this becomes a threat to their effectiveness, because the moment one becomes emotionally involved the objectivity of approach may disappear, and quite frequently does.

There is no social worker, nor any Sister engaged in the social apostolate, who has not at one time or another become emotionally involved. How do you reconcile now, not becoming emotionally involved, with the opportunity to give yourself to these individuals most generously? Well, I think the answer consists in this, that when you accept the other individual as a person and love that individual because he or she is a person—there need not necessarily arise this kind of personal, emotional involvement which is a threat to your relationship. You know the limits of sympathy and empathy. No one says that an empathic attitude toward a client or toward a child or toward a student, necessarily implies involvement. There is no contradiction, therefore, between being able to give yourself to individuals and to love them with this purified supernatural love, accepting them as they are and creating a tremendous attitude of rapport yet without becoming emotionally involved. Becoming emotionally involved hinders our work; hence we must be alert to the dangers of our apostolate, prudently and maturely handling interpersonal relations without involvement.

Father Evoy: Subject to correction from people who are expert in the field, I think that much of my apparent difference with Father Christoph on this point is one of semantics. At any rate, I would simply say that if you do not become emotionally involved with someone you are helping, there is something very seriously wanting.

Father Christoph: That is just why I used the word "empathic" relationship.

Father Evoy: All right. We are differing in words only, I think. I am fully aware that the wrong kind of emotional involvement can be a genuine hindrance, a real detriment in social work. A

Sister is not this youngster's mother, and unless she fully recognizes this she is not being realistic. Moreover, if she develops any kind of empathic relationship that leaves in this individual an unhealthy dependence on her, this is not good. On the other hand, unless this individual feels deeply that she does care about him as a person, in my opinion at least, she is going to be far less effective in her work with him than she should be.

But what I dread above all in the realm of social work is what might be termed "organized love" or "organized charity." I have real respect for the whole area of social work and social service, and I think you sense that we are both *simpatico* here.

The danger in the social work areas, then, is a twofold one. The peril of hurting people may come from either of two extremes. One of the extremes is that there would be the wrong kind of hurtful emotional involvement with someone. The other kind is that social work would become a cold, officious kind of functioning in which the individual is treated not as a person but as an object to be classified, categorized and dealt with accordingly. As far as this last mentioned danger goes, its logical reduction to absurdity is seen in the remark that, "It is only a matter of time before we can dismiss all our social workers and replace them with I.B.M. machines, which will do the classifying faster and more efficiently."

What needs to be emphasized is that your dealings with other persons must be on the basis of a personal relationship. It *must be*. It must be the kind of personal relationship in which these other individuals feel that you do like them, you do care about them, you are concerned about them and—I think it is not the wrong word to use—you *love* them.

Especially in your relationship with children should you be mindful of one well-established psychological fact. I wonder if even to this day you have an awareness of the impact that you have on the individual youngsters with whom you work. Do you wholly appreciate the fact that to the child you are dealing with, you are something of a colossus—a giant? Moreover, you are a giant who is in a position to crush or thrill a youngster simply by reason of the fact that in his eyes you like him or do not like him, you care or do not care about him. In placing such a tremendously great evaluation on your reactions to him, the child unwittingly teaches us all a lesson of the greatest import about our relationship to other people. We actually become our distinctive selves through receiving in so many ways from other people. And they become largely what they are through receiving from us.

Through social intercommunication we enter into other people and they enter into us. It is perhaps principally from the little child's social reactions that we learn to become really aware of the impact we have on other individuals. From these tiny persons we discover the fact that we enter into their being, become part and parcel of them, so that their view of things, their scale of values and their attitudes, are ours. But ours become theirs only after they know that we like them; that we want them; that we care about them. Nothing less than that, I believe, will do. Every one of us who has had teaching experience knows that it takes an average youngster in a class perhaps three weeks to discover, regardless of what is said, whether or not a teacher really likes him, really loves him.

The very size that a teacher has in the eyes of a child places her in a position to do almost indescribable damage, with perhaps no realization on the teacher's part that she is doing any hurt at all. This is one more area where we can slide imperceptibly into a lack of sensitivity in terms of our dealing with people. And Sisters, this can be done by us without any realization on our part that we might be particularly damaging with the children, simply because we are the giants and they are the children, and we forget the tremendous impact we have on children.

Father Christoph: This is spelling out in the case of children the tremendous sensitivity that we *have* to have towards other people. This sensitivity is indeed a sign of maturity. To accept people as they are, for what they are, is adult. You know, the

older I get the more I am convinced that there is relatively little
malice in the world. When people act, they act for a purpose and
for an end. Everyone wants to salvage as much of and for his ego
as he can. Everyone wants to feel important. Everyone wants
acceptance. So when people act in a manner which we may characterize as malicious, all I can think of is that they must be
driven by terriffic needs, and they are compelled to secure them at
any and all cost.

Father Evoy: Perhaps incorrectly, I infer from Father Christoph's
remark that we may go ahead and love others even when they
give the appearance of maliciousness, because in reality there is
no malice present. Now, while I normally would hesitate to mention this in his presence lest it go slightly to his head, Father
Christoph does happen to be a very generous, charitable, and
kind invididual. Nonetheless, I do not feel that it is necessary on
any score to exclude all malice from persons in order to regard
them as lovable. Augustine said, "There, but for the grace of God
go I." All human beings, I think, are capable of malice and I do
not feel that I have to explain away their malice in order to love
people. I am maintaining that the individual is lovable even
though covered by an overlay of real malice. In a word, I do not
have to find an individual "not guilty" in order to love him.

Father Christoph: Many of you are dealing with children who
have been badly hurt by others. Because of that they have developed within themselves, even at an early age, a crust or veneer:
"I don't care; I don't want anybody; I don't need anybody."
Actually, their history is simple: they were not wanted, they were
not needed. Rejection brings about counter-rejection. Hostility
engenders counter-hostility, and these individuals have felt the
sting of hurt because once they loved, or at least were capable of
loving or being loved, and were rejected. They survived, but they
could not stand a repetition of the original, so as their best
protection against being hurt that way again, they pretend and

act, and even cultivate a kind of indifference to the affectional approaches of others.

In dealing with these youngsters, the first thing you experience is their defiance, their indifference when you suggest that they do something because it is the nice thing or because God loves them or something of that nature. It becomes meaningless to them— they are on the defensive. Their defense has an ambivalent pattern, because they will do things to attract attention, which is perhaps the nearest they can get to acceptance and (notice) do it safely.

Because they are callous, cold and unresponsive, it is hard for you to find any affection in your heart for them. As a matter of fact, they even go out of their way to make themselves disliked, because they are afraid that if they ever should break down they may love you and allow you to love them, and if they do, they lay themselves open to further hurt. They cannot afford to be hurt again, and so they carry on in this fashion.

You should recognize that the vast majority of difficult individuals with whom you come into contact at the juvenile level are individuals who have been hurt. Therefore, they will do things that are mean and nasty, and they will in this way reflect that, "Sister does not like me because I talk out of turn; because I am obstreperous; because I am always fighting." They are afraid that if they *did not* do these things, you would still *not* like them and then your dislike would be because of themselves as persons. This would reinforce the fear that they have, or the experiences that they have, that they are a "nobody," and this is too crushing for their egos, so they automatically, without recognizing it, cultivate this kind of a pattern.

Then when you do reject them, you are just falling into the trap they have prepared. It is hard to accept these individuals, but they are still human beings. They still have the needs of every human being for love and affection. If you have the patience to bear with them, sooner or later they will lay themselves open and show a little more of themselves, expose their hurt because they want you to assuage it. Not to be aware of this causes those who deal with them to treat them as "things." You do the best you can. You make them behave. But you are never getting to the root of their problem—you are not correcting their defects of character and you are not remolding anything, you are just tolerating them.

Without any expert training in this field you can cultivate sensitivity. Father Evoy seemed to disagree, but I still insist that the individual acts and reacts to his needs. That is why I say I do not think there is much malice in the world. I did not say there was none. I think there is very little malice; so individuals by even vicious activity are trying to satisfy in some way, and the only way that they know how, their needs. If we have a more sympathetic attiude even to the villainy of individuals, I think we can accept them a little more and we may be able to help them.

Father Evoy: Really, I must say I do not disagree with Father here. His over-all position is that there is very little malice in the world. I could go even further, I think, and say there is very little malice even in the majority of sin. Does that make sense?

Father Christoph: Yes.

Father Evoy: Sins normally come from human weaknesses. Now I do not think that Father would say that all personal culpability must be removed before a person becomes lovable. This matter of judging another person's culpability is a most difficult one. As a matter of fact, even as confessors, we do not have to form with certitude the judgment that a particular confessed sin is clearly a mortal sin. We know as confessors what "gravity of material" is. In a given situation the person himself or herself says, "Really, I do not know whether all the necessary conditions were present or not: therefore, I do not know whether this was a full-blown mortal sin." Neither do I know. As a confessor I need not know

that. I am absolving from this sin sincerely confessed to the best
ability of the penitent. Where you would have unadulterated
malice in sin, I think the person *would* know. Where you have,
as you almost always do in the sins of human beings, one or the
other type of human weaknesses, is it easy to be sure of the degree
of culpability?

Perhaps that is why it is so difficult for us to understand the sin
of the angels. We keep coming up with the unanswered, "Why?"
The fact that in the case of the angels, sin was demonstrated once
and for all to have about it an attractiveness even to an angelic
intelligence, simply shows what can happen, but does not show
why. I would agree with Father Christoph that there is very little
malice in the world, and yet fully consonant with this is the fact
that man can do things that are morally imputable to him and
very seriously so, even things out of malice. Nevertheless, beneath
this unlovely overlay, he remains basically lovable.

Father Christoph: One Sister asked me the question, "How does
sincerity in facing the reality about people correlate with charity?" We have to be careful about bluntness. There is an attitude
current that you are mature if you face facts and do not mince
words—that if you call a spade a spade, you are an adult. I ask:
"Do you *have* to hurt people's feelings on the score of honesty?"
After all, if it is not our position to correct, and if we do not
know that this individual will accept it, we should overlook it.
If we feel that we may correct, then charity demands that we do
not hurt the individual's feelings. We get our point over as
gently as we can.

You know that the more I am aware of my defects, the
more I am hurt when they are called to my attention—and that
is because we are not animated pin cushions. The truth hurts,
too.

Father Evoy: At times I wonder if we do not confuse honesty and
frankness; I wonder if we do not assume that the person who is

not frank is therefore not honest. In genuine charity I must always be considerate. Now there are times when, out of considerateness, I think it better not to tell an individual something because it would needlessly hurt him. Am I being dishonest because I am not being frank with him?

5 *Religious to Religious*

Father Christoph: How do mature women get along together? Someone has remarked that no home is big enough for two women. If you reflect on relatives and the like, where a mother has moved in with her son or daughter, or where a married daughter has moved in with her family, there is always a conflict because you can have only one boss. This especially is true in the case of women. It seems every woman wants to be "boss," so there is a kind of basic psychological problem in the area of women getting along. The evidence of this is overwhelming in the business world. Women do not mind being under the leadership of men, being bossed by men, but women find it very difficult having women bosses.

In religious life rules are laid down, the outlines of which are usually well-defined. They require that there be a Superior at the head of the community and that the rest of the individuals in that community be subject to her.

Father Evoy: We already remarked how lonely some religious are. There are those who feel so alone that they exist as a stranger among strangers and the norm for their social behavior reduces itself to the question, "How does a stranger act with other strangers?"

You understand, of course, that I am not stressing the obvious, that there do exist religious communities which very closely approach the ideal in the matter of the relationship of one member to another. You are also aware, and I need not labor the point here, that there is tremendous happiness in certain religious communities. I am not so much concerned about that here and now. It is with its absence that I am concerned.

We can throw a bit of light on such absence when we advert to some of the things that can take place in religious life. To begin with it is wholly possible for a religious woman to have her relationship to God become a private, personal matter which is exclusive of all other persons. From her point of view it is a matter of "God and I, and I and God"—it is a closed system. Furthermore, she may in all good faith be living her life on the assumption that her love for God alone and God's personal love for her are for her the one and only way to work out her perfection.

From such a vantage point, other persons would only get in her way, would, in fact, somehow or other distract or deter her from the pursuit of her perfection. She does not even as much as surmise that this type of closed exclusive system is in reality a monstrous thing. Looked at correctly, it is as if a religious were to say, "I will simply love the God-man personally and disregard entirely His Mystical Body." She may not see the contradiction it would be to try to reconcile this position with what Our Lord said about His followers, namely, that they would be distinguished not by the fact that they loved God, but rather by the fact that they loved one another. This love for their fellows was to be the sign that they were His followers. It was a matter of, "See how they love one another."

Father Christoph: The distinguishing characteristic of Christianity is love; *a fortiori,* the distinguishing characteristic of a re-

ligious community should be love. I never go to a religious
community—whether I am there to give lectures or a retreat—
without someone telling me, "Emphasize fraternal charity." I do
not want to be told what to say, and I would resent a Superior
telling me to mention this or that or the other thing. But a
remark like this I do not mind, because first of all it is well-
intentioned and it is not too specific. Just, "Speak about fraternal charity." And I plan to speak on it, anyway.

But is there not something wrong with our attitude if there is
this ever present need? Why should we have to be told to be
charitable? Are not the members of our religious community our
own? We are bound to each other by a very real bond. We have
the same institute; we have the same goals; we have the same
authority placed over us. We are like-minded. If we are often so
like-minded, why can we not be like-willed? After all, love is a
dimension of the will.

Father Evoy: I have a slight suspicion, Father, that you are over-
stating the easiness of our loving one another.

Father Christoph: Did I not say that love was will-dimensioned?
That does not make it easy. I would like to comment on Father
Evoy's remark that since Christianity is to be known by and
recognized by the earmark, "See how they love one another," this
should be even more true of religious life. I believe he said in
substance that he was somewhat surprised that there is not more
real love in religious life, in the religious communities themselves. Would this be reasonably correct?

Father Evoy: I am not surprised, to be perfectly frank, at the lack
of it. On the other hand, I am pleasantly surprised at how much
I do find. Why? Because, Sisters, community life is not a natural
unit of social interaction, of social living. I do not say it is unnatural, but I say it is *not* natural for women to live *solely* with
women or, for that matter, for men to live all together with men

only. In such a social group all those natural helps flowing from blood relationship, as well as the sacramental helps which God gave to marriage, are absent.

In religious life you find yourself living according to a pattern quite different from that which you would follow socially in the world. Were you outside you would endeavor to pick and choose your companions. You would pass up this one and seek the company of this other one. In religious life you take them all. You may not pass up anyone. But you have not changed your human nature. Some of these individuals who are with you in religion are such that you would not naturally choose them for your friends and companions. Just because they are good persons, does not necessarily make them good company. Yet you find yourself living with them day in and day out. It is for these reasons that if you should do only what comes naturally, I fear you would not love very many of your companions. And if any community should slip almost imperceptibly into doing just that which comes naturally, I am afraid there would be precious little love in that community.

While people in the world must work at it to make a success of the society begun on the basis of personal attraction, and known as marriage, religious must work still harder to establish and to maintain a community atmosphere in which there is real love, one for the other. Sooner or later we find that any kind of living together socially is a task that is perhaps without parallel in life. And living together in religious community has its own peculiar difficulties.

This matter of loving one another in religious life demands that you give not just things, but yourself, or it will not work; because true friendship and genuine love can settle for nothing less. It is implicit in this statement that you give yourself even when you are afraid to do so. It means you give yourself when you do not naturally "cotton" to this person. You give yourself because she is your Sister, and because under God she is another member of the Body of Christ, and especially because she is, precisely as a person, worthy of being loved. You must continually work at loving others, because religious communities of women are not made up exclusively of persons to whom you are personally attracted.

That is why I feel that I have some difficulty with Father Christoph's remark. I maintain that this loving one another in religious life is a type of activity which is often admirable, on the score that it lacks any expediting foundation established by God in man's nature. In some ways at least, loving one another in the natural unit of the family has aids which are *not* to be found in religious communities. Would you agree or disagree?

Father Christoph: I agree. When I talk with individuals who have a problem along this line (and I do not care to what community they belong—whether men or women), I find myself making this remark, "Where will you find so many people, outside of religious life, so like-minded and so concerned about doing a good job and actually as charitable as religious?" The constant effort that we have to make to be charitable is extraordinarily rewarding, but we *have* to work at it all the time because as Father said, there are these natural antipathies. I do not choose in religion. I choose my companions only insofar as I became a member of this community, and then I am thrown in with this one and that one and the other. However, within the group there is a certain amount of choice.

But then the type of charity that I am supposed to extend to everyone is certainly not a result of just a fellow-feeling of kinship. We have the same interests and the like, but it is because they are my Sisters in religion that I am to love them, not just because they are people. I remember our Tertian Instructor telling us once in an exhortation, "The life of a priest is a lonely life. You have to learn how to live alone." He then went on to speak about the loneliness of a priest. After the instruction, for some reason I had to go down to his room and I said, "Father, I don't think you finished that instruction." He said, "Why?" And

I said, "Because we are priests, and we are also religious. Does not being a religious compensate, and should it not compensate, for the loneliness that is intrinsic to the priestly state?" He said, "That is right. Remind me to tell them tomorrow because here we have something that the average diocesan priest does not have." But we *do not* make enough of it as religious. As religious women you entered religion, not to seek your salvation by yourself without the aid of others, but in cooperation and with the help of others.

Father Evoy: Sisters, I have the impression, at times, that people assume that priests and religious are lonely because of their state of life, and that had they chosen another state of life, specifically marriage, this whole feeling of loneliness would have been completely unknown.

We have to be most realistic about this. It is true that as religious you have given up the potential that marriage had to diminish the feeling of loneliness that occasionally, at least, is yours. But the assumption that marriage of its very nature removes completely and wholly from individuals all feelings of personal loneliness is certainly not substantiated in fact. How many individuals have returned from their honeymoon, surprised to find that their experience of loneliness, which had preceded their marriage, to a large extent still remained? Their surprise was that marriage did not once and for all remedy this feeling of being alone. Marriage does not completely wipe this out, and this has been testified to by men and women throughout history.

It would be unrealistic, then, for religious to assume that the experience of loneliness or "aloneness" is exclusively theirs, and due moreover to their religious state, and accordingly is something that would not be there at all had they chosen the married state. This side of the grave, man is never so completely fulfilled by another person or by any other source as to lose entirely his "aloneness." It was to this, I think, that Augustine was referring when he said, "Our hearts are made for Thee, O Lord, and they will be filled only in Thee." Man, by reason of the fact that he is living in this world, is still at least occasionally aware of some lack of personal fulfillment by another, and perhaps this is never for even a short period wholly removed from him. It would be just as erroneous for religious to seek in their relationship with other persons the prospect of complete removal of these feelings of loneliness as it would be for two people to hope that marriage would somehow or other accomplish this same thing, so that once and for all they would never again feel lonely.

Just as the actuality of marriage often falls short of the ideal and, therefore, fails to remove this loneliness to the extent of its full potential to do so, so religious life is not always operating at the ideal level and likewise does not realize its full potential for reducing these feelings of "aloneness."

I do not believe that it really will be news to you when I tell you that there are communities of religious women in this country which are divided into factions. Does this astound you? The splitting of a given community into segments may be done on any one of several bases. For instance, you might have the Superior lining up with one group while the remainder of the community might be over on the other side. You have even such things as divisions in religious life between the "haves" and the "have nots," or between the "ins" and the "outs." There are other grounds for separations, as, for instance, age. There are divisions rooted in educational groupings and flowing from educational advantages. Let me be more specific in this last area. There are certain members of religious communities who know that they have been passed over, while they witness the younger members being permitted to acquire the advantages of training and adequate preparation for their proper fields. There are religious holding down positions today who face with dread the inevitableness of displacement by a younger person who is now receiving the academic or professional training currently demanded for the position, and, lacking which, they can no longer hold down such a position.

You do not have to look very far in religious communities before you find a group of younger Sisters who get along very well together, but who do not really talk to the group of those they consider their elders in the community. These "elders" are often the middle-age group, among whom are those who have already been replaced by the youngsters and who, as a result, at times feel bitterness, hurt, jealousy, and envy. A great many things rankle in them. Among these "elders," particularly, are to be found some who know what it is to feel alone.

Father Christoph: Here I am. I am lonely and no one comes around. Maybe I am demanding too much and giving too little. Maybe I drive people away by my attitude. As a mature individual, one of the marks of my maturity is to accept what *is* when it cannot be changed. You know the little prayer of the Alcoholics Anonymous. Let me translate it into a more Catholic context. "Dear God, give me the grace to change the things that must be changed; to accept the things that cannot be changed; and the wisdom to know the difference." I want the serenity to accept that loneliness which is mine, because sometimes it is going to be there. But remember it is a sign of maturity to accept what is, and what cannot be changed. So instead of being bitter about my loneliness I can at least make a virtue of necessity. On the other hand, as a member of the community I have an obligation to go out of my way to do what I can, if I see someone who is lonely, to try to be more companionable.

There is no way I know of in which we can screen candidates for a religious community so that we get only the type of people that mix well. Now, let us face it. Some are socially awkward, social misfits. They get into the community and they have a hard time, and they may make it hard for others. But you have to live with them.

Father Evoy: I have been asked in this connection, "Is not the isolation of an individual from the rest of her community often a conviction of her own and not brought on by the members of her community?" I would have to answer "Yes" and also "No." You see, when an individual withdraws from the community, she stays away from others. She has a long face and usually does not invite anyone to come close. What is your reaction to her as a member of your community? Your inclination at least is to look at her, shrug your shoulders, and say, "I am going to go with somebody I can talk to, and not someone who may snap my head off or be cold or probably turn and walk away from me." In that sense, something of a vicious circle is started. If you withdraw, you pull yourself away and repel people from approaching you. You begin to feel and to say that people do not like you.

This is not paranoid. This is accurate. *They do not.* Why should they? You will not let them. You do not give them the time of day. Why should they like you? You remain forbiddingly distant from them. Psychologically, at least, you turn your back on them and they know it. Hence the answer to our question becomes clearer. In reality, as a person withdraws she often pulls herself further away from approachability. She reduces in herself social availability. She is not *there* anymore. Since she is not there, others like to be with people who are there. And people who leave and rebuff others tend to be disliked, and to be left alone.

Nevertheless, it should be recognized that the Sister who noticeably withdraws from the community withdraws because she feels she must. She has to withdraw because she has been wounded, because she has been hurt. To the extent that she stays safely away, she begins to receive negative attitudes from others in the community, for whether they realize it consciously or not, they are disinclined to approach her. Is it not true that when we encounter a person who is most friendly we tend to reciprocate in this regard? There is a counter-pleasantness that we show to this person. When we walk into the presence of another who is cold and distant, do we not also tend to reciprocate by pulling back and staying away?

Father Christoph: So it is something of a vicious circle.

Father Evoy: Yes, and in terms of the community factions and divisions we were just treating, I think that many of the individuals in one faction do not invite anyone's approach from the other group. At least this appears to be part of the factual picture. Once this is the case, just waiting the thing out is not going to heal the breaches. One is forced to ask, "What, if anything, can be done in such a highly charged situation?"

By way of answer, I should like to recount for you that some time ago a certain Sister who was in what might be called the younger middle-aged group, and comfortably close to her own group, was also deathly afraid of the "older Sisters." On this particular day she was walking in the yard when she noticed, over on a bench, with a sphinx-like set to her features, one of the older Sisters. The latter was just sitting there looking most unapproachable. This younger Sister hesitated in the struggle with herself and finally said to herself, "I don't care. I'm going to do it, anyway." And she walked over to the older Sister and said, "Hello!" The older Sister looked up, glanced around, and seeing no one else about who could have been thus addressed, answered, "Hello." They began to talk, and little by little the features of the older Sister began to thaw. After some twenty minutes in close conversation they were very comfortable and pleasantly relaxed. The older Sister paused for a moment and spontaneously asked the younger one, "Why did you come over and talk to me?" The answer came immediately, "I just wanted to see if you were real."

What I did not tell you, because I know that I do not need to tell you, is this: When this younger Sister walked over, she really needed her religious garb so that her shaking knees would not show. She was that afraid. She could have been shattered if this elderly Sister, who to her was one of the formidable ones, had turned and rebuffed her one way or the other. Had this happened, she would have actually dragged herself back into the house, and you can be sure it would have been a long, long time before she would get up the courage even to contemplate doing this type of thing again. But she dared to do it that one time. Because she did, she achieved most satisfying results. The reason she succeeded so well is not too difficult to grasp. Sisters, we maintain that the basis of our coexisting harmoniously is our love for each other.

Now, if we love each other we simply must communicate. If we are not communicating, if we are really not talking together, it is difficult to understand how we really love each other. Or if someone maintains that even without communicating we still love each other, I candidly admit that it is a type of love that I do not understand. Our example shows clearly among other things that, at times, to talk to other individuals, to cut across or knock down walls that are there in religious life, takes courage, tremendous courage.

What I am going to say now, I say subject to correction. I think that perhaps many of the younger members of the community have greater strength to tear down some of these psychological walls than have most of the older members. For that reason, maybe the younger ones should go fifty-two percent of the way so that the older members will have to come only forty-eight percent. This is, as I said, subject to correction. Nonetheless, it seems to me that many of the Sisters who, at least in their own estimation, have been bypassed, and as a result are hurt and bitter and feel that they have been treated unjustly, are scarcely in a position to make the first move. In addition, they feel now that they are *not* contributing to the community and are not even fulfilling any useful function in it, and so are not disposed to come even half the way.

After all, the feeling that she is not really contributing anything, that she is not doing anything useful, and, moreover, that she is not really needed is very, very hard for a religious woman to accept. Often enough, the resulting bitterness, resentment, and stand-offishness is not felt primarily toward this or that particular younger person, but rather toward any one of them, because she happens to be "one of them" who have taken over and displaced the older ones. On the other hand, it is not inconceivable that the older ones *do* have a real foundation for a grievance, because you and I know that experience can be a valuable teacher.

I think it goes without saying that there are people who learn from experience and there are people who simply experience but seemingly never learn. The supposition here is that these older people who have had a great deal of experience have learned something, and that at least a part of what they have learned could benefit the younger Sister and make her a better instrument in the office she is fulfilling in the community. How often are they asked by the younger ones to share this experience?

Father Christoph: I think there should be mutual respect for everyone in the community. It must be pretty obvious to practically all of you that the division that Father speaks of between those who have had all the educational opportunities and those who have not is a real thing. I can sympathize, but I must also remind those who have borne the heat of the day that they were good "plug-horses." They did their job with inadequate training and preparation and now that someone better trained and better prepared comes along, they must yield. I can understand the feeling of being pushed aside. If the common good is the thing that the older Sisters deeply appreciate—and they should—then because it is the end of the institute to improve its way of achieving its end, they should be very happy to have more competent people doing these things, representing the institute. They should welcome the fact that they are supplanted.

I come along with my Ph.D. degree. That does not make me a better religious, and that does not make the one whose place I am taking inferior to me. This is part and parcel of the price we must pay to be effective in our apostolate. We have to have preparation, and thank God we are not now being sent out after one year of novitiate, and maybe one year of college. It took this older Sister fifteen years to get her A.B., and another six to get her M.A. Today Sisters have better preparation. There should be mutual respect for each other's contribution.

On the other hand, the younger generation—those who have had all the opportunities and who have capitalized on them—should have a tremendous amount of respect for those who have gone before them and who are *bene meriti,* who have in their own way been giants, because they tackled such huge programs with sometimes little preparation, but with tremendous confidence in God. And they did a pretty good job. This should beget mutal respect.

It is only when we are living for ourselves and are very self-centered that we become envious and resentful of the achievements of others. So Father Evoy is successful! "Well, hooray for my side! We've done it." I vicariously enjoy his reputation. I feel good because one of ours has made it. One of ours has accomplished something. Again, it does not make any difference that I do not even have an education. That is not important.

The important thing is that one of your Sisters is making her contribution to the common good, and by the same token, then, the lowliest individual in the community—the one who has been set aside now because her eyesight is gone or her hearing is bad, and who no longer teaches and does not have something to do to enhance the prestige of the community—yes, the lowliest participates in Sister's achievement.

Even those who are no longer physically able to make their contribution in work can make their contribution in prayers. We are all members of active communities. But normally each active community has two groups of contemplatives—the novices and the retired religious who are unable to contribute actively. The effectiveness of our apostolate depends on the cooperation of everyone, and especially on the prayers of these.

Someone has to lead, someone has to come out in front, someone has to be more important, but whether or not I am the one out there should not be my concern. The important thing is that we are working together to achieve this end. So religious should be very conscious of the respect they owe to each other.

I have a little problem with small communities. So many of our religious houses in the West are small, and this poses a real difficulty. I know of a house in which there are three Sisters. One is in her eighties, another in her forties and the third in her twenties, and I think that is unfortunate. Now, the one in her twenties came to me and said, "I have nothing in common with them outside the habit that we wear, the Office we say, and the fact that I am teaching in the same school."

You know what we have here? We have the equivalent in society of the grandmother, the mother, and the grandchild, have we not? Superiors should recognize when they make assignments that these things may have to be done this way in special instances, but it is nice to have as a companion-Sister one who is more or less your age peer. I like to be with people about my age—they understand my attitudes, etc. Hence there should be some regard by Superiors for compatibility as far as age is concerned; otherwise, it does make community life unnecessarily hard. You say that the woman in her twenties can look with admiration on this other woman in her eighties. Yes, but the eighty-year old woman is talking about Sisters and events that happened before this young Sister was born, and this can be boring to the young. There should be some age compatibility if possible, it seems to me.

Father Evoy: Unquestionably. I might add one distinction which I think Father has taken for granted. A person chronologically old is not necessarily psychologically old. A person even as early as her fifties may be able to talk freely about things that happened thirty or forty years ago but about absolutely nothing that is current. On the other hand, a Sister in her seventies may be as contemporary as this morning's edition of the newspaper.

Sisters, what needs to be stressed is that everything, including the personnel in the convents, should be considered from the point of view of increasing and enhancing the love of the Sisters for each other. Harmonious living together does not just happen spontaneously. We mentioned the rents in some communities. There are breaches and gaps and there are walls we spoke of between one group and another. I think we can live together for years and years, but these factors tending toward disunity will not naturally incline toward taking care of themselves unless we do something about them.

It seems important to reflect back on and emphasize one point. Since my doing something about this means personally approaching another individual, I can never take the personal risk out of it. Every time I do it, it is at least a risk if it is not a gamble, because I have only a chance of getting away with it. To go up to this other individual means to drop my guard and leave myself open. As such, I can be cut down completely. This individual can confront me with the equivalent of, "What do *you* want?" and I think it would just about finish me.

As we said earlier, I can love a person only insofar as I know that person. Now, as far as I can judge, when Our Lord said, "A new commandment I give unto you, that you love one another," implicit in that was that we get to know one another. I do not think I can really love the girl baby who has been abandoned on the bank of the Yangtze Kiang, because I do not know her. I can have some feeling for such infants as a group, and about their abandonment, but I do not love them in any real sense, because I do not know them. I do not think I can love abstract humanity. I love Joseph, Mary, Bill, and Lillian. I love individuals, but I love them only insofar as I know them. Love happens to be something that proceeds from one person and terminates in another person. Obviously, we are using the term loosely when we speak of loving things.

Certain statements have been made in this area that would lead us to believe that we could increase our love for someone simply by willing its increase. Frankly, I know of no way of directly increasing our love for any individual, but because of this close relationship between love and knowledge which I just mentioned, we can seek opportunities to increase our knowledge of this other person, and to that extent the increase in our love will take care of itself.

Notice that my *motive* in trying to get close to this individual, at least as close as she will permit me to get, is love. Often my love for Christ must be my principal and even sole motivation for my efforts to get to know another person. But my activity, thus motivated, is going to result in an increase of my love for her, to the extent, of course, that she is willing to let me come close to her.

Let me see if I can clarify this. This individual whom I now approach largely from love for Christ, may be someone I have been living with in the same community for many years. One reason I do not really have much love for her is that I have never come to know her. Now, while it is almost solely my love for Christ that takes me closer and closer to her, provided she will let me come close, I will come, I think invariably, to love her also for her own sake. You will have no difficulty in seeing that we must, in our generosity and out of our love for God, start to do something about loving each other. What we do, it seems to me, is not directly to turn on our love in some way, but rather to try to get to know each other better.

You remember the song, "Getting to know you, getting to know all about you . . ." from *The King and I*. This may very well be, it seems to me, the threshold to getting to love someone. How do we get to know each other? The only way I know consists in the endeavor to get close to someone and takes the form of a genuine effort to listen to, attend to, and notice a particular person. If we could do this, I think we might be able to mend many fences in religious life that have been broken down. Perhaps I should talk of rents in the community fabric, rather than fences. At any rate, if we went about it correctly I see no reason why we could not repair these tears in the fabric of our community (social) life.

I do not consider myself unrealistically idealistic when I say I see no reason why love could not be the one salient characteristic of any given religious community. My basic reason for this statement is that no matter how much I might be tempted to wonder whether I am being too optimistic, Our Lord did not think it was optimistic. He said that this was the way people would know that these persons were His disciples—that they had love one for another. Note that Our Lord said this was to be something which was to be so evident and manifest in them that others could see it. Since He expected it, it must be within the order of our possible attainment.

It is peculiar how often we are almost driven back in our considerations of the mending of rents in the body social to the point that we are not what we should be unless we love God; and, moreover, we cannot love God unless we love each other. It is that simple. No matter how we spell this thing out, it comes back to that same thing.

Father Christoph: May I push that a little further? The love of which Father Evoy has just spoken should be also characteristic of our regard for other religious institutes. "Who are these up-starts—this other community? We were here first. We are the largest; we are the best." Suddenly we find, not so much the desire to excel *A.M.D.G.*, not so much to do something for the kingdom of God, but rather that we cannot afford to be second best to the Sisters of the other community who think they are pretty good, so we are going to prove that we are a little better. Sisters, today the apostolate is so important and makes so many demands upon everyone that there is room for all of us.

With over one hundred thousand Sisters teaching in the United States, it is difficult to determine accurately how effective or ineffective they are, but I suppose a case can be made that Sisters could be more effective. But if it is God's work and some-one else is doing it, let us give her all the support we can. If we are doing it, we should expect the cooperation of others. There is room for everyone—there is work for everyone. We should be very pleased when we hear that some other organization, some other religious community, is going to start a school, is going to start a hospital, is going to undertake this work or has so many novices. We *should* remark, "Thank heavens someone is getting the novices."

There should be that largeness that extends beyond the limits of particular good and embraces the common good. There is the common good of the community of which you are a member, and there is the common good of the whole Church, and this latter should be of most concern. This should come before the common good of the institute. So there should be the generous out-going spirit for the good works and accomplishments of other religious communities. There is no room for envy and jealousy. It is not only unbecoming—it is un-Catholic, and frankly immature.

Father Evoy: We must be most realistic. When we love each other, we love each other as we are. You love a person as she is. You do not say, "Sister, stop that. Change. Start to be cheerful and alter your whole pattern of behavior and I will consider loving you." You wish she would change, but you must love her as she is and the "as she is" might include the fact that she feels very bitter toward a number of persons, including even you. This means, in effect, that when Sister in your judgment is resentful, forbidding, and withdrawn, you go to her at a personal sacrifice because of your love, despite your feelings and your inclination to give her a wide berth.

At this initial stage of approaching such a one, your love is largely in terms of will, because you have not made the break-through yet to human feelings in this love. You must operate in terms of what you *should do,* rather than what you feel, in order to love her. And by loving her I mean genuine acceptance of Sister and not anything whatever in the line of tolerance. Please, tolerance is for animals, *not* for human beings. We do not tolerate human beings, because to tolerate, at least in the strict sense of the word, means to take a condescending, superior, patronizing attitude, and no matter who I am, I may never licitly look down on another human being. To do so would, in effect, be to look down on one of Christ's members and would also be to look down on one who has the same inviolable human dignity as I. This other person is also at the apex of God's visible creation.

Father Christoph: "Do I love by just saying it? I know I do not feel it." No. You love by willing it, but you know, willing is in the domain of doing. You do something about it. I love—I have to do something about it, and so I do the things that love demands. Now, I do not *have* to feel it. It is unfortunate that many of us do not have the affectional side of our nature as well developed as we have other aspects. So I may not even feel my love for Almighty God, and this is a genuine problem with many people. "I don't feel. Do I love? I am more conscious of hurting my neighbor than I am of hurting God—that is, I have a feeling of shame and sorrow if I have caused someone to have a long face, but if I were to offend God, I do not have these same feelings."

Remember, we say in moral theology that our love of God has to be appreciatively the highest, not affectionally the highest, because this is not always possible, since the affectional is more noticed in our inter-personal relations. The proof that my love of God is genuine, even though it does not have the affectional aspects found in the love of my neighbor, is the fact that no matter what happens, I will not offend God. Unfortunately, the feeling element is sometimes almost entirely absent.

Father Evoy: I think this still might sound a little theoretical, as though we were speaking from a philosophical approach not too meaningful to you. But we are talking to you about the real order and not just about theorizing; and that is why you expect us to communicate to you, as far as possible, that which is drawn primarily not from reading or from reasoning, but from our experience. Specifically then, what experience have we had in this particular matter that we could pass on to you which would fit within your framework of loving people?

Sisters, I can give you only my own experience, covering an average of several hours per day over better than the past twelve years. It is largely in the area of dealing with individuals who have come to me in a counseling relationship. Let me begin by saying that in this experience I have clear evidence that I still belong to the human race. Why? When these individuals first come to me, I find certain ones strike me as being interesting and attractive persons, while others do not make much impression on me one way or the other, and there are some few others who make an unfavorable impression on me. It may be that these last mentioned somehow or other are felt by me to be threatening or that I experience them as pushing or crowding me. I am not sure. It might be that for some wholly unrecognized reason, I simply react to them with uncomfortable feelings or dislike. This initial experience with many, many individuals cuts across the entire gamut of feeling reactions in me from the positive to the negative. This kind of reaction, I think, is the accumulative indication that I still belong to the human race.

Now the important consideration here is that as these individuals proceed to let me come closer to them, to let me see more of the real person in them, they almost invariably include in this display of the real self the record of the unlovely aspects of their personal and moral history. What has been my reaction to such revelations? My experience, without any exception, to the best of my knowledge, is that as I have come to see more and more of the real individual—and this despite whatever heavy overlay there might be of socially and personally unacceptable behavior, I find the following. I could say that I find something in each of these individuals that is lovable, but, I think it would be far more correct to say that as my knowledge of the real person increases, I discover that the person himself or herself *is* lovable.

As the counseling proceeds I am not sure what words would best describe my subsequent reactions and my attitude toward these persons. Perhaps I might attempt a description. I find myself spontaneously becoming more interested in each of these individuals as an individual; caring about the person, and especially about the person as this *particular* individual. I find that it really begins to matter to me what happens to this person, and while my feelings can vary notably with the person concerned, I think that it is correct to say that as my knowledge of the *real* person grows, I find that also my love for this person spontaneously increases.

Sisters, this is not theory and not book knowledge; this is drawn directly from experience, and among other ways in which it has proved beneficial to me has been the fact that it has enabled me much better to understand, in a way which formerly I did not so fully appreciate, how God can love *every* person individually. He knows every one and He knows each one as no one else knows that one. Even God cannot love a vacuum. He loves that person, who, as that person, is lovable. He constructed that person intrinsically lovable, and as I in my own small, finite way come to know more and more of this individual, I also discover that this person is lovable. And Sisters, in my own experience, I have not found a solitary exception to this.

This real lovableness, I want you to understand, seems clearly to allow for degrees of difference. There are certain individuals who are my special friends, just as there are individuals with regard to whom I am much more aware of my love. Moreover, there are individuals that I love in a particular way. But when I get through looking at all the variations on love, I come back to the one point, that love of another person always says a real acceptance of this other person, insofar as this individual makes this possible by letting himself or herself be known to and by me.

For years we have known that love generates knowledge. So,

for example, when two people love each other very much they are frequently unable to conceal from each other what they are feeling and experiencing. The woman who loves someone very much often knows what he is going to say before he says it, and knows when he is concealing bad news. But what we have not reflected upon is the point being made now. To come really to know a person is to come to love that person. I am convinced on the basis of my own experience that any given person will be found to be lovable and actually become loved by us if and when there is a real increase of our knowledge of the real person who is this individual. To state it succinctly then, it seems that not only does love beget knowledge but it also seems correct to say that knowledge begets love.

As I mentioned, Sisters, this does not in my experience exclude people whom I at first disliked. There were indeed people whom at first I was aware I disliked and admitted, at least to myself, that I disliked them. Later on these persons did not prove exceptions to what I am saying.

Father Christoph: Well, I do not think that we have any disagreements, even when some time back Father Evoy apparently disagreed with me. Because the question was, "Can you will love?" It is an act; you have to will it; you have to do something about it. Father adds that the more you know the person, the easier it becomes to love the person.

Father Evoy: So the position I am taking is that I go about the business of loving someone by trying to move in to further and further knowledge of him. And how do I do that? By going out toward him in whatever way I can. This means, as well, the opening to this person of my own doors so that he can get to know me.

You are well aware that genuine love never operates on the basis of giving *in order to* get a return. But as far as we know human love, whenever we love someone, we *want* a return of that love. This is not the same thing at all as giving in order to get. Rather, this is a giving of self without any guarantee of return, but a giving which is accompanied by the desire for a free return. Love often does bring a return of love. This area seems to be so important that we should develop it somewhat.

As I spell out what we actually do in order to get to love someone, does it include trying to work up feelings of love for that person? Do we endeavor to work up an act of love in our will toward that person? We begin with the recognition that we may have no positive supporting feelings at the initial stage of our loving someone. We know also that we do not *have* to feel it. Our first act, as Father Christoph indicated, is an act of will which takes us, in whatever way is possible and prudent, closer to the knowledge of this person.

Let us be even more specific. As a member of this community you do not really know a particular Sister. Your first act is to say to yourself, "I'm going over and talk to Sister." You are fully aware that this is a testing situation, and that you may get deeply hurt in attempting to talk to her. Nonetheless, to the extent that you are willing to go out and repeatedly try to get close to others, I think that you can successfully crash the fear-originated walls between many religious and get through to most of these persons.

Now, Sisters, since I am spelling this out for you in terms of my own experience, I would be less than fully honest were I to conceal from you that there is one characteristic of my own dealings with people which may not be verified here. For the most partt the persons to whom I talk come to me. You understand? They have come to me first and in this sense have thereby taken the first step toward coming close to me. But when you decide to walk over and talk to Sister A, who stands aloof, you know that she has in no sense invited you to do so. Moreover, if she has been displaced from a job or otherwise by-passed or forgotten, you might suspect that she is sensitive, at least on the score that her opinion has not been asked and that her knowledge has not been sought. In addition, she may well feel that she has been through all of the mistakes that these newcomers are making and could have shown these people how to avoid such mistakes, but frankly, no one has asked her. So when and if you dare to walk over to her and break the ice, no one need tell you that this is a perilous thing to undertake.

Father Christoph: The supposition is, which is true—you cannot love what you do not know. So you have to know before you *can* love. But of course, as Father said, it works the other way: once you love, you can also know the person more. There is something lovable in every one of us. When we do not love it is because we have *not* found that thing.

Father Evoy: Jean Guitton, in his *Essay on Human Love,* points out a real danger to religious women. While Guitton is not speaking exclusively about religious women, he is including them in his treatment of unmarried women. His remarks to which I am referring, are, in my judgment, somewhat too strong and yet, as I mentioned, he does point up a real danger. The burden of his remarks is that if the unmarried woman fails to love, she can, with the passing of the years, readily become bitter, severe, and even masculine in her personality and filled with regrets for never having loved. He goes on to say that this is the reason why, among unmarried women, sanctity is more characteristic of youth than of old age.

This is a very severe indictment. Yet, Sisters, I think that this points to the real peril, that if a religious woman does not love other human beings she can dry up into a most unlovely, shriveled-up person. She can gradually change until she finds herself cut off from the warmth and reassurance of personal companionship, facing life alone, cynical, skeptical, suspicious, unloving and unloved, and perhaps, in the eyes of her fellow religious, even quite unlovable.

You are fully aware that there is always danger involved in loving someone. Here and now it seems well to point out that genuine love inevitably means a form of personal involvement. There is no such thing as an *impersonal* love. The type of involvement found in genuine love must be one of donation of self, when and where and in the manner such giving would be for the good of the one loved. To be loved is to be fulfilled, and to love and be loved in return is still more personally fulfilling. If every love is a personal love, so every real friendship is a particular friendship. The difference between love and friendship is that love can be a one-way thing even though desirous of a return, whereas friendship always involves a mutuality of love.

Friendship exists where a person's genuine love for another is returned by that other. The personal involvement is in terms of caring enough to want to benefit, enrich, and better the other person. A friend is one from whom you do not have to conceal. Your friend is one with whom you share. The deeper the friendship, the less need be concealed. A true friend accepts you as you are, for better or for worse, and you neither have to prove anything to him nor do you have to meet any kind of standard of expectations he has established for you.

Father Christoph is fond of quoting Horace's classical definition of a friend, namely, *"dimidium animae meae"*—"the half of my soul." The other definition, an *"alter ego"*—"another I," is also very well known to you. In as far as you regard a friend as "another I," you need not conceal from him. But because, in another sense, this other person is also his own "I," which is not yours, he can by the act of giving himself to you enrich you with that which you do not have, just as you by giving yourself to him can complete his being.

Sisters, Father Christoph and I are both conscious that we must keep this development very close to reality; hence it is fitting that we look still further at the practical aspects of the actual happenings in a person's efforts to love another member of the community. Remember I said that the initial difficulty is greater because you are not always approached by the other individual and, at times, you feel that an advance on your part might be interpreted as an invasion of the other person's privacy.

This area needs to be studied closely. For instance, how can Sister X be reached when she withdraws from you? Not only is there a wall of ice present at personal meetings, but on passing you in the hallway or elsewhere she looks down or turns aside from you. With a chosen few she is amiable and has personality plus. However, you find that if you join the group she just does not see you. Conversation is never directed toward you by Sister, though others in the group readily accept you. As far as she is concerned you do not exist. What are you going to do in such a situation? In this area, I think all of us agree, that you do what you can to get to know her. Now, starting from this point, I frankly admit that I, myself, lean perhaps too far towards the safe side in terms of anything that might be regarded as a violation of the personal privacy of someone. For that reason, perhaps I would be more inclined than some others not to press, pressure or crowd another in any way whatever. But what of you? Regardless of what you do, you can know an individual only insofar as she lets you know her. If you have the courage to approach her time and time again, without making yourself a nuisance, you are not only admirable, but close to heroic. True, she cannot hurt you now as deeply as if she were your friend, but still she can hurt and hurt you incomparably more than any mere thing in existence can because she happens to be a person. Moreover, she has a greater potential to hurt inasmuch as she happens to be a person about whom you care, as far as she will permit you to.

Father Christoph: You cannot force a person to accept you. No matter how much you want her acceptance, if she is not going to accept you there is nothing you can do about it. You try—you can keep coming back to her and she will begin to recognize you, know you and learn more about you, but you *cannot* make a person like you or want your company. I would, after making a number of attempts, be inclined to say, "Well, I'll be friendly but I'm not going to embarrass this individual, because it is pretty obvious that she is not interested in me."

Father Evoy: Some time back when we were discussing this matter, one of the Sisters said, "I see no reason why I should tell my personal affairs to every Sister who is curious enough to ask. I think busybody religious should find something more important to do than going about the community asking questions that are none of their business." I agree with her perfectly. Actually, I do not know why the subject came up, because I surely hope that we did not give the impression that a Sister should go about telling her personal affairs to every Sister curious enough to ask. This is not a matter at all of letting a lot of people know about your personal life; rather, it is letting persons come close enough to you to know you and, according to your ability and desire to do so, to leave yourself "open" to be known by certain individuals. By no means do you have to answer the questions of any "busybody" about your personal privacy.

There is the possibility, at least, that the one who takes the attitude that she is not about to tell her personal problems to everyone could be a trifle on the defensive. It could be that anyone approaching her in an attempt to get close to her would be automatically decreed by her to be a "busybody." Aside from this possibility, I agree wholeheartedly with her that a busybody religious should find something more appropriate to do, like knitting, for instance.

Father Christoph: I agree. It could be a defense mechanism. You go walking around like an accident looking for a place to happen and someone says, "What's the matter, Sister? You're down." She is not a busybody! You have given every evidence that you are unhappy, and out of solicitude Sister says something to you. If you do not want that kind of solicitude, then do not go around with a long face, because we thus invite this type of concern and it would not be reasonable to call it "busybodyness." But it is true—you do not have to expose your soul to anyone and everyone who is curious. That is ridiculous.

I would like to add the following by way of a corollary. I have reference to the spirit that should exist among religious. Usually there is an *ésprit de corps* in the religious family as such, but not infrequently things that should not be divulged to the public are broadcasted. To put this more clearly within the framework of maturity—everyone of you has been a guest in the home of a relative or friend when some very small child began to tell a story to the guest, which was a great embarrassment to the father or mother. The child treats of things that you should not know and you are embarrassed. But we expect this from children, so we smooth it over as much as we can and have a good laugh with the parents and generally forget these things. Now as mature individuals we ought to keep what belongs within the bosom of the family within the bosom of the family.

Not infrequently, little problems will come up within the community, such as differences of opinions among Sisters, or between the Superiors and Subjects, or even criticisms of Superiors, which are then divulged to the laity and, I might add, to the scandal of the laity. Our love for each other should have about it a kind of cohesive loyalty, and as a result of this we do not relay to the laity, to externs, what does not properly belong to them. We all know this.

But frankly, we do not all possess prudence, and the fact of the matter is, things are said. This brings me to another point, namely, that not infrequently we take out our disgust, our impatience, our hostility, on a fellow religious. We save the best for the externs and we give what is left over to our fellow Sisters, and sometimes what is left over is not very much. We can understand this, but we may not excuse it.

In the world, men and women who are employed must perforce, in order to keep their jobs, smile and be pleasant with the people with whom they deal, even though they are disgusted with them. They may have a tendency to unmask themselves

when they come home and take it out on their family. This kind
of thing is possible in religion, also. We, too, have to present a
demeanor, attitude, and appearance that sometimes belie our
inner feelings. This is not hypocrisy, because we have an obligation to share our best with externs. But it is a sad commentary on
religious life that, as a consequence, we give very little to our
fellow religious. Real love for our Sisters says we should contribute to recreation. Recreation ought to be a refreshing experience.
We ought to be gay, happy, cheerful, pleasant, and to save the
best and not give our Sisters just what is left over.

Why is it we have a smile and a good word for every extern
with whom we come in contact, and our Sisters have to bear the
brunt of our impatience, our anger, and our hostility? Are there
not Sisters who have a tremendous reputation among the laity
for being mild, gentle, gracious—everything you would expect to
find in a religious woman—but who are "hellions" in the community? There are. I said that even though this is not wholly
excusable, it is readily understandable.

Sister perhaps had had her face frozen in a kind of a smile for
eight hours, and when she gets home she says, "Now, I am going
to be myself." But what kind of a self is she? She is impatient.
She is demanding. She takes out her hostility where it is safe. We
always do that. It is safe to take it out on members of the family,
and I always know that the Sisters have to accept me—they cannot remove me from the community, they *have* to put up with
me. So I am grumpy. I am impatient; I am unkind; I am sharp; I
am short; I am not thoughtful and I will not go out of my way to
help anybody, because I have been helping everybody all day
and I am through helping people. Well, this is where we have to
extend ourselves. We have to give and save the best for the
family, and our religious family comes first.

Father Evoy: When a member of your community has more time
for a youngster or other extern than she has for you, this spells
out in unmistakable terms what you would not like it to spell

out. Time given to one is often the measure of the presence or absence of love. At any rate, this is the way many people regard it. So when characteristically she does not have the time for the rest of you that she has for this extern, when she is a most pleasant, agreeable person with the extern and quite the opposite with you, what other conclusion can you draw? So I say that to you this says something very clearly that you do not like it to say.

There is a further aspect that I would like to mention here. I think externs should soon discover in their dealings with you that they will not be permitted to say anything derogatory about your Sisters in your presence. They learn that. If they do not learn that, there is something radically wrong. This is by no means to say that you should not be able to listen to reasonable criticism of yourself, of individual members of the community, and of the community itself. But if anything is unfair to one of your Sisters you are adamant on the point that you will not hear anything ill spoken of the one you love. You should be known for this characteristic. Loyalty to your own should be something that other people regard as your hallmark.

Father Christoph: There is a matter right here relating to communications between members of the same family who love one another. Even though this is primarily concerned with Superiors, it still is something which is between religious and religious. I am sure we are all familiar with the section of Tanquerey's *Spiritual Life* devoted to tepidity. But you know there is something that relates very closely to tepidity from the socio-psychological point of view which Tanquerey does not mention. He talks about the languor in the religious life, the distaste for spiritual reading and all the other things that make up the life of a religious. Something very important, I think, is overlooked. The enthusiasm, the generosity, the tremendous will-to-do of religious youth very frequently changes into the indifferent, "I don't care attitude" in or around middle age. I submit that it is not due primarily to lack of appreciation of the spiritual life, but it is a problem of morale.

By this I mean that morale in great measure correlates positively with the knowledge of the over-all objectives. The more I know what is going on, the more I am able to throw myself enthusiastically into that which is going on.

I offer Mass out at an Air Base. We have no war going on at the present time. All I hear about is the low state of morale, because the airmen are doing things and they do not know why they are doing them. They are orderly, and they do not know why they are orderly. There is red tape and they do not understand the reason for red tape.

If we were in the midst of a war, we would not have this problem at all. We expect secrecy. We expect that people in charge of the different operations cannot, for obvious reasons, divulge information, and so during a time of war a soldier accepts the fact that he is not in "on the know." But in time of peace, the same thing happens and he does not have any enthusiasm because he asks himself, "So what does this mean to me?"

In proportion as my Superiors and others keep me aware of what is going on in the community, keep me abreast of the approximate and remote objectives of our activities, I can throw myself with generosity and enthusiasm into the work. In proportion as they keep these things secret, and do not divulge them to me, I feel like a robot. I feel I am not regarded by them as a person. For the sake of morale, I think it is extremely important that Superiors every once in a while call the community together and say, "Listen, this is the situation," and let them know.

Most towns have a United Crusade. Well, in our city we have a large thermometer placed on a prominent downtown corner, and those in charge of the drive show by the thermometer where the drive is at every moment. Everyone is watching that thermometer. Everyone hopes that it is getting closer to the top. If it needs a little more and there are only a few days left and the citizens think they have beaten the bushes for every nickel they can get in the community, they still can come up with ten or twenty thousand more than they expected because there is enthusiasm. Their thinking is, "We are getting to the top. We are making our goal. Let's try a little harder."

The importance of participation, to the extent that it is possible in the knowledge of aims and goals and movements of what is happening in the community, what is happening in the institute, is seen in that it contributes to high morale and enthusiasm. These things have a tendency to bolster morale and make us proud to belong to our institute, and make us put our shoulders to the wheel with much more generosity.

Father Evoy: Sisters, you will recall our saying earlier that perhaps one of the greatest single barriers to happiness in religious life is fear. I would say it is for the most part a fear of getting close to others, loving them, and feeling and expressing genuine affection for them. Undoubtedly there are other sources of unhappiness, but this merits our close attention because it produces in a religious something of an incapacitating condition. The individual who says, "Nobody will ever get close enough to me to hurt me," is also implicitly saying, "No one will ever get close enough to warm me, to comfort me, to buoy me up as a person."

Father Christoph: This is not the only source, but it is the pattern in the past, I believe, of much religious training, particularly in the novitiate.

Father Evoy: You are going to find, if you have not already done so, that if any individual who really cares for you and really experiences the impact of your love, were ever to suspect strongly you loved her *only* for God, she would as a result become nauseated and even physically ill. I mean that literally. When Our Lord said, "A new commandment I give you, that you love one another," He did not mean that you should love a person just for God or love only God in that person. No. He meant that you should love her for God and love her *personally for her*. So often

we are afraid really to love another human being. This above all
is the fear that tends to paralyze.

So often we are afraid to love because we sense that this would
be a dangerous thing. It happens to be true, Sisters, that the
more I love an individual, the more that person can hurt me. It
is also true that the more that same individual can fulfill me. As
we have already implied, to tell young religious that there is
something wrong and improper about loving another human
being is simply hideous.

6 *Superior to Subject*

Father Evoy: I hope we do not give the impression that we are discriminating against any one group. When we treat person to person relationships found in religious life, we endeavor to evaluate them one at a time in terms of the maturity that *should* be there. Accordingly, we will treat first the relationship of Superiors to Subjects, then of Subjects to Superiors, and thirdly of person to person in the religious life. Later still, we will say a few things about the maturity called for in the relations of religious to those outside of the religious community. The first thing to keep in mind as far as the impact on us of Superiors is concerned is that it really makes little difference how old we are in religion in terms of years. Neither does it matter much how old the Superior happens to be. The point is that there is one person in the community who can thrill or hurt each of us as no one else can, regardless of age and other considerations, and that one is the Superior.

The one thing that is found all too often in religious communities of women throughout this country is that, on one score or another, not enough Superiors are really felt by their Subjects to be motherly. Very recently someone has talked about the all too common preoccupation of Superiors with brick and mortar construction and referred to it as the "edifice complex." Many Superiors suffer from it. Whether or not that enters into it, the fact is that Sisters across this country in large numbers report that they do *not* feel their Superiors are motherly.

I am reasonably sure Father will agree when I say that far too many Sisters, on the other hand, fail to regard their Superior as a mother in the sense of feeling toward her as one should toward her mother. Implicit, of course, in this absence of feeling of the Sisters is a non-motherly attitude of the Superior. It seems important, then, to start with the fact that many Superiors at least do not give the impression to their Subjects that they are motherly.

I think that this failure of a Superior to appear motherly can be understandable on a number of scores. To begin with, it is at least possible that a given Subject would simply be impossible to please in this area. Frankly, Sisters, we must face evidences that there are in some religious communities across the country one or more individuals who are practically impossible to satisfy in this regard. It is understandable, also, why a Superior might give the impression of not being motherly on the grounds that she would be unable to devote considerable time and attention to her community because of other demands. In all reality, many religious Superiors must be concerned about building, about reconstruction, and particularly about administration and all of the multiple facets of a large community. As a result, there is necessarily less time left to be given to her Sisters in religion.

Because you are women you know far better than we ever could that a Superior can still be motherly, and her Sisters in the community know that she is, even though she has very little time to give them because of the press of these other matters. It is not even primarily a matter of time. Why, then, do some Superiors appear not to be motherly? Some Superiors seem not to be motherly, perhaps because they are afraid to be motherly. It is as simple as that. They are afraid to be warm, affectionate, and accepting toward their religious Subjects. Why?

Some are afraid that were they to be really motherly there would be an end of discipline in the house. They might fear that given such a comfortable mother-daughter relationship, there would have to be resulting disobedience, since certain people would be bound to take advantage of such a comfortable relationship. There is indeed a possibility that should a Superior dare to be a warm motherly person, someone might well take advantage of it. This is *always* a possibility. If, however, she is afraid that, as a result, there will be an end of discipline and her religious house will become a loose, free-wheeling community, does this not say something about her own security? If, on the other hand, her fear is that word would get out to higher Superiors that there is no real religious discipline in the house, does not this also throw a question on her motivation?

There seems to be a rather prevalent conviction in places that unless a Superior is rather impersonal toward her Subjects, she loses her power really to correct them when such correction is required. The fallacious nature of this type of reasoning is immediately evident when you check it against your own experience. You know immediately that the one person in authority who cannot correct you without hurt is the person who, you feel, does not love you. If you knew that a Superior really loved you, I think that if you would ever take anything from anyone in the line of correction, you would certainly take it from her.

Father Christoph: Is this not true because a mother who loves her child will correct that child? Yet the child certainly does not think the mother loves her less because she is corrected.

Father Evoy: Loving them and being so nice to them that they cannot dislike you are by no means to be identified. They are not at all the same thing. Many women can fool men rather easily, but they cannot as easily fool other women. This holds for women as young as those attending college. Another woman cannot fool them. She loves them or she does not. She accepts them or she does not and it does not really matter how nice she is to them.

On reflection, is it not something of a travesty on love to feel that you have to be so terribly nice to them that they cannot disobey you or cause you any trouble? Is not this buying their friendship? So we are almost forced by our own reflections back to the topic of which we have just spoken, that we do not mind taking corrections from one whom we know loves us. Is that correct? If she does not love us, any kind of correction or any kind of check on us has the opposite effect. The lesson to be learned here is unmistakable. A Superior should reflect that if she *really* loves her Sisters as their mother under God, then she is free to do just about anything that she wishes. If she *really* loves them, the community is not going "on the rocks." The Sisters are not going to lose all sense of discipline. In fact, the surprising aspect of this whole matter is that there should be a well-grounded fear that discipline might suffer where the Superior was afraid to love her daughters with a warm, motherly, personal love. The Superior should be reassured on this one score. If, to the best of her ability, she does love each of them personally as their mother, then she is free to do almost anything she wants and the community will, as a result, suffer in no notable way.

Father Christoph: The fear of Superiors to give themselves to others is an important point. Frequently, this is based on the feeling that everything in religious life is cut and dried. A religious woman said to me recently that apparently the ideal Sister in her community was cold, aloof and distant. Now, that is *not* the ideal any place. Can you imagine Christ as being cold, aloof and distant? If you love the community, your Superiors, and your companions, you need not worry that your attention to or your affection for them is going to break down discipline. This is an unjustified fear. A religious Superior has the obligation, an obligation above and beyond that of anyone else in the community, to see that religious observance is maintained in that house. That is the duty of a Superior. But, *the law of charity is the way.* Because human nature is as it is, there must be some regulations set down and there must be someone put in charge to see that the regulations are reasonably observed—but all within the framework of charity.

The Superior, as a mother, has to expect that her subjects are *not* always going to measure up to her expectations. They are human and they have weaknesses. We do not check our weaknesses at the novitiate door when we enter a religious community. We have those same weaknesses sometimes throughout life. The same tendencies "to chisel a little," to "get by" with mediocrity on occasion, to break a rule here and a rule there, so long as we are not "cracking them" so often and so loudly that the religious house sounds like a boiler factory, are a part of religious life. We *are not* perfect.

Now there is a difference between a motherly solicitude to see that the rules and regulations are kept and a kind of police surveillance under which you are constantly observed. This latter is a servile observance directed to the Superior and there is nothing of the love of God in the servitude of the Subject under these circumstances. Remember, you do not destroy human nature by getting into your religious habit. You are still the same individual with the same tendencies. The tendency to resent surveillance normally manifests itself in a certain amount of satisfaction in deceiving the people who are watching you. So motherly solicitude to protect, guard the rule and institute and to make this particular house a model for the whole institute is not going to be achieved by being a Sherlock Holmes watching the movement of every Sister and spying to see if there isn't something which you can correct in her.

A Superior has to be big enough, at times, to overlook some of the obvious defects and failures on the part of individuals who do not observe the rule. We are sometimes just too tired to do what the rule calls for and, if the Superior comes and "bawls us out" under those circumstances, we take umbrage rather than correction. However, as Father said, if the Superior is very considerate and if she loves her community, we do not feel unduly upset when called to task. To feel an initial hurt at correction is human. But it is a sign of maturity not to brood or feel resentment as a consequence.

Father Evoy: What kind of love in a Superior declares itself to be genuine toward you and at the same time does not really trust you? Frankly, I do not understand this kind of love. As a religious, to be trusted by your Superior means more to you than you could ever put in words. Were you to try to express it, I think you would probably put it in something like the following expression. Without your understanding exactly why, when your Superior, by her behavior and whole attitude, tells you that she trusts you, it gives you the feeling that you are indeed trustworthy, and, moreover, that you have the competency to do that which she trusts you to do. In a very real sense this trust of hers is something that enters into the completion of your very personality.

Father Christoph: When religious are found to be untrustworthy, is it not often because they are not really trusted? If the attitude is, "I don't trust you," the Subject tends to act in a way in which she has not been trusted. By this, I mean if she is judged to be untrustworthy, why not act as if she is that way, namely, not trustworthy. You may say that this is an irreligious way to act but human nature has a tendency to manifest itself in this fashion even among religious. Superiors should not test virtue to the limit.

Father Evoy: There are many applications and ramifications of this matter of trust or lack thereof on the part of Superiors. For instance, I know that in many religious communities, Superiors feel that they should, for instance, monitor the mail of their Subjects. In many religious communities Superiors do have the *right* to open and read the mail of even the older Sisters. Now, I know of *no* religious community in which a Superior *must* do this as a general practice. Am I wrong?

Father Christoph: I am somewhat disturbed about the matter Father is treating. Sisters, there is not one person here who, if she wants to get a message to Timbuctoo, cannot get it there. What is the need to be so severely exact, as far as Superiors are concerned, in keeping this one rule of opening and looking over the mail? The care with which this rule—if it be a rule—is observed and the lack of concern about other rules, suggests curiosity about, rather than maternal solicitude for, Subjects.

Father Evoy: Is that a rule? I mean, is it a rule that the Superior *must* do it, or is it simply that she has the *right?* As Superior, I have the right to question Father Christoph about every telephone call that he makes. I say that I have the right to do so. But it seems to me that it would be simply unthinkable that I exercise that right until and unless he has proved himself unworthy of trust. Just because I have the *right* does not mean that I must always discharge it in each and every possible instance.

Sisters, nature at times cries out for a little privacy and human nature does not radically change in religious life. I know, for instance, that all I have to do to make sure that I get the maximum amount of cheating in any class is just to walk into that class and say, "No one in this class cheats. I cannot, in conscience, trust one individual in this room, so I am going to see to it that in this exam no one is going to cheat." If I were a member of that class, I believe I would consider it a matter of principle, something of a challenge, to find a way to cheat somehow or other or else consider myself to have failed in meeting a personal challenge.

Father Christoph: It becomes a kind of a game. In religious life that does not mean that there should not be some regulations with respect to writing and some regulations with respect to the use of the telephone. That is pretty obvious. I notice this particularly where I am telephoning a community of religious women. There is usually one telephone, *one* telephone number, and when someone is talking lengthily on that telephone, I get a little annoyed. I wonder if there are time limits on the use of the telephone. So we are not talking about reasonable regulations. We are talking about the exaggerated surveillance which is based upon a principle that is never voiced but must be there: "You can't trust a woman."

Father Evoy: There is another kind of trust which we do not ordinarily think of when we talk in terms of a Superior's attitude of trust toward a Subject. For the most part we take the term "trust" as having the connotation of giving another person credit for honesty, good will, and dependability in the sense that she will do what she promises to do and what in her judgment would be the right thing to do.

At the moment I am talking about "trust" in quite a different sense. As I am using it now, it has reference to the evaluation by the Superior of a Subject's competency. You will readily perceive that the lack of this kind of trust can be extremely hurtful to a religious Subject. At the same time, it is quite conceivable that it would never even be recognized as a lack of trust by the Superior.

Distrust in this sense is an attitude of the Superior which at least implicitly says to her Subject, "I think the world of you, and I am going to give you the protection you need. Now, I want this particular thing done, but of course, it is too much for you to do." Recall what I said earlier to the effect that your Superior is so big that she can hurt or thrill you as no one else can. Her importance is now seen to extend even to your own evaluation of yourself. If she says, without any question at all, that she thinks you can do something, you tend to say to yourself, "I can do it." If she says, in unmistakable language, "Look, dear, you couldn't possibly do this. It's far too big for you," you may resent that evaluation very much but as a result of it there will be something of a question mark in your mind with regard to your ability to do it. If you run into enough of this, by the time you get to be, say forty years of age, even though you have college degrees and unquestionable competency and ability, should someone give you a new responsibility, you might well panic. You just know that you cannot do it. You have been told all along by people who love you, "You can't. You are not capable." This devastating type of thing can be done by a Superior within the framework of her love for a Sister, without ever being recognized by her for the debilitating thing that it is.

You see, this is *really* another area of trust. True, it is not the kind of trust which a Superior would feel toward her daughter in the matter of such things as phone calls, letters or conversations with someone and on the score of which it would simply never occur to her not to trust her daughter in religion. In this latter, more commonly used meaning of trust, her attitude is, "I can trust you anyplace. I know I can." This attitude would remain unless and until there should be reason in a particular case, to question it.

Yet, closely related to this is this other type of trust in which a Superior would say to herself, in reference to one of her Subjects, "I assume that she *can* do it unless there is evidence to the contrary." Do you see what I mean? Who is to say whether or not Sister can do it? The Superior's attitude, at least, is that of course she can do it. How do you know that a Sister can teach when she walks into the classroom for the first time? You do not know. She goes in there and sinks or swims. But if the Superior's attitude is that Sister has the ability to go in there and "carry it off," what a tremendous difference that makes.

You see, Sisters, what we are really talking about is the Superior's acknowledgment that her daughters in religion are adults. The love which is proper for her to have towards these daughters of hers is a love for them *as* they are—as adults and not as children.

Father Christoph: If you treat Sisters like children, they will behave like children. I told you that they would be trying "to get away with things." There is something more devastating here.

Subjects take the evaluation of Superiors as their own, and if you
treat subjects like children, they begin to think and act like
children and they never will become or act like mature women.
They will *never* feel capable of making decisions. They will have
to be led by the hand the rest of their lives, and certainly this is
not the ideal of religious life.

Guidance can take on the aspect of a fetish and this is true on
the part of the very good Superior who has a tremendous concern
for her Subjects and wants to lead them and to develop them
correctly, and make them saints. Because the Superior will usually be in charge of younger members of the community, she feels
that she has something to do with the molding of the religious
temperament and the religious character of those under her
charge. So she "over-guides" and interferes, as a matter of fact,
with the workings of the Holy Spirit.

There is yet another kind of Superior who *has* to be in the
vanguard of every idea, of every movement and everything that
is done in the community, and this type of guidance is a protection for her own inadequacies. The more adequate one is, the
less one fears competition. Superiors are human. They are not
necessarily the most adequate individuals in the world. The incidence of genius is about one in thousands, according to some
recognized authorities. The incidence of leadership material out
of which we can make Superiors, as I mentioned earlier, is certainly not one out of five. Yet we have to have so many Superiors
because we have so many houses, and as a consequence, let us
face it, sometimes women of mediocre talent and of mediocre
ability are placed in charge of the community because someone
has to run the houses.

The one named is put into office, not necessarily because she
has the most talent, but principally because she has shown some
evidence of being able to lead a community. Sometimes among
these individuals we find men and women, specifically now, Sisters, who are afraid of competition, and so their guidance takes

on the dimension of a compulsion which they always can justify
in terms of the fact that they are to lead the community.

Father Evoy: A Superior can be very motherly and trusting of
her daughters *as children* and, moreover, permit externs to trust
them *as children*. This is something which is most regrettable.
Recently, I saw where a Monsignor in the Middle West wrote an
article for the Catholic paper, in which he said, in substance,
"Please don't give me another one of those pictures of the Sisters
being taken out to the ball game together or any other place as a
group, because as far as I am concerned, it's in the same category
as the picture of the group of orphans being taken out in a group
to something or other."

The burden of his remarks was that this kind of condescending
and sponsoring attitude to these "poor, helpless Sisters" which
would appear to be implicit in such a thing as taking them all
out in a group to the ball game, is not fitting at all. If the Sisters
are going to the ball game, fine and good, but they should not
have to be taken out there and paraded in the form of a group-
charity. If a Sister should want to go with a companion to the
ball game and can get the requisite permission, I see nothing
whatever unbecoming about this and so I see no real reason why,
occasionally at least, a Sister should not be permitted to go to a
ball game should she be so inclined. It seems to me that there is
nothing anymore wrong with her going to a ball game than with
her going to a concert or a play. In fact, it might not be a bad
idea to begin to educate the public along these lines.

This whole attitude of regarding the Sisters as a group of older
children is far from wholesome. There are Sisters who can stand
shoulder to shoulder with any woman outside in terms of education, in terms of ability, and in terms of maturity. Sisters should
rightly resent being treated as helpless children. In this connection, I would much prefer to see a Sister obtain permission to
buy some extern a dinner rather than the other way around if, in
her being treated to dinner, there was the slightest implication of

any belittling, condescending attitude toward Sisters. For a number of reasons, I very seldom go out with externs to dinner. I appreciate, however, that for many people an invitation to dinner is the most fitting expression to a priest of their gratitude and friendship; and they can be deeply offended by a refusal that is not handled with real consideration.

However, personally, I know that all I would need to make sure that I would turn down an invitation would be to have someone say to me, "We like to take some of the Fathers out and get them a good meal and buy them a drink once in a while. We have to do some charity in this world." This would certainly do it! Never would I go near their home, because if I am not welcome there as a Priest and as a Priest judged by them to be honoring their home, then I do not belong there. If, in such an invitation, I caught something of a patronizing attitude toward the "poor Priests," I should most certainly never go there. For this would savor of the thing of which I have just been talking, being regarded as grown-up-children. Sisters, I think that many Superiors are really motherly, but most unfortunately, their motherly concern for their religious Subjects is one of overprotection, and lack of trust, one which, in a word, is directed to them as children rather than as grown adults.

Father Christoph: To return for a moment to the example already used, there is a reason for watching and keeping a surveillance over the mail of novices as well as young religious, because it takes a certain length of time before young men and young women learn that you do not write or gossip about certain things because they are family affairs. These young religious should be checked so they do not retail to the public—and your relatives and friends are public—things that are completely domestic and should be kept domestic. I know Subjects who have come to me and have said that they resented deeply the Superior's remarks about matters contained in letters. It would not be something unbecoming or embarrassing, but it would be upsetting to them that the Superior should have taken notice of information which was purely a bit of domestic news. Your sister writes about an argument she has had with her husband, and your Superior says, "It's too bad your sister and her husband can't get along," or something like that. Well, is that the purpose of reading the mail? No. The purpose is to preserve good order. Superiors have an obligation to see that the rules in general are observed in the community, but if to do this they have to peek in the keyholes, stand behind doors, if they monitor telephone calls—these things have been done—it is treating the Subject as if she were a child.

Father Evoy: Sisters, if a religious going on a trip were told by her Superior, "Wait, Sister, until I write your name and destination on an envelope and pin it to your habit so that you won't get lost," it would be ludicrously clear to everyone that she was being treated as a child. But is not the equivalent of this often done when, no matter what the religious Subject tries to do, the Superior invariably says, "Look dear . . . this is the way to do it. You don't do things this way, etc., etc., etc." Is not this treating the Subject as if she were a child? Unfortunately, it not only annoys her, but it also pulls the carpet out from under her. She is not a child. Perhaps there is no place else in the world where individuals are systematically kept in adolescence as long as they are in religious life. A religious resents, and rightly resents, being treated as a child. Sisters, very candidly, I think you can see the wisdom of what Our Lord did when He made only men confessors. Although there are abundant exceptions to this, we often have evidences of the non-guarding of confidences by Superiors. How many times Superiors have been told things in confidence by Subjects who later on have discovered that these things were "passed on."

As a religious you want your Superior to love you and to love you as you are. This is why you resent being loved and treated as a child, because you are *not* a child. If she is

loving you as a child, she is not loving the *real* you. Chronologically, at least, you are an adult. You hope you are at least becoming an adult in the community. You also want your Superior to
trust you in every way as long as you are trustworthy and especially do you want her to safeguard confidences of every type,
whether you give them to her yourself or someone else does. You
want so much to be able to assume that these things go no further. Unfortunately, Sisters, I think that there is not one of you
who does not know that such is not always the case. Sometimes
strict confidences *do* go further.

Father Christoph: Treat them like women! Presume maturity
until the individual shows that she does not possess it! Then let
us examine our consciences as Superiors to see if we are responsible for the failure of this individual to show maturity. Here is a
woman in the world between the ages of twenty-six and thirty.
She is the mother of a family; she is reasonably self-sufficient. She
makes independent judgments with respect to the internal running and management of the home. She is "the boss," and she has
responsibilities and she fulfills them. If she were not, God help
the human race, because women with families find that by the
time they are twenty-six to thirty, these responsibilities are thrust
upon them, and without too much training they manage to do a
pretty good job. Why cannot we, as Superiors, presume that those
who have dedicated their lives to God in religion are not per-
petually immature? Let us start by treating them as we would
women in the same age bracket out in the world and see if, in the
process, we cannot uncover a lot more maturity than we suspect
is there.

This means that we project a tremendous amount of trust
and that we believe women are capable. This means that we
believe that women do not have to be told, in the process of
performing a function, every aspect of activity that is associated
with that function. It means that we give them a duty and all
necessary implied permissions to complete it. She who wishes the
end, wishes the means. The presumption is that if an individual

twenty-six, twenty-seven, or twenty-eight years of age is undertaking something, she has certain ideas of how things should be done. Superiors should not ride on her back, or as the expression goes, "breathe down her neck." Give her enough "elbow room." Give her an opportunity to show her ability and even to make mistakes.

There is an element of conceit in this whole matter. Remember, I am not saying that Superiors are conceited. I am saying objectively there is an element of conceit when the Superior tells you how to do everything. The supposition is that she knows all the answers, and knows how to do it, and her way is the *only* way and the best way.

We ought to be willing to allow the Sisters to make their own mistakes and fumble around a little. To do so is humbling for the Sister. It makes the Sister realize that she does not know everything, and it does develop frustration tolerance in her, and, indicates to her that she may have been a bit brash in her manner of handling the situation.

Father Evoy: Are we maintaining the position that religious should be treated as adults even if psychologically they are not yet adults? Before I answer that, be assured we are very aware we are not actually out on the firing line of convent life and so are able to make these statements. It is true, Sisters, that we are not out on *that* firing line. Neither of us is the Superior of this particular mission or house, and neither of us experiences the relationship to this particular member of the community who in one way or another proves difficult. We are aware of that. On the other hand, I think that you recognize the fact that Father and I have sat at the feet of hundreds of religious women and they have been our best instructors. We have been on *that* firing line. We have not derived this material solely from books. To that extent, I think we are about as close to an appreciation of these problems as men can come and in this way, quite close to the real order.

Let us assume that there are certain individuals in the community who are not at all adults. One characteristic of your dealing with an adult is that you are able to give her responsibility. You can, in effect, trust her to be able to do this thing without having to "breathe down her neck." It may be that a given individual, as soon as she is given any responsibility, is going to fall flat on her face, if you will pardon the expression. But unless she has the opportunity to fall flat on her face a number of times, how is she ever going to learn not to fall flat on her face?

It is very clear that we cannot teach someone a sense of responsibility just by telling her about responsibility. This is something which she must learn. The acceptance and successful carrying of responsibility is something that is learned, as any difficult art is learned, by correctly and repeatedly doing it.

I would say that the only way a young religious is ever going to do something as well as, say her Mistress, is to be permitted the luxury of being able to make her own mistakes. If such is the case, she can, in time, acquire the perfection which her Mistress has, or even surpass the performance of her Superior. No religious is constructed with built-in wisdom which of its very nature is infallible. She will make her mistakes, and the only way she can learn this particular aspect of the art of living, called the exercise of prudential judgment, is by repeatedly doing it correctly. This is the only way, for instance, one can learn to play tennis. One will not get it from reading a book. This is the only way one can learn to develop any art. There is no other way a person can learn to speak or sing. An art is mastered by doing, and doing it again, correctly. The mistakes of a young religious must be corrected. She will correct some of her mistakes herself; some others her Superiors may, in all charity, point out to her. But she must be given the opportunity to do the things in which she runs the risk that she will make mistakes. When we consider the notion of "correctly doing" we find this often means *corrected* doing. This correction may come either from self or from others; at any rate, when a Sister fails, she should try to find out when, where, and why she failed, so as to correct and then go on again.

Let us assume, for the sake of example, that a Superior can do this particular job better than any youngster in the community. If she continues doing it successfully and lives to be eighty-five years of age, she is going to have members in the community in their forties and fifties who still cannot do it because she can still do it better. They have never had the opportunity to do it. As something of a corollary, Sisters, it is hard to see how you can lose by trusting the individuals under you as far as you can.

You will recall Father's remark that guidance can become something of a compulsion. It is well to note in this connection that the tendency to manipulate, and to be a managing sort of a person, can have a psychological explanation. This managing pattern can correspond to a very real need even in a Superior. Such a one, in order to feel adequate, has to give herself almost constant evidence that she is adequate. This she might do by keeping the individuals in her community not only in a position of reasonable dependence, but in one of almost slavish subservience. Moreover, she could do this without ever having even a strong suspicion that there was any self-seeking or self-gain in it. She could see it all as being for God, and lawful by reason of the fact that she was conscientiously trying to be the Superior that she ought to be. This whole business of using religious authority to deprive an individual of much of her individuality and reduce her to unbecoming passivity is a catastrophic thing. Still, you can see how a given Superior could, in all good faith, become so preoccupied with guidance activities as to overlook completely her first and principal duty to her community, which happens to be to love and respect each member of her community with her whole strength. If she does this most important thing, loving and respecting them to the best of her ability, these other things can be wanting and somehow or other, I think, this community will survive. But lacking a warm, motherly, personal love, all of the techniques in the world will come to naught because this Superior is going to be presiding over a community of affectively hungry persons.

Father Christoph: A Superior may say to herself, "I am responsible to God, to the Church, and to the institute for the well-being of this particular community of which I am the Superior." With that reasoning she can justify ruling with an iron hand. She can also justify being very personally involved in every decision any Sister in the community may make. But there is nothing in the law of God or man that says responsibility cannot be shared.

Every individual Sister is responsible for the good deportment and for the high standards of religious observance in the community. Superiors, Visitors and the like, on their visitation to a convent may say to the Superior: "Poverty and other rules are not being observed in the community." But the Superior herself cannot guarantee the observance of rules. The Subjects have to do it. The Superior only *shares* the responsibility with the Subjects. Superiors must have the capacity and courage to delegate. The other day I saw a cartoon. There was apparently the president of the organization with a broom in his hand, sweeping the office. A couple of the members of the board were talking to each other and one said to the other, "Smith would be a great executive if he would only learn how to delegate." Maybe Sister Superior does not sweep, but she might just as well. She is superintending the operation immediately.

At times, do you, as a Superior, just presume that the individual cannot do the next operation without being told? To allow the individual to exercise her own initiative is a sign of confidence in that individual. It is also a sign that you do not think that *you* are the only one who knows how to do something. It also indicates that you are a good executive. You can share the burdens of your office.

The Superior should presume good will. As the years pass, I appreciate more the problems that the individuals have in doing things, in following out regulations and the like. We should begin with the presumption that we have nothing but good will with which to deal. That may be hard at times, but I think it is a valid assumption, especially among religious, and so Superiors could reasonably presume that there is good will. Superiors should not be unduly concerned about the productivity of Subjects. The Subjects, it should be assumed, are doing what they should do, what they are able to do. They should not be overburdened, that is pretty obvious. But there never should be a projection of one's own capacities into another. Occasionally I find myself saying, in regard to a younger man, "I do as much as he can do. What's the matter with him?" I have no right to say that even to myself. It is not right because I do not know his makeup, his physical strength, his psychological problems, etc.

There is a tendency to project, and frequently Superiors use, as their norm of efficiency, their own proper capacities. I used to say, and I still maintain, that I would prefer a Superior who has had some experience with illness, who has herself been ill. I say this because I have seen evidences of Superiors who could not understand illness because they never had been ill. That is one area, I think, in which you have to have personal experience before you can know what it means. This is part and parcel of what I am saying, that you *have* to presume good will.

The presumption is, that since she is a religious, she is doing the best she can. Maybe the best she can do is less than mediocre, but the presumption holds that this is *her* best.

Father Evoy: I agree that the presumption does hold. This point should be emphasized because well-meant but mistaken conduct of individual persons at times appears to bear a remarkable resemblance to ill will. There are areas in which the behavior of certain religious and even an occasional policy in a community would appear to flow from ill will. Let us take one area of a community policy to illustrate. Robert Louis Stevenson, the wellknown novelist, once said that to write was to endure the pangs of childbirth. After all, men know little about birth pains, but those who have worked for a higher degree will say that graduate studies should be close to that experience. On several scores the undertaking is a most taxing one before the individual ultimately emerges with the degree.

Now, when the graduate students finally make the academic grade, they are feted, honored, and warmly congratulated. I think that almost without exception, everyone somehow or other is wined and dined. There are numerous celebrations with friends and relatives. This is the picture for those outside of the convent.

What is the picture for those in religious life? Here we find, frequently, a highly strange phenomenon. Religious women have returned to their convent after having attained their degree, and the reception they received was about as far removed from that of their non-religious confreres as one could imagine. The policy would seem to be, now that they have their degree, they must be very careful, lest they become proud. So they find that when they have finally attained their academic goal and are somewhat spent as a result of the taxing nature of the "long haul," they are put aside for a time.

The one who has just received her degree feels that she is walking around under a cloud. She may be assigned to do housework for a time or something else that would be thought fit to keep her from falling into the clutches of pride. So many of these actions are well meant. They look as though they must proceed from ill will. They are actually thought to be for her own spiritual good. What is frequently not realized is that they are in the poorest possible taste in terms of genuine love for this fellow religious. It is almost unbelievable the things that have been done to Sisters in misguided efforts masquerading as charity and other religious motivations.

Sisters, these things have occurred in this country. When we think about this we are first of all amazed that anyone could possibly confuse humility with being humbled. No one else can make a person humble because no one else can make a person virtuous. God made us *free* beings and the service He wants from us is ultimately a free service. If any one of us is not giving Him a free service, he or she is at best a kind of sanctimonious slave.

Father Christoph: Father Evoy gave us the example of someone getting a higher degree and then being sent to the kitchen upon her return to her convent. I actually knew a community in which this was always done. For one year after one earned her higher or highest degree, she was sent back and literally put to work in the kitchen, and that was supposed to keep her in her place. Now, I became aware of this situation because there was one rebellious soul. She did not believe in this type of discipline. She was not an arrogant, proud individual to begin with, and she thought that it was just ridiculous to presume she was proud. When she approached her Superior and made this remark, etc., the Superior said to her, "Well, the very fact that you are indignant over this assignment is an indication that you are proud." And Sister rejoined with this remark, "Well, I am indignant over the supposition underlying this appointment—not the fact that I'm going to work in the kitchen. I'll work in the kitchen the rest of my life, but I don't want to work in the kitchen because I have a degree. I don't want to be sent to the kitchen because I am proud."

As a matter of fact, going to the kitchen is not going to make the Sister humble. But, as Father said, it is not an infrequently recurring pattern in religious life that those who have the ability are stymied in the efforts to express or to use their capabilities because they are sometimes a threat to the existing regime. Let us face it, there are individuals who do not want anyone to be their equals because they fear being supplanted. So a threat is present when the younger religious come up with new ideas and have these new advantages. This threat to the power and prestige of the "elders" is met by condemning roundly the ambitions of people who have new ideas. They blame it on education and on the worldly spirit the young religious picked up in the course of getting a higher degree.

None of this need necessarily be true. We ought to presume that individuals recognize there is an unequal distribution of talents and that some individuals are going to be brighter than others. Therefore, we should presume that some should go on for higher degrees, that some should become Superiors, and some should not. But we should not accuse persons of being proud and ambitious in the worst sense of the terms when they strive for excellence and try to be the best in their particular field—all for the love of God and the good of the community and the furtherance of community activities. There ought, therefore, to be a happy balance between the desire of the Subjects to do the best they can, and the desire of the Superiors to give their Subjects the best opportunities so that in the best sense of the word, the community will exploit talent wherever it exists. We should encourage ambition. We should encourage initiative, and we should not think of it as a threat to the existing order or traditions of the community.

7 *Subject to Superior*

Father Evoy: Now we will take a closer look at the area of the relationship of Subjects to Superiors. It might help a bit were I to endeavor, in imagination, to put myself in the place of a religious woman in her relationship to her Superior. To begin with, let me recall Father's remark that it is a rare woman who can exercise authority over other women. We are not talking exclusively about religious women in this regard. Father and I have both checked this out with women in the various branches of the armed services and in the business world with pretty much the same findings. In general, we find that women will take a *great* deal from a man, but very little from another woman. It throws a bit of light, perhaps, on the universally recognized difficulty of finding a good dean of women or a good housemother for college girls.

By way of application of these findings we are making the point that just because the Superior is a woman it is more difficult for her to govern harmoniously. In a sense, there is almost a parallel here to what is true of a student seeking entrance into a medical school in this country. In all honesty, Father Christoph and I both have to tell a girl ambitioning to become a physician that she will have to be better than the boys to get into medical school. If she is only on a par with them, the chances are that she will not gain admission because these schools favor the male students.

The parallel is clear. To be a good Superior of a religious community, a woman must be better at it than a man. It is harder for her religious Subjects to take obedience from her, because they are taking it from a woman. The intelligent woman Superior knows this, and it puts an extra burden on her, a burden which at times is pretty heavy to carry. The Superior is a human being and she remains such when she is made Superior. She is a woman, as well. As Superior she is not only the person in authority, but also the mother, under God, of all these, her daughters. We must be most realistic about this.

Now from my fantasied place as a religious woman I view my Superior. Assume that I am an intelligent person, and reasonably objective. Now, I reflect that every mother in the world has the obligation to exercise authority and often to exercise it over the young women who are her grown-up daughters. This certainly appears to correspond closely to the role of the religious Superior of women. It causes us to question our position that the exercise of authority over women by another woman is so difficult. At the same time, it recalls to our attention how frequently we have found mothers who, having had no particular difficulty exercising authority over their girls when they were small, admit themselves completely baffled at how to deal with the same girls once they are in the period of adolescence. It must be recognized as well that every Mother in the world has helps in governing the young women who are her daughters which the religious Superior does not have. She has a biosocial aid in the form of a natural tendency to love her own which the religious Superior does not have. Moreover, by the time the mother in the world is in the position of authority over her adolescent young women, she has had a good deal of training and much experience in exercising authority. She is not placed over her young adult children until she has been exercising authority over them for many years. She has had, in a word, a good deal of seasoning. She did not suddenly have to start exercising authority over them when they were already young women. This is a very important consideration. Even then, as you are well aware, armed with such a back-log of experience, there is a definite chance that she may not do a very good job of exercising authority over them once they reach the age of adolescence. There is a relevant and interesting point here which, in passing, I will simply mention for your consideration. I refer to how frequently we find the inability of a girl, once she has reached the age of adolescence, to accept a foster mother of any kind.

In my imagined role as a religious woman, I look closely at my Superior and very frankly find that she is not without imperfections. In her actions, I see mistakes; in her personality, shortcomings, and in her I see a lack of wisdom. This is a pretty objective picture, I think. Then I ask myself whether, in view of these things which are so apparent to me, I can honestly feel and act toward her as an adult daughter should toward her mother. A little sound reflection tells me that of course she is imperfect. She *has* to be. Moreover, the exercise of authority by anyone other than God must be imperfect. By reason of the fact that a Superior is a human being, she is limited in her knowledge, both of the Subject as a person, and also of some areas in which the Subject will be engaged under obedience. The most unrealistic attitude would be to expect her not to be imperfect. Hence to expect the exercise of authority not to be lacking in perfection is simply to be unrealistic. It is such things from which dreams are made.

On further reflection, it strikes me that it is precisely because she is imperfect, because she is a mere human being and is fully aware that the exercise of her authority is at times replete with imperfection, that she needs my love and loyalty. If she were letter perfect, she might be able to get along pretty well without me. But she needs me because, among other things, she knows she is not infallible and not certain. It is only reasonable to expect that, at times, she feels unsafe and insecure. Notwithstanding, she *has* to act, to make decisions, and often she cannot put these off until she is certain. This is one reason why she needs the comforting and reassuring love of those who count in her life. As long as I become her Subject, I become, also, her daughter and so one of those in her life who happens to count.

As a religious Subject I want my Superior to love, trust, and treat me in all things as an adult. Very good. But I am forced by looking at the facts to admit that it is relatively easy for me to disregard the very significant fact that this is, and must be, a two-way relationship. It is a two-way street. The other individuals in the community feel a little different when the Superior is present, and she knows they feel this way. As long as she is Superior this will be so and hence in a certain sense, she will be a lonely person.

Some Superiors appear to be less lonely than others, but it seems that every Superior is a little lonely, no matter who she is, simply by reason of the fact that she is Superior. All she has to do is walk into a room where other members of the community are and immediately the atmosphere is not quite the same. Moreover, sensing such change, she is only too often not perfectly comfortable in joining a group. She does not want this electricity in the air. In a sense, she does not have the same companionship that you have. She does not have the same freedom of association that you have.

Father Christoph: This business of Subject and Superior is obviously a two-way relationship. I, as a Subject, am supposed to give my Superior a little freedom and a little of my concern for her, also; so the attitude of the Subject should be one of consideration for the Superior. Because I think this area is so tremendously important, I wish to add a footnote to the remark of Father Evoy's about the loneliness of a Superior. I do not care how friendly you are to your Superior, you are always conscious of dignity and of her role, so when she tries to be one of the com-

munity, she simply cannot be just another member. When she
talks, everyone else keeps quiet. This is respect. I do not want it
otherwise. But do you see how that cuts her off? She does not
have all the satisfaction you get out of community life. She cannot afford, as Father said, to go to the ones to whom she would
naturally gravitate, because immediately she is accused of starting a cabal, a division in the community, or not having a universal interest. So her position is a little difficult. We have to give
Superiors credit for good will and due concern for the interests of
the community. Even when they have very obviously proved
themselves otherwise, it is best to leave the judgment to Almighty
God. Indeed, rash judgments are not uncommon as far as Subjects are concerned when they are thinking about Superiors and
the attitudes of Superiors.

Father Evoy: Yes. We have already stressed the point that her
daughters have the right to their Superior's love and whatever is
called for by that love. But, as their mother, she also has the right
to their love, and to all the loyalty that true daughters should
have to their mother.

These religious Subjects, as we mentioned, have a definite
right to assume that every confidence given to the Superior, their
mother, will be safeguarded at any price. Here again we must
remind ourselves that this is a two-way street. Very candidly,
sometimes religious daughters do not act as if that were the case
at all. The Superior does something, and immediately some of
those who are most insistent that she may not divulge a single
confidence proceed to criticize her roundly for what she has done,
on the score that she has been unfair, unjust, or unwise. True,
the Superior has given no explanation for something she has
done which directly affected one or more Sisters in the community. Those who are criticizing her have simply assumed that they
have the entire story, and they are in full posssession of the
relevant facts in the case.

When looked at in this light, it is not a very pretty picture, is it? As religious Subjects, we insist that Superiors must safeguard all confidences, so as never to reveal anything that even approximates a confidence. Yet, since she has not said why she is taking this particular action, we assume that we know why she is doing it and proceed to judge her accordingly. Many a Superior has said to herself, and perhaps even to someone else whom she can trust, "Thank God, I can put my finger on Sister N and know that if the worse ever comes to the worst, I could go to her and without any explanation whatever simply say, 'Sister, I need to move you in order to solve a problem in the community. May I? I can give you no further explanation,' and she would answer immediately, 'Certainly Sister, you may move me. Where do you want me to go?' "

Father Christoph: Then everyone in the whole house or province says, "What's the matter with Mother Provincial? What's the matter with the Superior General? Here is a Sister perfectly content and doing a wonderful job. What does Mother Provincial do? She takes her out and puts her over here." As Father said a moment ago, the major Superior may have information that she cannot divulge. The Subjects expect all along that every confidence is regarded as inviolable, but they will not give the Superior credit for having an intelligent reason for her action. They do not conclude that perhaps she *may not* talk.

As Father says, it is a two-way street. You have to be fair to Superiors. Superiors are not just arbitrarily moving Subjects as one moves checkers on a checkerboad. There is lack of faith in the confidence and competency of the Superiors when the issue is not even raised by Subjects that there might be good reasons for what has been done. Do you know all the facts? We have no right to presume that we know all the facts. "Well, I talked to Sister X and I got her side of the story." How do you know her side is the right side? You know that when I am personally involved, I can do a pretty good job of making myself look good. This is something each of us should reflect upon.

It is true that our Superiors are not infallible—they do not claim to be; they do make mistakes, but we should not presume that they are acting arbitrarily or capriciously in moving individuals. The presumption *should* be that there is some justification for what has been done and that they may not tell. So give them *always* the benefit of the doubt. In fact, that is small credit to you—just to give them the benefit of the doubt. Better, presume that they are acting wisely. In the last analysis, these things seem to work out so that eventually, ten or fifteen years from now, you will get the whole story, and you will see how wise the move of the Superior actually was.

Father Evoy: When I assume that this was a stupid move on the part of the Superior I am claiming, in effect, that since she did not give the reason, she did not have a reason. On the other hand, I am insisting she should never divulge any information she receives in confidence. Is that consistent? Is it fair? Is it mature?

I can be fair if I say that, as far as I can see, this did not appear to be too shrewd a move, but then I really do not know all the facts in the case. Actually, the longer we live in religion the more we realize that the Superior very often is not free to explain. She may not talk. Her hands are tied. If you want confirmation of this, go to a counsellor of the Superior and ask her whether or not it is true that very frequently no explanation of any kind may be given for some decision without an unauthorized revelation. She will tell you that this is indeed correct. Only too often, no explanation of any kind may be given. So, Sisters, we can be unfair to Superiors, terribly unfair to them without realizing that we are.

Father Christoph: Father Evoy said that Superiors are lonely. You are entitled to your own friendships with certain individuals; you are entitled to associate with the people in the community you like, whose conversations you enjoy and whose interests are your interests. You know, if Sister Superior does that, how is she labeled? She is criticized for not having universal charity. The two or three with whom she "runs around" are regarded as kind of a cabal or "kitchen cabinet." Why cannot Sister Superior have her friends? What is wrong with that? There is always the danger that there may be a cabal—that there may be a select group and that they are "in on the know" and that *no one* outside of this group, not even the counsellors, know what is going on. There is the danger that they can usurp the place of the counsellors of the Superior, but this need not be. Are we to presume that it is so? Certainly not without adequate evidence.

I have been challenged on this a number of times, and I really do not know the answer when asked, "How does a Superior have her own friends without being suspect on that score?" Very often, this is one of the penances of being Superior. In other words, if you choose to visit with a Sister in the community who is your friend, you are liable to be accused of not being interested in the whole community. Charity demands that we *do not* make that type of judgment of Superiors, but *we do*.

One more reason why the Superior is lonely ties in with the last. You, as Subjects, can always turn to someone. To whom can the Superior turn? She has five Sisters under her and everyone of them comes to her with her problems and is upset, *really* upset, if the Superior does not solve the problems. Every one of these five Sisters has a problem that she does not want the Superior to discuss with any member of the community. So to whom does Sister Superior go for counsel? Where can she turn? You know it has been said that you have more than the ordinary number of holes in your head if you *want* to be a Superior. This is one of the reasons.

Subjects have an obligation under God to make the governance of Superiors as easy as possible. Honestly, I do not think there are very many Superiors who can say that every one of her Subjects is so minded. Some of them seem to have a peculiar capacity to keep the Superior in a turmoil. They are never satisfied with anything; they are unhappy about everything, and are always challenging the Superior as if she had the divine capacity to solve all problems.

Superiors have to listen. But let us face it, sometimes that is all they can do. They cannot always do anything effective about a problem. They did not choose the Subjects they have; they can do their best to make their representations to higher Superiors, but that is all they can do. Again, this loyalty to Superiors demands that we respect them as women of integrity who are trying their best. Sometimes even people of integrity slip. If it is any consolation to you, the saints committed venial sins. So your Superior may be very saintly, but she may slip up once in awhile. However, we should not roundly condemn her because she is human. Give her a break!

Father Evoy: This is going to have the appearance of a tangent. I come back after being hurt, in reality after being crushed by my Superior, and I go to someone who is a real friend of mine in the community—someone I think I can trust—and I tell her about it. I say, "Sister Superior hurt me deeply. She deliberately and maliciously singled me out in front of several others and really cut me down." Remember I am telling this to my fellow Sister. I am not going to an outsider. I am revealing this to just one of my own Sisters in religion. May I, with a clear conscience, say that to her?

Father Christoph: You may tell your neighbor that your Superior hurt you deeply. You may tell her that much.

Father Evoy: But I said, "She deliberately and maliciously singled me out."

Father Christoph: How do you know?

Father Evoy: Precisely. And that is why this is a rash judgment! Yes, as I said, this was only apparently a tangent, because when I said that she "deliberately and maliciously" did this to me, whether I knew it or not, I was being disloyal to my mother. On the other hand, since the person to whom I was speaking is my Sister, there is something wrong if I may not tell her that I felt I was just crushed by my mother. I may, indeed, do this. Perhaps I have to do this. I must get it out or I am afraid I may explode.

Father Christoph: There is no disloyalty there at all. As Father said, you have to have some kind of release and it is far better to talk to one of your companions when you are deeply hurt than for you to tear the veil off Sister Superior.

Father Evoy: All right. I could understand a Superior who would be severely tempted to say, "If these, my daughters under God, do not love me and are not loyal to me, what is the use of even trying? I might as well forget the whole thing." I think you can understand that. I can understand it very well, because *you* are all she has. She is necessarily alone in many areas. It is so easy to forget that she, alone, carries the major worries and burdens of the community. She, alone, has the real, intimate sense of these responsibilities. The others can try to share her concern, but ultimately she, and she alone, is the responsible person. It is she, and only she, who lies awake some nights worrying about things important to the community which are going badly. If you are not loyal to her, then what has she, under God, in terms of human affection, or in terms of anything tangibly comforting, reassuring or bolstering? What?

This gives rise to a relevant question. If I should happen to find a community in which not a *single* member is loyal to her Superior, I seriously wonder about it. In fact, I wonder very much about it. There is something suspect. If no one of them is loyal, then in effect, no one really loves her Superior. My concern here is not with this defect on the part of the Subjects, but rather with what it would seem to say about that particular Superior. We tend to love people who love us. If a Superior is unloved by all her Subjects, I cannot help but question whether she really loves them. At any rate, love seems so often to be a counter re-action. You tend to find it much easier to love the individual who loves you. Your own experience tells you that it is not really hard to love a person who really cares for you; who is really concerned about you, and in whose life you really count. In fact, you might find it difficult not to love such a person. In view of these considerations, the Superior who must truthfully say to herself, "None of my daughters loves me," perhaps should re-examine the whole situation, and see if her community is really that different. To begin with, in religion you have the cream of the population. You *have*. Sometimes, I am afraid that Sisters begin to wonder if Father Christoph and I think otherwise because of the critical things we must say. Mind you, I am not saying that the finest people you know are *all* in religion. No, but I am saying, in general, you took the cream right off the top. You took persons of generosity, of high purpose. You took persons who were capable of loving; those with the highest motives. These are the ones who came into religion. This is the group you have.

It is only being realistic to recognize that religious life has no monopoly on personality. The assumption is that everyone enter-ing religion is a good person, highly motivated. I may not equally assume that they are always the easiest persons with whom to live. A good person can be a very difficult person with whom to deal. At any rate, if an *entire* community is found in which not one of the members loves the Superior, we must wonder why. Should she not go back to inquire whether she is, perhaps, mak-ing it almost impossible for them to love her? If she is, regardless of any impressions she might have to the contrary, she does not really love them.

She may, indeed, be making it nigh on to impossible for them to love her. Such could readily be the case because the impact of the Superior on them is so great that if she did not love them, I doubt that they could really experience any considerable love toward her.

At any rate, if I may refer to something outside of the convent, I must say that I have never yet encountered a child who really was able to love a mother whom he felt did not love him. True, he would want her love. He would like very much to love her, but he could not manage to love the mother he felt was rejecting him. Time and again the experience of many persons has been that the personally emptying effect of such a rejection is just too great. The experience is that there is nothing left to the person with which to love. So it would seem, also, that here in religious life there is something in you that is destroyed if your Superior seems to regard you as if you were a "nothing." You feel hollowed if you sense that she judges you to be without personal worth. As a result, you tend to feel you are worthless. Because she sees you as a "nobody," you begin to see yourself in the same light.

Now, if you feel that she does not love you, then I do not think you are going to experience any real warmth of love toward her. Notice I am talking about a specific kind of love you have for her. When you take consideration of your conscience-bound duty, must you love her even if you still feel that she does not love you? Regardless of how she sees you and regards you, you still have the obligation of loving her with whatever love you can manage to elicit, because she is your mother and, as such, has the right to be loved by you.

The love which you have toward her must be characterized *at least* by loyalty to her. You simply will not hear of anyone saying anything against the one you love. You will not tolerate it. This certainly is one of the characteristics called for in the behavior of a Subject toward her Superior. No one, especially externs, should ever be permitted to say anything unkind, belittling or unfair about your Superior, and permitted to leave with the impression that you were condoning this type of thing.

It is so easy to be unfair to a Superior because, in a way, she is a natural target. At times, it strikes me that Superiors are regarded by many as not entirely unlike coaches of various ball teams. If a particular team loses, who gets the blame? The players? Almost always, the coach takes the brunt of it. If the team succeeds, who gets the credit? Right. The players who starred or who were outstanding in the game; not the coach. I wonder if there is not a parallel there. If things are going nicely in a community, people tend to praise the individual generosity and competency of the members of the community; if badly, the Superior is said to be clearly to blame.

Father Christoph: That is so, I think, because the Superior is the mother of all. In a family, small children vie with one another very frequently to get their equal share. For them their share is *equal* share—not equity, but equality. Today when a family is expecting a new arrival, the smaller children are frequently informed of the needs of this new arrival in order to preclude jealousy as far as possible. It does not always work, because you sometimes have a two-year old or four-year old jealous of a newborn babe. Perhaps in your own families you have had experience of this or have had members of your family tell you about it.

Now Sister X goes with Sister Superior. Sister Superior enjoys the company of Sister X. How is this regarded by other members in the community? If she goes off with Sister, we have the beginnings of a clique. Or the criticism is made that it is not because Sister Superior needs some recreation that she is with Sister, but that the two are talking about the rest of the community; or, at least, Sister X is monopolizing Sister Superior so that Sister Superior does not have enough time for the rest of the community.

Is it not unjust and unfair on the part of the Subjects to think in this fashion? Does not Sister Superior have as much right to choose to be with this Sister rather than that Sister? If she is tired and wants some recreation, is she not entitled to it? Father said that a Superior's life is a lonely life. We are the ones who make the Superior lonely because we will not allow her the same rights that we demand. Is that not immature?

Father Evoy: Would you say that materially, at least, this is a lack of loyalty?

Father Christoph: It is if I accuse the Superior of having her own cliques and neglecting the rest of the community. That is a lack of loyalty. What is basically wrong with the individual is the feeling, "I own my Superior." Just as the child does not own all her mother's time, neither do I own the Superior's. Sister Superior has a right to leisure; she has a right to self-improvement; she has a right to some quiet. Yet, from the time that she gets up (at least in a large community) until the time she goes to bed, she is at the beck and call of twenty, forty, fifty, one hundred or more Sisters, and she can be pretty tired at the end of the day.

You know we can be so immature about this. One goes to Sister Superior and taps on the door to ask for an audience. After a very brief discussion, Sister Superior dismisses her. "She has *no* time for me," thinks the Subject. Why does the Sister think that? Because she is so full of herself that she believes her concerns are the only ones of great moment, and she demands that her Superior look at them in the same way. But the Superior cannot, because she does not have that much time.

We demand time that the Superior cannot give. We want equality when the Superior, realizing that she has ten Sisters waiting for her, must give extra time to Sister Y, and cannot give the ten equal time. But do not think that she is not being a mother! She is being more of a mother when she gives Sister Y this extra time. If we are large enough and mature enough, we will realize this. This is equity. Sister Y needs this extra time. Sister Y would be in a sorry state if the Superior had not been more indulgent to her.

Father Evoy: You do not live in community life very long before you observe certain things. Among them is a danger which must be pointed out in connection with this matter of the loneliness of Superiors, about which we were talking. Reflection on this loneliness may mistakenly elicit in the mind of an elder retired member of the community the thought that since her Superior is so lonely, her dedicated mission now should be to remove the Superior's loneliness. So with the best of intentions, she becomes Sister Superior's "one-man plague." The Superior does not have time to turn around. This elderly religious is there at her door morning, noon, and night, to "rescue" her from her terrible loneliness —until the Superior could scream.

It can be terribly difficult for the Superior to handle this type of thing because she knows that she can so easily hurt this good elderly Sister if she says anything. Yet, very often it becomes unquestionably clear that no such indirect method as giving her hints or clues will work at all. So the Superior is faced with the most unpleasant task of having to tell this overly-solicitous person in some way or other, as nicely as she can, the age-old message, "Don't go away mad. Just go away, please."

If you happen to be one of the elder members of the community, you should reflect that you are not really capable of relieving the loneliness of the Superior. You may feel that a type of "Be kind to Sister Superior" attitude would benefit the community, but you should be very much on your guard against a "Be with Sister Superior all you can" pattern of behavior or even attitude.

We are talking not just about possibilities here. Actually, many a fine religious Superior has been practically driven out of her mind by the persistent standing at her door of some member of the community who really had nothing else to do. This well-intentioned, unemployed individual, with perhaps the best of intentions, was simply creating one more problem for the Superior. A far more sensible attitude would be that of going to Sister Superior's door only when necessary and showing one's kindness toward and consideration for Her in terms of not constantly "getting on her back." I find it very difficult to understand *what* kind of important business could take *any* Subject to her Superior's door on an average of more than once a day.

It is difficult to face the fact that you can be unfair, terribly unfair, to the Superior without realizing it. You can be very unreasonable. For example, take the time of permissions. All of you line up at the Superior's door, and when it comes your turn you are hurt because she did not talk to you for at least twenty minutes. You are aware that she knows very well that only yesterday you were visiting with your family. She did not even ask about your brother or your married sister. So you are hurt, deeply hurt. It does not even occur to you that you should not in all fairness have expected her to mention them or spend extra time with you at that particular moment. If she had even said, "I am glad to see you back," she might well have had to put aside very pressing business just to take the time to say that much.

Let us assume that you have been deeply hurt, and many a religious has, because she did not inquire about your family. When you look at the more mature attitude here, I think you will agree that it has the following aspects. Since one's own family matters very much to her, a Sister would be happy if Sister Superior would at least mention them, but out of consideration for her Superior she would not *expect* such mention. Why? Because she would assume that *if* the Superior were free at the present time from other pressing considerations, she would ask about her family because they are *her* family. She trusts her Superior enough and has enough confidence in her to understand that if her Superior does not ask about them, her Superior has a reason for not doing so. This special notice of her own family by a Superior is something over and above the duties of the Superior. It is something in the line of a bonus. If Sister Superior manifests her interest, fine. She is delighted. If she does not get the bonus, she would not go up to the Superior and say, "Sister, when am I getting this bonus?" She has no *right* to it. A bonus, of its very nature, is something that is given over and above that which is due the recipient.

Father Christoph: Is there not, Father, an element of selfishness in that attitude of expecting and demanding? Again it comes back to a lack of maturity.

Father Evoy: Perhaps self-centeredness would be a preferable term, since it does not have the blameworthy connotations of the word, "selfishness." I am interested in my relatives. Were I a woman, I think I might be much more interested in having my Superior inquire about them than I would be and am, as a man.

Father Christoph: We have been stressing the dimension of the material aspect of the Superior toward Subjects. If the Superior loves me, she shows an interest in me. Now, we had better not push this too far in terms of how important to her our concerns are. My problems may be overwhelming to me, but I may forget that in a community of twenty, thirty or forty Subjects, perhaps each Sister has just as large or larger problems than mine. I become indignant because Sister Superior does not give me all the time I want to discuss my problems with her! Perhaps I only want someone to listen. Let me exemplify by a parallel. I wake up in the morning with a toothache and it is really bothering me. So, without any telephone call, without any appointment, I go down to the dentist. The dentist has two people in the chairs and four other people in the waiting room. I cannot understand why he is not taking me next. Does not everyone know that my tooth is driving me out of my mind? Why should I have to wait? I forget that these people may have had appointments for over a month, and that if I spend ten minutes in the chair now, I may be robbing someone of ten minutes for which he has been waiting a month. The point? We become so wrapped up in our concern that we forget that the Superior has to be concerned about all. This is possessiveness on the part of the individual.

I have heard the complaint that Superiors do not have time for their Subjects. The Subjects are wrong to the extent that they feel their problems are the sole concern of Sister Superior or Mother Provincial or Mother General. They are being unfair and unrealistic. The Sister Superior has a twenty-four hour assignment; she is Superior twenty-four hours a day; but we have no right to presume that we are entitled to any one of those twenty-four hours. She has a right to privacy. She has a right to spiritual and intellectual growth. How many Superiors have time to read a book? And, frequently enough, it is because they are imposed upon by their Subjects. So let us not think because the Superior locks her door and has a half hour that she is going to call her own, that she is being unfair to us Subjects.

Father Evoy: In community life we sometimes resent it if a Superior has very little time for us because, as we mentioned earlier, she is so preoccupied with administration, building, and this type of thing. We do so rightly up to a point, but again we may also unwittingly become unfair here.

Father Christoph: Did it ever occur to you that at times we talk to others about the restriction Superiors place on us but never expose our attitude to the Superior herself? Very frequently, because of the past patterns of behavior of Superiors, we just presume we will not be permitted to do certain things. We complain about the crippling attitude of Superiors with respect to our initiative. Why do we not bring these things to the attention of Superiors? You know what we do? We sit around and talk with fellow religious about what we may not do and about the restrictions Superiors place on us. We never go to Superiors and tell them these things. The place to complain is where something can be done. There are frequently too many cliques in communities and divisions down the middle; not necessarily because the Superior has her own group, but because individuals do not like the way things are run.

Maybe some of their complaints are legitimate, but all the complainers do is create a disturbance in the community. They are known in Canon Law as *perturbatores pacis*—"disturbers of the peace." They create an atmosphere of low morale. They are complaining, they are criticizing adversely and they never make their voices heard where something can be done. This is extremely unfair to Superiors. You may find fault with your Superiors among your companions who may not feel the same way you do about them. But if you say enough about Superiors that is derogatory, eventually the ideas catch on. You brainwash your companions; and this is most unjust, and unfair, and certainly irreligious.

There are two other attitudes, I think, that the Subject should have toward Superiors. We have talked about loyalty and all the connotations of loyalty. Gratitude and appreciation also should be there. We have labored the point that when I, as a religious, operate and function in a given capacity I want the seconding, the full moral support of my Superior, provided it is something that should come to her notice. I always appreciate a kind word from my Sister Superior. But you know, I have heard individuals say of their Superiors, "Why do I have to thank her? She is my Superior and she has to do it, anyway. That is part of her job." What kind of mentality is that? She is supposed to do it, but she might not have done it. So when the Superior goes out of her way, when she shows her kindness and generosity and graciousness, we also ought to be big enough to notice it.

Superiors are human and if I want a "pat on the back," do you not think that they may need that just as much as I do? It gives them the stimulus to do more and be even more generous. Unfortunately, gratitude is one of the vanishing virtues. We demand things and we think we have a right to them, and when we get them, whether we have them by right or by gratuity, we accept them casually and never realize that Sister Superior could have refused them. So the generosity of Superiors should be matched by the appreciation and gratitude of Subjects.

Father Evoy: Father, does a Superior *have* to love her daughters?

Father Christoph: Well, I do not like the word "have to" because "have to" supposes a kind of formal obligation in the relationship.

Father Evoy: All right. But does she not have such a formal obligation? Could you not say, "Because she is Superior, she has the obligation of being a mother to them?"

Father Christoph: I would say it is the same thing as, "Does the mother *have* to love her children?"

Father Evoy: Precisely.

Father Christoph: She *should,* but sometimes she does not.

Father Evoy: But because she *has* to, does it cease to become worthy of commendation? Does it cease to be something for which a person should be grateful? Just because she *has* to? Our Lord said, "A new commandment I give you, that you love one another." Yet, He rewards our keeping that commandment. Even though we do what we have to do under obligation, He appreciates it.

You are religious Subjects and you are also women. Now, Sisters, I am going to be very frank here. You do not use any kind of cosmetic make-up. When, therefore, you are tired or you are not well, you look it. Hence you may say and it seems to me, rightly so, that if your Superior were genuinely interested, she would notice how you look. But what of the other side of the coin? Your Superior is also a woman and she does not use make-up, either. When she is tired or ill, she shows it. Do you notice it? Does she not have a right to expect that you would notice it? If she is tired or ill, and consequently shows it, should she not expect that you would say something about it? When you stop to look at it, this is simply *one* way of spelling out your love for her.

Sisters, I think that it is true that a Superior to a large extent, can make or break a religious community. Is it not also true that the members of the community, in a real sense, can make or break the Superior?

8 *Wellsprings of Behavior*

Father Christoph: It has been frequently remarked that the obedient religious would do absolutely anything she was told, short of sinning. This harks back, I think, to the famous letter of St. Ignatius on Obedience. The title modern psychologists have given this type of obedience is "cadaverous obedience" because St. Ignatius wrote that you are to be like a corpse or an old man's staff that serves him however he wishes to use it. The words Ignatius used may give the impression that you are not a person, that you are a thing. Some false ideas, therefore, relative to the nature of obedience, have gained currency on account of expressions which have been misunderstood.

Obedience does not mean that we are wooden. Even obedience of the intellect does not mean that we regard the position taken by the Superior with respect to things that are suggested or with respect to things that we are told not to do as being objectively the best thing. For the religious Subject it means it is the best for her spiritual development, but not necessarily the best objectively. So on the score of obeying, to restrain yourself from any effort, from engaging in initiative, from doing things on your own is *not* the correct idea of obedience. It has been claimed that Ignatian obedience demands a certain type of passivity in the one obeying; that religious are animated sticks. Nothing of the kind!

Let us get the context of the total situation. The letter on Obedience was not written on the spur of the moment. It was the fruit of Ignatius' original meditatons on the submission of the intellect and will to the Church. Ignatius lived in a period where there was rebellion against submission to the mind of the Church. St. Ignatius in his rules for thinking with the Church (better translated as "thinking *in* the Church) says, in effect, that if the Church says something is white and you think it is black, you still say it is white. It would take us too far afield to analyze this statement, but it has a bearing on obedience.

When St. Ignatius wrote this letter to the novices of Coimbra, he had primarily in mind the tumultuous conditions that were existing at the time, and the rebellion of so many people against submission to the Church. His letter, and the expression "submission of the intellect," must be interpreted entirely within the conditions under which St. Ignatius wrote. We have no right to interpret his writings out of context. So the question arises immediately, "When would submission of intellect be unhealthy and/or against faith?" First of all, no one can ask you to submit your intellect to accept anything as true which is contrary to faith or morals.

This does not refer exclusively to that which the Church has defined, for all of the dogmas of the Church have not been defined formally. So in matters of faith and morals, no one can expect you to give your intellectual assent to anything that is contrary to faith or morals. Again, the Superior can expect only your assent of the intellect in those areas in which she is competent to command, and she is not competent to command in all areas. Moreover, the assent of the intellect does not mean you agree intellectually, as in the well-known case where religious were commanded to plant the cabbages up-side-down. Can you agree intellectually that this is the acceptable way, the best way, or even the correct way to plant cabbages? You can give your assent to the command, but do you know to what you give your assent in this particular case? You assent to do what the Superior wants you to do. You can say, "This is the best thing for me as a Subject operating under obedience." You do this, *not* because it is the best thing for the cabbages, but because it is the best thing for the end proposed, which obviously is a test of obedience. By the way, this is not a very wise test, but if there is such a test of obedience, then I can give intellectual assent to it on that score.

Father Evoy: May I put it in slightly different words? This assent of the intellect must be reasonable at all times. Very candidly, Sisters, one is *never* permitted to commit suicide either physically or psychologically. She is not permitted therefore to violate her intellect. For her to say black is white or white is black is to violate a very essential part of herself. She must be true to herself. She cannot, therefore, say that she sees black when she actually sees white. She must, accordingly, find some reasonable way to give the assent of her mind to the directive of her Superior, so that in so doing she is not in the slightest way violating her intellect.

It makes a good deal of sense for her to turn over certain operations of her intellect and will freely to God within the structure of religious obedience that comes down to her through her religious Superiors. When she is then told to do something under religious obedience, she may do it even when she is not able to agree that the thing appears to be either wise or correct. She does not have to say that black is white. In fact, she may, even laudably, tell her Superior what her judgment of the correctness or wisdom of this thing is, after which she will do exactly what the Superior says. Thus, she is not violating anything and is certainly not saying what to her is, really is not, or what to her is not, really is. She is simply carrying out the orders as well as she can. She does it freely because of her original commitment to God within the framework of religious life. There is no personally violating difficulty whatever about that commitment. It does

her no violence even should her Superior persist in thinking that
black is white. It could be that after she and others have pointed
out to the Superior that such does not appear to be the case, the
Superior might still insist that black is white. Given even such an
extreme case, she can almost smile and say, "All right, if it makes
her happy, let her think it." Now, Sisters, with reflection it is
clear to all of you that any serious consideration of religious
obedience necessarily gives rise to the place of initiative and
ambition in religious life. These in turn must be evaluated over
against the importance and proper area of conformity in religious life. First of all, then, we will say something about conformity in religious life.

Father Christoph: Within the framework of religious life, I am
supposed to develop as a unique personality. When we enter
religion we have a tremendous amount of enthusiasm. We are
generous and we are eager to be good religious. Then we are
subjected to a regime in which we are given the ideals and told
how to achieve them. Emphasis is placed on conformity. "Do this
and you will become perfect. Do this and you will be an ideal
Sister." There is justification for some type of conformity.

One sociological law says that whenever you have numbers of
human beings together, you must have regulations. Laws multi-
ply in proportion to individuals, because the relationships mul-
tiply. Let us put it this way. Two individuals decide to work for
the love of God. They are two women. Each can do as she pleases.
They have a common life insofar, we will say, as they live in the
same place, assist at Mass together, eat their meals together. Now
they can lead perfectly beautiful lives of love and service of God
and yet not do anything else in common.

Suppose they add to their number, one dozen, two dozen, three
dozen, or four dozen other women. There are bound to be some
regulations, and regulations involve conformity. Let us suppose
further that the two women did not even have time to eat together because of circumstances or on account of the particular

work they chose to do. So one ate her breakfast at seven; the other ate hers at eight. Can you envision this group of women, thirty or forty of them living together, each eating breakfast at a different time? This does not make good sense, so there has to be some designated time for breakfast. You cannot expect to have ten priests come to your convent to say Mass in order to accommodate the desires or needs of Sisters who are getting up from four to ten o'clock in the morning.

So there has to be a regulation regarding Mass. There has to be conformity within the framework of the rules and the constitutions of your own institute. It is within a framework of a particular institute that there should be the development of an individual personality, but along lines laid down in the institute. There is the conformity that makes for order, efficiency and common life, and a conformity that fosters regimentation and stultification.

Father Evoy: So right here we are introduced to a danger which is peculiar to life in religious community. We have pointed out that obedience not only is not an evil, but is in no way a violation of an individual's own person or own integrity. We have also indicated that religious obedience of necessity dictates a certain conformity of behavior in religious life. This conformity, which is a good thing, and an essential thing, in a community, is something which can slip almost unnoticed into the abuse of an ultra-conformity which can be most hurtful to the individual members as well as to the community. The hurtfulness of such conformity is particularly evident in reference to initiative and ambition in a religious Subject.

It seems well to clarify the two words "ambition" and "initiative." Would we use "ambition" and "initiative" as interchangeable terms? Ordinarily not. For the most part, the exercise of initiative refers to self-determination of ways and means in carrying out what one is given to do. Besides, it ordinarily would be understood to call for a certain amount of ingenuity in doing things. "Ambition" is usually understood in the sense of the hunger, the striving, the impulse in a person for the more, the better, the higher, the greater, the newer. "Ambition" also says a certain amount of ingenuity, but it is more concerned with the striving for a goal rather than it is with the planning of means to end. In that sense, I think we could say that initiative is always presupposed in ambition, but the converse is not true. Ambition need not be implicitly contained in initiative. This is so even in view of the fact that initative can well call for a certain amount of originality. It can call as well for imagination and even a search for better ways of doing something. But it is ambition that wants to obtain the higher—that wants to do more and to do it better. Furthermore, the urge of ambition normally will not satisfy itself by doing very well the task of the moment.

Father Daniel Lord once upon a time recounted the following little episode. There was a knock on his room door one day, following which Father LaFarge entered and asked, "Where does the one leave off and the other start?" Father Lord, with something of a double take, replied, "Where does what do what?" Father LaFarge then remarked, "Sorry. I thought I had made it clear. Where does obedience leave off and initiative start?" When he asked that, he framed a question which I think every religious should ask herself from time to time. I am not talking principally in terms of available time. I am talking in terms of an *attitude.*

So before we develop ambition, let us look for a moment at initiative in religious life. A genuine danger lurks here. Under the protective umbrella of alleged obedience, a religious can, if she is not vigilant, convince herself that she is operating maturely when she is simply doing what she has been told to do as she has been told to do it. The hazard is in the danger of her becoming something resembling an animated sponge without self-determination or self-direction worthy of mention. In a word, it is possible for her to go ahead in a passive, routine fashion, carrying out the things assigned to her in the way she has been told, with her

own initiative operating at the very minimum. If almost complete lack of initiative characterizes her work, I think further
reflection will show she simply cannot operate as a fully adult
person while caught in this rut. This point we hope to develop
for you presently.

So much for initiative at the moment. I wonder, Sisters,
whether you have ever gone to confession and said, "Father, I
accuse myself of not being ambitious." Very frankly, I never have
done that myself, but I think I honestly might have, since I am
interested in mentioning in confession important areas in which
I fall short of what I should be. Obviously, if and when I were to
find myself ambitious in the sense that my over-all search was in
terms of *me,* characterized by self-centered efforts in the interests
of "Number One" to feather my own nest, I might well accuse
myself in confession of being ambitious. This kind of self-seeking
ambition is clearly out of keeping with the ideals of religious life.

I would confess it, not because it is ambition, but because it is
the *wrong* kind of ambition. But we also fall seriously short if we
lack the *right* kind of ambition. We are apostolic communities.
We can be apostolic in the full sense of the word, only when both
as individuals and as religious communities we utilize our God-
given talents to the full in His cause. The distinction which I
have drawn between ambition and initiative is a good theoretical
distinction. In practice, however, initiative and ambition are
often so closely inter-twined that it seems more practical to treat
the two of them together, with full recognition that what we say
at any given time might refer somewhat more to the one than to
the other.

Now, as we promised earlier, we are going to explore further
religious obedience. Once we stop to analyze the nature of obedience, we discover that when initiative and ambition are lacking
in the individual religious, obedience in that person finds itself
handicapped to the point where it can be "hamstrung" in its
efficaciousness. Such an analysis of obedience will show first of all
that the exercise of authority is essentially imperfect. Its imper-

fection flows from the human equation necessarily involved in its operation. The Superior herself is still a mere human being with a limited fund of knowledge. Moreover, she has at best a limited understanding of her religious Subject over whom she is exercising authority. Again, the expectation is that she has only a partial knowledge of some of the specialized areas of work of her religious Subjects, in which, nevertheless, they are functioning under her direction.

Accordingly, it would be preposterous, from a mature point of view, to expect the exercise of authority to be lacking in imperfection. It must contain imperfection. This is the way God has set it up. Viewed very maturely, in fact, the last thing in the world that should surprise one would be a lack of prudence and wisdom in the commands and directives of a Superior. Even though, like all things human, the exercise of authority is marked by imperfection, the important point is that it cannot be exercised even at its best unless the Superior is informed about those matters required for her wise governing. In other words, the Superior must have the body of information needed in order to govern as wisely as is possible.

And Sisters, much of the information she can obtain only from you, the Subject. There is a closely related consideration here. You know that, generally speaking, you tend to work better where your spontaneous interests lie. On the other hand, your tendency is to work less well in those areas which run directly counter to your interests and inclinations. Let us assume, for the sake of an example, that I know only too well that I am naturally disinclined toward laboratory work, and my over-all inclination is to be dealing with people, not with things. I experience an involuntary shudder when I consider that Superiors might put me in "thing work," instead of "people work."

We recognize that there is, perhaps, not a single individual in or out of religious life who likes every aspect of his work. Furthermore, we know that a religious Superior cannot always give every Subject the kind of work toward which she is naturally inclined. The work of the community requires at times that naturally distasteful tasks be carried out by certain persons. This, we fully accept. What we are concerned about is that a Superior might never be given the opportunity to evaluate and place her religious Subjects according to their inclinations and God-given talents, because the Superior *has never been told.*

Are we assuming that with the Superior's office comes a grace of state which has, as one of its components, a bit of omniscience, or some type of mental telepathy which enables her to read minds and to look into the inner sanctuary of one's personal interests?

Here is an example. Suppose Sister X loves to be in the laboratory while Sister Y is desirous of working with people. Neither one tells the Superior this. Is she supposed to guess it? Suddenly she has a particular vacancy in the laboratory. She looks at Sister Y and says, "I think, Sister, that you should work in the laboratory." Sister Y has never told her. If she had told her and then she judged, nevertheless, that she would have to put Sister Y in the lab, she then has the knowledge requisite to govern wisely in Sister Y's case. On Sister Y's part, she has a clear conscience in the matter and so can undertake this assignment, willingly, without hesitation, even though it is naturally distasteful to her.

Over and above the fact that Sister Y could have failed by never having told her that which is necessary for her wisest administration of authority, there is yet another related area in which Sister Y could be wanting. It may seem to her that there are certain things which would help the community to be more effective in its over-all functioning. Some of these might be best undertaken by Sister Y personally; some, by other individuals or by the community as a whole. These are things which are over and above that which has been laid down by obedience. As a mature religious a Sister should not take it lightly that she has never bothered to tell her Superior these things.

Father Christoph: Just to add a little to what Father has been saying. There was a period in the history of religious institutes when it was regarded as a kind of a small crime to give a Sister or a religious the kind of work that she liked to do, because this meant there was no virtue in it. Well, you know, after all, religious communities ought to be run efficiently. Motivational studies have taught us that interest, ability, and efficiency go well together. Let the individual do what he likes and can do because he will do that best.

The idea that if you, as a religious, are going to find some enjoyment in your work, you should do just the opposite kind of work, is strange indeed. That belongs to some bizarre type of thinking, a puritanical attitude which held that anything pleasurable was simply to be avoided by religious. There was a time when individuals in religion were told, "Do this because it is good for your humility. It will break your will so it will be easy for you to conform, and you will be more pleasing to Almighty God." It did not matter if you were teaching something about which you knew nothing. Actually institutes were cheating the children attending classes in their schools. That did not matter because this was good for *you.*

For the most part this, thank heavens, has disappeared, although occasionally I hear evidences of it in my work among communities of religious women. The idea that you should be doing something that you dislike because it is more virtuous, is in itself, a lot of nonsense. When I do something I happen to love to do, I can be very holy and most pleasing to Almighty God, and I can still be doing it for the love of God. If it is something I do not like, I do it also for the love of God. What is the difference? One is harder, yes, but not necessarily better suited to one's religious objective. The work that I do for the love of God and enjoy, may actually be more fruitful. It is not the merit to which I should give consideration, but the end for which I work.

We live in the twentieth century, not in the Middle Ages. We live in an age where we have to exploit, in the best sense of the

word, the talents of individuals. We do not have enough people
to go around, and so we choose the best individual for a given
job. To thus exploit the individual to the best, there must be
allowances for initiative and creativity. Unfortunately, historically, the attitude of a religious was considered to be excellent if
she were passive and merely receptive to any commands that a
Superior gave.

This whole slant on obedience seems to be due to a misinterpretation of the letter of St. Ignatius on Obedience. This attitude, as we noted, has been called "cadaverous obedience." That
is the last thing in the world that St. Ignatius wanted his Subjects
to have and to be. You know, he told Xavier, "Go to India."
And, as far as I know, he left it up to Xavier how to get there. Is
that "cadaverous obedience?" If it had been cadaverous obedience, then Ignatius would have had him boxed and sent him
there. As Father mentioned, the word ambition often has a
pejorative connotation. The Latin root of ambition means to go
around something, *ambigere,* to move around a thing. According to this pejorative connotation, ambition has been linked with
pride and excessive self-love. But, as Father pointed out, there is
a good connotation to "ambition." We should want to do the
best we can for our community in the best possible way. This
ambition should never be stifled but rather fostered by Superiors.

Father Evoy: As we go on in religious life, we discover pretty
clear-cut talents in various members of the community. Fortu-
nately, this often comes to the attention of Superiors. I wonder if
Superiors have given enough attention to the thought that such
God-given talents are signs of what God wants for a particular
person. Talents are given to be used. Have Superiors sufficiently
considered the fact that one indication of God's will for a particular religious Subject is the special gifts she has been given by
God?

Father Christoph: This is one thing I think Superiors should reflect on more. In religious life there is a studied effort to make the Subject realize that a command given under obedience is an expression of God's will, and this is true. But as Father Evoy says, the presence of this particular talent may be and *should* in fact be regarded by the Superior as evidence of God's will. Superiors do ill, it seems to me, in failing to see and take advantage of the natural talents of the Subject. You know, when Superiors do "exploit" talent, the individual is inclined to be more generous in making use of her talents because personal morale is strengthened.

If, in selecting a Sister to do a task, there is a choice between two or three individuals, one of whom is able to do it much better than the others, it would be unfair to the community to put the poorest one in that particular work. It is a sign of maturity on the part of the other two to recognize that this one is best suited for the undertaking, and so instead of being downcast because they were not given the work, they look for something that is more in keeping with their talents and also will fill the gaps in the community's program, whatever and wherever that happens to be. But let me remind you that there seems to be a positive correlation between a lack of ability and the overestimation of one's potentialities. Many are unrealistic in their own self-appraisal. My own experience in the classroom has led me to expect that the individual who is inferior is often surprised at low grades, which indicates there is habitual overestimation of one's abilities. "I like to do this. Therefore, I am able to do it." This is the type of individual, I suppose, that might misconstrue some of the things we are saying here.

Father Evoy: We are at one in recognizing that one bane of teaching is the person who is at best a "D" student and cannot understand why she does not get "A's." This indicates defective ability to evaluate self correctly. It is hardly surprising that the same kind of defective self-critical ability is to be found in religious life, since it happens to be one of the by-products of a pattern of ultra-conformity. I would not want to be misunderstood on this point.

By no means am I saying that ultra-conformity is an over-all characteristic of religious community life in this country. My concern is only with the danger that a pattern of conformity which by and large is wholesome, can slip unnoticed into ultra-conformity. Actually, ultra-conformity can have such devastating effects on the members of the community that it is difficult to exaggerate the damage that it can do. Because this mockery of proper, reasonable conformity is so peculiarly liable to invade religious communities I think that we ought to spell out some of the hurtful effects that it has, so that religious can be on guard against it.

Father Christoph: The simplicity that flows from uniformity, I think, is one of the reasons why, in the young religious and even in the older religious, there can be a certain neglect of the element of initiative. If we allowed postulants and novices more initiative, there is always the fear that we will not get the required minimum amount of uniformity. That is why, I think, things are spelled out for them.

Father Evoy: You are really spot-lighting a danger there. There is a danger that a Superior could almost unknowingly slip into insisting on over-all undue conformity, because of her feeling that such was required for better government. It could appear to make government easier. But that easiness comes at a tremendous price to the community. This ultra-conformity has the over-all effect of producing individuals accustomed to not thinking for themselves, to being passive, to being to a very little extent, self-determined. All but the very minimum opportunity to think for self may be denied one.

There is a corollary to this thing. If we look once again at the impact of a parent's judgment of a child, we can catch something relevant here. For instance, if a father says repeatedly to his child, "You will never be able to hammer a nail straight," even at the age of forty that son will probably feel still unable to hammer a nail straight. In view of our previous statement that religion has the characteristic of being a recapitulation of life, the deadening effect of this same pattern of "big people" evaluation is immediately seen.

We are emphatic about a point mentioned earlier. If religious women from the earliest years of their community life are being told quite effectively, "You can't do your own thinking; you can't do your own important deciding," the result will be dreadful. When they reach, let us say, their forties, the effect on them is going to be a feeling of basic inadequacy and incompetency in these areas.

It is always going to be difficult, I think, to encourage independence of the right kind in young religious, because of the conformity required in religious communities. But granting this difficulty, it is something that must be seriously striven for in view of the almost unbelievable potential of ultra-conformity to turn out religiously garbed, partially dehumanized persons. Extreme conformity can be dehumanizing in the frightening sense that it produces individuals who are not really responsible for themselves. These people, in fact, could not dream of making any kind of decision or serious judgment for themselves. They cringe pitifully even at the prospect of having to do so. It seems to me that this danger needs to be declared openly because it is so easy for it to slip into religious community life. The peril is there. Unless we are vigilant against it, we can turn out religious so crippled by passivity that in God's service they somehow continue to exist, though actually incapable of really being themselves in any significant way. Objectively, it is a travesty on God's creation.

As Father Christoph mentioned earlier, we are particularly concerned at this threat to those who are wholly dedicated to God's work, lest among them might be found this type of debilitating, stultifying, dehumanizing—yes, and in a real sense, depersonalizing pattern. If personality means anything, it refers to the uniqueness of the individual. If we rub or blot out this individuality so as to make all of the persons come out of the same mold as non-thinking, non-deciding, frightened individuals, we have produced a monstrosity.

Father Christoph: We reduce everyone to a dead level, rather than elevate each to the status of being a person making a genuine contribution to the good of the institute. Again, this reemphasizes the need to give the individual as much room as possible for the developing and exploiting of her own abilities.

At the same time, we are fully aware of the difficulties involved in permitting such freedom to individual religious. Liberty has always come at a price. This freedom is well worth the granting, despite the risk involved. Among the foreseeable difficulties in giving religious such independence is the assumption that certain few individuals will come up with "bizarre ideas" because some of these individuals are going to be imprudent. But strange as it may seem, this should not appear an insuperable difficulty to us. In recent years a socio-psychological phenomenon called "brain-picking" has been developed. A group gets together under this formality and discusses a particular problem. They do not care how ridiculous the ideas are, because the point is, no matter how bad any idea is, it may cause someone else to take off from there and come up with a genuinely good idea.

Father Evoy: Yes, and in the light of this, it seems that frequently in religion today there is too much concern about a spirit of independence, especially in the younger religious, and not enough concern about unhealthy dependence. There is not sufficient concern about the habitually thoughtless, other-directed personalities developing almost personality-less under the impact of this stifling, killing thing which must be labelled "abject conformity." As a matter of fact, I am almost sympathetic to a question that has been raised in this area. The question is,

"Should Superiors occasionally command their Subjects to make their own decisions and to be responsible for themselves?" I am not at all sure that this is the correct way to do it, but I find myself sympathetic, at least, with the over-all intent of this kind of thing.

We have already mentioned in our book, *Personality Development in the Religious Life,* some of the damaging effects of unhealthy conformity on youngsters in the world outside. You are aware that there have been attempts to account for rather extreme conformity in religious communities on the grounds that it is required in these religious bodies since they are so many military regiments of Christ's army, fighting for His kingdom. It would be a real fallacy to regard the exercise of obedience in religious life as somehow paralleling the exercise of obedience within a military body of the country. Within such a military body all that is required, for the most part, is external observance, which means the actual carrying out of commands. The military wishes them carried out without any notable evaluative operation on the part of the subjects. Military obedience is fulfilled simply by doing what one is told.

This is one reason why younger people are preferred in certain areas of the military. The presumption is that they will carry out orders without the strong inclination to insert any of their own critical thinking about the wisdom of the orders they receive. In religious life, on the contrary, we never settle completely for the externals. We may never renounce our own responsibility for what we do. This refers not only to what we are but also to what we do. What we do is always understood as taking place within the framework of religious obedience. We might ask the question, "But, is not a religious always a dependent?" The answer, of course, must be distinguished. In the sense that dependency means childlike and befitting trust and submission toward the commands of the Superior, yes. In a sense which would in any way lessen the person of the Subject, or take away from the Subject the responsibility for herself, no, absolutely not.

Dependency, therefore, must never be permitted to become

depersonalizing or demeaning to the individual religious. Nevertheless, this dependence is built upon and actually permeates the whole of religious life under obedience. There is, I believe, a ready temptation for a religious to avoid doing her own thinking and deciding, on the score that this is somehow or other not in keeping with religious perfection.

She might put it this way: "I couldn't make my own decision because this would be doing *my* will, rather than God's will." I think the unsoundness of this position will be rather strikingly evident when we recollect that God wants a service according to the nature He has given us, even in the religious vocation which is ours. He has made us free. We are to continue to operate as free persons, even under obedience. Since we remain free persons, even in religious life, we may not renounce what we are and accordingly, our exercise of obedience must be suited to our nature, which is free.

We are to be free not only in the sense of lacking some kind of external coercion, but also in the sense of being capable of making decisions, and of being able to determine for ourselves the validity of something. I may permit no one to violate my intellect or my will. Still another facet of damage to a religious due to the wrong kind of conformity is a regrettable social immaturity. In the eyes of adults in the world, religious are at times judged to be somewhat socially deficient. Indeed, to the extent that we are active religious, we are for the most part also professional persons and it is a sorry encomium when religious are judged not really capable of dealing as professional equals with externs.

Father Christoph: Maybe too much stress is put upon a pattern of behavior that is somewhat artificial. We are too well aware of the sameness that appears, especially in religious women. This is manifested perhaps in their posture, the things they do, their actions, the way they present themselves to externs. Granted that part of this is certainly dictated by a sense of propriety. But within the pattern of propriety, it seems to me that there should be room for individuality. Religious life does not, and should not necessarily mean, that you lose yourself as a person. This deadly conformity implies that religious think alike, speak alike, and have the same inflections and intonations, the same attitude toward reality. There ought to be an area in which the individual can be herself as an independent person.

Father Evoy: Religious at times are kept from really being as effective as they should be with externs, apparently because of their lack of social development. They are not comfortable in their relationships with other persons and especially with men. There are religious, you see, who fear to talk to a man even on the phone, let alone in the parlor. They are *most* uncomfortable with a man. Probably some of this originates in the fact that in their early religious life undue stress was placed on the point that a man can be a source of temptation. Certainly, because you are women, a given man could be a source of temptation just as he could be for a woman in the world.

Perhaps a great deal of this social uncomfortableness is due to the fact that for many a religious woman, a man remains something of an unknown. She has talked to priests in and out of the confessional, but often there has been no comfortable, informal, social experience with them, and besides, she regards priests as not just mere men. The opportunity of close contact with men has not been given her. The Sisters have not had the opportunity to get to know men, hence communicating with them is an unaccustomed and an uncomfortable experience. But many of you must be directly in personal or professional contact with men, either because of your relationship to their children, or on some other score.

Father Christoph: Let us take the example of a home and school association or whatever you may call it—the Catholic counterpart of the P.T.A. Look at how many religious women just hate to go to meet the parents. This is due in part to the fact that some religious do not know how to hold up their end of the conversation, or put people at ease, or be urbane. They do not really understand how to be friendly without failing to be deeply religious and committed to their vocation.

We must mention, I think, that in the training of young religious, Superiors and others can fail to see that their guidance can assume the dimensions of an obsession. Besides, there is at least the possibility that such guidance would be needed more by the Superior than by the one being thus guided. It can fulfill, primarily, a personality need of the Superior. This is a great danger in religious life, both for the religious man and the religious woman. Since we have given up the role of parenthood, it seems that some of us have a need to help someone, and so we take these people who are not in a position to refuse our guidance, and we direct them and thus satisfy this parental impulse, to the extent, sometimes, of directing them the rest of their lives. We interfere; in fact, we treat them like children and we keep them children because we need to.

Father Evoy: At times it may even be in keeping with the psychological needs of the older person to "play God," and accordingly to take over and so completely dominate another human being, that in a sense, the older person seems to be correcting God's original creation. And the older person's psyche can furnish her with a full window-dressing of justification for so doing.

Father Christoph: Some time ago a religious Superior told me a story indicating something which she said happened all too frequently in her community. The Superior who told me this was an older member of the community and highly respected in her community, and, I think, a woman with a lot of common sense. A Sister in her forties was told by this Superior to carry out a project on her own. About two hours later, this Subject came to the Superior, distraught. She was completely upset. Why? Something that she wanted all her life happened to her and now that it happened to her she did not know where to begin or what to do. She was told to do something all on her own. She was not given a road map on how to do it. She was not told every detail of the operation. She simply broke down and cried!

She came to the Superior because she could not take it any longer, just sitting in her room trying to figure out what to do. "All my life I wanted to do something on my own and now that you have told me to do it, I can't. I don't know where to begin. At my age, isn't it embarrassing and humiliating? I have never had an opportunity to exercise initiative, and now that you give me the opportunity, I don't know what to do. I am afraid. I am afraid to make a mistake." The Superior said, "Well, you've done these things before." The answer came back, "Yes, but someone has always been around to lead me."

Is that a mature attitude? Is that how we expect a woman even thirty years of age to act? Yet sometimes the misunderstanding of religious obedience and of humility and submission to the mind of Superiors, and a strict adherence to the letter of the rule and constitutions leave an individual robbed of initiative, devoid of incentive, struggling against low morale because nothing can so defeat high morale as not acting one's age. It is only when we are in situations calling for decisions do we sometimes realize how childish are our attitudes toward life, toward our obligations and toward our work. This is because we have a false idea of religious obedience and the limits of honorable ambition.

Father Evoy: There is another major deterrent to both initiative and ambition. I refer to a silence which is killing. Silence coming from whom? Well, the most important individual involved would be one's Superior, but next to that would be her fellow Sisters. I can show you the type of thing I am speaking of by means of an example. One of our own men had traveled some distance to give a sermon for a special occasion. He went with about half a dozen other priests from his own community. When he returned, he walked into my room and said, "I don't think I will give a sermon again as long as I live."

He was most discouraged and deeply hurt. His reason? He explained it. "I did not prepare and I did not give this sermon for any of these other priests, but I worked very, very hard on it and did as well as I could, and I think I did a good job. Do you know," he said, "that I traveled all the way home with them and not one of them as much as said to me, 'Nice job!' or referred to it in any way? I'm through." This makes sense to me and I think it also makes sense to you. For if we love one another, should we not care what the other individual is doing? If we care, what is the matter with expressing this to the individual concerned?

Father Christoph: In fact, if you care, you will express it because you *do* care. What Father says is all too common. There is not one Sister here who has not had the experience that Father has described. Expressing approval, admiration or congratulations is called for on occasion. Particularly is this so if someone prepares a program, whether it is a choral group, or a TV performance, whatever kind of public presentation it may be. Sisters, it strikes me as strange and suspect when no one comes up and says in her own way to Sister, "That was lovely. That was well done. That was . . ." You know, the way you personally would express it to her.

There is something more involved here than applauding or giving the individual a pat on the back. You know what really hurts is when you do something for the community and only a small segment shows up. When "ours" do things, be present if possible. They are not doing it for themselves. Show up, even if you do not like it. I think that "ours" have a right to my support, a right to my concern, an interest that it be a success. It is most disheartening when someone puts out for a community of twenty-five persons, and only four or five of them show interest in it. It crushes. What happens to the ambition? What happens to the initiative? What happens to creativity? What happens to generosity, charity? "No one cares, so why should I care?" Now as Father said, you do not do it to get the approval of Mother General, Mother Provincial, Mother Superior or your companions, but it makes it a lot easier to do it again if someone says in her own way, "Nice going, dear."

Father Evoy: Over and above the occasional events calling for personal commendation are some things in everyday living. Occasionally you pick up a complimentary remark about one of your Sisters. It is not necessary, for the most part, to go out of your way in order to pass along a compliment. But when you do get the chance, say, "I heard a very nice thing about you today," or, "So and so said she enjoyed your class very much," or, "Somebody said you were a very conscientious nurse," or whatever it happens to be. Telling her is never out of place, and is called for at least occasionally.

Why do more religious not do it? It does not cost one much, and it means so much. No matter what you are doing, Sisters, you do need a certain amount of this kind of thing, especially from your fellow religious. It seems to me that it is not just that you need their reinforcement, but you need to know that these persons care. This kind of expression usually says clearly to you that the person does care.

It means so much that they care. Perhaps this is why a hurt from them can be so painful and so depressing. Both of us can understand, and we are sure that you can, that occasionally an individual religious, after being "quashed" by a fellow religious, especially if she is a Superior, will say, "Never again. I will never again open my mouth because to do so is just asking to have myself labeled as a 'problem child' in the community, or one who must be disciplined, and kept under surveillance of one type or another. I will not run the risk of getting myself categorized as a troublemaker, as someone who is bothersome and refuses to conform."

Under the smarting impact of this kind of experience, we both recognize that an individual could very well say, "Never again. If they want me, they know where I am and they can get in touch with me; but I will not volunteer anything." Even though we can understand it, we still must say this is not the ideal. This is not what we would want to see. It takes a courageous, unquestionably brave individual, at times, to have the courage prudently to go back again and again. Put very frankly, this means that one would become, in the service of Christ, something of a human gymnasium dummy.

It means that after a religious has been "slapped down," she picks herself up as soon as she has recovered sufficiently, and again approaches a Superior or someone else, when wholesome ambition dictates that she do so. To do this repeatedly requires almost incredible courage. Even while I am making this point, I am aware that this same pattern of going back again and again after being hurt could be employed by one in the community who is so lacking in ordinary prudential judgment that she might be bringing the rebuffs on herself. Indeed, a religious could in this way acquire her needed "martyr-kicks." Whatever the case, even for these individuals, tremendous courage may be required, although these people would prove very wearing on Superiors.

But this willingness, periodically, to make overtures to Superiors for the purpose of enabling them to govern wisely, is something of the utmost importance. Clearly, we are talking about an ideal, but an ideal which is most consonant with the real order. The ideal, on the whole, would be realized if every member of the community were to say, "I am going to try, with reasonable frequency, to keep my Superior informed about my own abilities and interests, and also about possible improvements in and for the work of the community."

Unless, in a given religious community, this ideal is, in large part, realized, a segment of Christ's Mystical Body is going to suffer. This suffering will be due to the lack of effectiveness and the lack of impact of these active religious on the body, social and religious.

Father Christoph: There is a genuine difficulty here, because when the individual wants to do what she can do, there has to be enough incentive to make her do it. It is a matter of push and pull. The push is the motivation; that is something within you. The pull is something outside you, the incentive. Incentive is the thing that draws on this motivation, that causes you to operate.

What are the incentives out there? The incentive that you are doing it for God ought to be enough, but unfortunately, as much as I live in the presence of God, God is not tangible to me. You do not do it for the Superior, but if the Superior does not notice it you may find yourself saying, "What is the use?" I do not do it because I expect or want the Superior to commend; that is not the incentive—the thing outside of me that is eliciting my activity. But being a human being, when I do something and it is not noticed by my Superior, I feel crushed. I think to myself, "What do you have to do to have the Superior notice that you are trying?" Perhaps all I need or even want is to be loved, to be appreciated, to feel wanted, to have my activities seconded, to have someone say, once in a while, "Nice going."

Does it mean that I am a less religiously orientated person when I need this type of seconding? *No!* It only means I am a *genuine* human being. I have a right to expect that those who portion out the activities of obedience will have the graciousness to see that when I do what is commanded, I get commended for it. Remember, you do not do it for the commendation, but if you do not get any at all, the time may come when you cannot do it any longer because you are weary and want to give up. So your ambition and incentive are sometimes stifled by the lack of appreciation on the part of people who count in your life. And Superiors count very much. Companions also count.

I once heard a Superior say, when it was suggested that members of the community should be asked about certain things, "Why should I ask the members of the community about anything? I have the grace of state. I was put in this office and therefore my decisions are certain." I said, "They are certain, but they are not infallible." The Superior who will not listen to any suggestions, effectively dampens any enthusiasm. She puts cold water on the fire of ambition, and she has a community of individuals who are like the four animals in the Apocalypse who say, "Yes. Yes. Yes." She surrounds herself with individuals who agree with everything she wants and second her every idea. Do you think she has a good religious community? She has a very subservient, low-moraled, servile community from which she will not get a new idea in a decade, because the initiative and ambition in members have been thwarted and crushed.

Father Evoy: Father and I could employ our time speaking of the religious houses all across this country in which initiative and ambition, far from being thwarted, are actively fostered by both Superiors and fellow religious alike. But we would judge that you are already aware of these and that they meet with your unqualified approval and commendation. It is our purpose to do what we can toward advancing this state of things. Our aim is to point out the faulty interpretations of the spirit and rule of religious life which have unfortunately led to a suppression of human beings in this all-important area.

It seems to us that we are quite realistic in working on the assumption that, once there has been an unmasking of unwholesome patterns which have been masquerading as properties of religious life, at least a beginning will have been made from which individuals in religion will be able to work toward whatever correctives will be needed. It is of the utmost importance then, for religious to be acquainted with the psychologically and spiritually wholesome patterns of religious life and to be able to discern precisely what is defective in those insidious patterns which have, at times, grown up and flourished in religious life.

Father Christoph: Therefore, there are a few types of religious patterns of which we have to be careful. One is having no ambition and no desire to strike out on our own to do the things within the framework of religious obedience that should be done; and another, somewhat akin to it, is retiring from the active life in middle age. I do not think that you will find, percentage-wise, more individuals who are in semi-retirement at middle age than in religious communities of men and women.

Do I make myself clear? We find men who at the age of forty-five or even forty are not producing—are not really doing much. They justify their existence by doing the minimum, but they are not pushing any more. There is no great enthusiasm to achieve. There are women, around the same age or even younger, sometimes only thirty-five, who apparently feel that they have done their work in life and from now on they will do a kind of minimum. They are the type that no particular house wants because it is known that they are not going to do a real day's work.

Why is it that people retire at a relatively young age? They can do it effectively in religious life because there are so many ways of being retired, you know, not the least of which is for health's sake. There are individuals who *do* lose their health and this is no reflection on them. I am talking about the individuals who are "taking care of their health," individuals from the age of thirty-five and forty, and certainly a number of them from forty-five on, who, seemingly, are saving their strength for the work of their community. When they are going to do it—no one knows. They have actually retired.

Now sometimes this retirement is due to the fact that the individuals have lost their desire to do anything because the human elements, the commendations, the satisfactions which are needful to feel like a mature human being are simply not there. They give up by not caring whether they do anything any more, so they just do the minimum. Sometimes it may be almost completely their fault, but more often it is a combination of their own attitudes and the fault of Superiors who have not encouraged them to be ambitious for the better things.

Father Evoy: It is also a real possibility that a religious could say, "Ambition isn't in order for me, because I have a very limited amount of talent. I couldn't do things very well, anyway." Gilbert Keith Chesterton, the English man of letters, once said, "Whatever is worth doing is worth doing badly." We forget that. *If it is worth doing at all in the first place, it is worth doing as well as possible.* If it should happen to be poorly done, it is at least something accomplished, and something is better than nothing. Rather than holding back out of fear that you would not dare, that you could not attempt something like this, the more mature thing would be to go ahead. It is far more mature on the score that you are doing what you can, as well as you can, as far as you can, under obedience.

Father Christoph: Because we in religion put a premium on perfection, there is a tendency to reject anything less than perfect. This is a defense mechanism that we cultivate because sometimes we are tilting with a windmill—we are fighting with a shadow. It is not a fact that people outside think we are inferior. But every once in awhile we hear the remark made that we are inferior or that our work is inferior, so in order to prove that our work is equal to secular or non-Catholic groups, we have an almost irresistible impulse to excel. We are not satisfied with doing just a good job. We have a ghetto mentality that forces us to be always on the defensive and to prove our superior excellence.

And, I may extend this remark to say this also goes for competition between institutes and congregations within the Catholic Church. There is an element of this that is good, but there is an element of it that is bad. The element that is bad robs the individual of a desire to do, because he cannot do as well or better than. So this fetish of perfection and excellence can be overdone and it robs us, therefore, of the desire to achieve. Again, it is a threat to ambition.

Father Evoy: This can crystallize into the crippling myopia of, "What is wrong with this?" Such a hyper-critical point of view can paralyze all action. For example, had Father and I waited until we could do a *perfect* job, we would never have mounted the platform, and we would never have put anything in writing. This attitude of looking exclusively at "What is wrong with everything?" can be a devastating thing. I am reminded of a professor I once had, a very brilliant man. He never wrote a single line because he said he really did not know *all* about his field; and of course, he was correct. There were many gaps in his knowledge. Note that this attitude kept him from making a lesser, but very valuable series of learned contributions. But he kept putting these off while he waited to make *the* definitive contribution. After all, who can make *the* definitive contribution to anything?

So this unhealthy preoccupation with perfectionism is a thing which, in a very devious manner, can militate against the ambition befitting a mature religious. There is one other thing on which I would like to comment here, in passing, because it is something that can also put a damper on suitable ambition. The impression can be given that a good religious should not do *too* well in her studies. In a sense this is just the opposite side of the coin of which we have been speaking.

This position finds justification on the score that it is apparently easier to remain humble and avoid vanity and pride if one has non-brilliant, sort of run-of-the-mill, grades. It is obvious that this could be a very destructive thing because it might keep an individual from doing her best for Our Lord. It smacks of the temptation in Our Lord's parable, to bury one's talents.

There is still another factor here which has an important relationship to the cutting off of ambition and initiative. I think the day comes for almost every Sister when, with something of a shock, she first says to herself, "I'm not going any place. I'm not going to be a Superior. I'm not going into administration. I'm not going to get another degree. I'm there! For the rest of my foreseeable life I will be doing what I am doing now. Even though the places and circumstances change, I will be doing this

same kind of work." This is a perfect culture for the development of discouragement and depression. It is so easy for her to
feel, "I have been doing this same work for many years now and I
don't see that it has had any profound impact. People with
whom I have worked long and hard have gone away pretty much
as they came to me. What, then, is really so important about
what I am doing? No one seems to care a great deal about it. Just
as long as I show up each day on the job, very little is said. If no
one else really cares, why should I continue to care?"

Father Christoph: For a period of years you are going some place
and you have something to anticipate. Then all of a sudden you
have "arrived." Wherever and whatever it is, since you have
arrived, you are not going any place. You started out as a postulant and looked forward to being a novice, a junior professed,
and then a professed. You were getting an education. You were
assigned to get a degree and you earned your degree; now where
are you going? Look at all the Sisters who are going to work with
youngsters for the rest of their lives. Their future is pretty well
crystallized.

You feel you do not have what it takes to be a Superior, so
there is a threat to your sense of being someone in this area and
that there are no further goals for you to pursue. Humanly
speaking, it is correct that there are no further goals and this is
where religious motivation *has* to take over. Doing the same
thing over and over again can create a deadly monotony. There
is not enough variety in community life to satisfy accessory needs
and, as a matter of fact, we are not situated so some of these
needs can be satisfied. A woman out in the world does the same
thing that you are doing and she is going to do it for the next
thirty years. We will say she is unmarried, and has her own
apartment. She has a little hobby that she has developed: she has
a stereo and she collects records; her record library is her life—it
prevents her from going stale, from becoming stagnant. She did
not realize it when she began, but now she is an avid reader of

catalogs of music. She finds out it is not enough to have a record. She must see live musicians, and, when once she never thought of the opera, now she goes to the opera frequently.

But see, she has these opportunities. You do not have those opportunities to develop this or that particular type of hobby. Here is where it becomes essential that you supernaturalize your actions and your motives. You are doing this now for the love of God. This can be for you something that grows, something within you that makes you want to continue for the next twenty, thirty or forty years, doing this or that, not being oppressed by monotony, unless you can say that constantly doing good becomes monotonous. This problem has to be faced and you have to face it more than religious men or priests because once you have achieved your degree or whatever it was, you are "there." After you get "there," then where do you go? There has to be something out there to draw you. What is out there to draw you? I think it was Sir Hilary who, when asked why they climbed the mountain in Tibet said, "Because it is there." It is there and someone had to conquer it, because it is a challenge. You must always look for a challenge in your work.

Why do you continue to do your work? Where do you engender your enthusiasm? There has to be something, and what is it? Ultimately, it is the love of Almighty God. So you have to inject the supernatural into your lives—particularly in the area of the work you are doing. This is especially so since work is not always very rewarding or satisfying. As I mentioned, you do not have the many satisfactions that others, not religious, may have in doing the same kind of work. Moreover, there is less opportunity for self-glorification; there is less opportunity to be noticed. When commendations are made, they are usually made to the institution rather than to the individual. When commendations are made and rewards are given to a non-religious group or non-religious organization, more often they are given to individuals.

Father Evoy: There is another attitude sometimes to be found in religious which can be a real deterrent to ambition of any kind. This attitude characterizes certain individuals who are primarily concerned about getting all of their rights and privileges. It is the mentality which says, "I must be vigilant to get all my rights and as many privileges as possible from the administration and give only what I must." It is the kind of attitude that the late President Kennedy was inveighing against when he said, "Ask not what your country can do for you; but ask what you can do for your country."

It seems almost beyond belief that such an attitude could insidiously have slipped all unnoticed into a particular religious, as a result of which she would regard authority and administration as "those people up there" with whom she must have as little as possible to do and from whom she must be careful to obtain everything possible. In her eyes, any religious favoring those in authority would definitely be a "company man."

Do you see what this type of thing could do to an individual's ambition and initiative? For a religious woman, initiative and ambition are mainly a matter of attitude, rather than a matter of time. I had better explain this, although I suspect you know to what I am referring. For the most part, you go from your year's work into your summer jobs and if you should happen to have a couple of days off, you clean the house from top to bottom. You then go into your annual retreat and if you get a breathing space at all, it is so small that I think the unions in this country would view it not only with astonishment, but even with alarm.

The first thing you know you are back, tired, starting the next year. This is why I say that for you, time is not the all-important thing in your initiative and ambition. The additional time which is available for the expression of your initiative and ambition is almost non-existent. The difference between these and their opposite is fundamentally a matter of attitude. This difference in attitude can be spelled out in this manner. It is the difference between merely doing well just whatever you are told to do and the wanting to do whatever you *can* do. It is the divergence between the mere willingness to do what you must do, and your wanting to do what you can, as well as you can, in any way that you can.

It is an aspect of maturity to recognize that a religious has an obligation arising from her religious commitment to develop to the utmost every talent she has. She may not, without moral culpability, simply bury these talents. Hers is a strict obligation arising from her religious state following upon her vows, to do the best she can, to realize herself in every beneficial way for Our Lord. Her religious commitment was a presentation of the whole person to God, nothing held back. To deliberately restrain a talent in deep freeze would be to make a mockery of her vows.

Father Christoph: We are stressing the point that ambition is something with which we should all be fired. We want to do the best we can for our community in the best possible way, and this ambition should never be stifled, but rather be fostered by Superiors. The founders of religious communities were *tremendously* ambitious people. Their activity was limited only by the things with which they had to work and the people who followed them. The correlative of this ambition is making room for initiative and creativity. Again within the framework of the religious institute, Superiors should encourage this intiative and creativity.

Father Evoy: The exposing of relevant reality dictates here that we point out one pattern in which Superiors appear to be really encouraging initiative and ambition, while the picture in reality proves to be otherwise. I refer to the Superior's *attitude* toward something proposed. The Superior says, "Well, what are you talking about, I gave my permission; I approved of it." She did.

Because she was asked, "Sister Superior, may we take in this particular cultural event?" she answered, "Must you ask for this kind of permission? Well, I guess I may as well give in. All right." Word-wise she said, "Yes," and everything-else-wise she said, "Not again! Not again! You are not still on my back with these unusual requests!"

Sisters, the *attitude* of a Superior when someone proposes something, can plunge that individual into an iced feeling so fast that I think there is no stop watch that could time it. There is a consequent, immediate refrigeration of the one who has made the request, and very often it takes great virtue for her to go through with that for which "she has received permission." Her temptation would be to say to her Superior, "Forget it. Just forget the whole matter. Forget I even brought it up." To this temptation, of course, she would never yield. This is the type of thing I am talking about, which on the face of it looks fine, because if you just take the words themselves, then permission was granted. But the attitude of the Superior which comes through with tremendous impact could be stated tersely as, "Please, not again!"

Father Christoph: You know, an interesting facet of that, Father, is that usually institutes do allow for expression of one's initiative. But—especially in communities of women—the Superior is the interpreter of the rules and she says, "Yes, you may do as you please." But you do not do as you please because if you fail to do what the Superior wishes you to do, you feel that your conduct is reprehensible. The rule says that with reference to this you are free. The Superior says it, too; but the attitude conveyed sometimes to the Subject, seems to be prohibitive and so initiative is stifled. For example, "You may have the afternoon free, Sisters. You may do whatever you wish." Not one in the community makes a suggestion. This is not unusual. They are waiting for the Superior to express what *she* wants because they have an idea already of what she wants. They feel she is giving them this freedom with one hand, and taking it away from them with the other. You have so little free time, such small areas of freedom. This is the time when the Superior ought to encourage the Sisters, those who work with her, those who work under her, to indicate their preferences. There is so much unexpressed creativity in religious women. Subjects and Superiors alike, I think—because it affects both—should sometimes examine their consciences in this particular because they do not do what they could so easily do in making their unique contribution.

We all do a number of things together—we pray; we eat; we scrub floors and we "polish the polish." We act like automatons. This whole area of the lack of expression of initiative and ambition should be of the utmost concern to us. You cannot get away from the fact that in many communities you find individuals who, to use the secular expression, are "going along for the ride." They are individuals who will satisfy the minimum requirements to remain in religious life and who will not extend themselves. They take orders, do their work—even well—but that is the limit of their contribution.

Part of this is due to the fact that there does not seem to be much of a reward for doing one's utmost for the community. In fact, it has been traditionally recognized that those who do the most are the ones called upon to do more. This is more or less an application of the truism, "If you want something done, ask the individual who does not have time to do it." So there is apathy sometimes, too. Let us face it, self-preservation is the first law of nature even in the religious life.

Religious at times see themselves as being exploited if they cultivate their talents and accordingly they have tendencies to prepare themselves reasonably well for a particular office, but they are *not* going to over-extend themselves because of this inequity which they perceive. You can say that this shows a lack of appreciation of their religious vocation, but they are human beings. We are in the real order.

Father Evoy: I am going to give at least the appearance of taking issue with Father Christoph on this point. Understood in the right sense, I would like to say that preservation of one's life is not the first rule in religious life at all. In fact, it is almost something that should be implicit in the living of one's life. By this I mean that it ought to be taken for granted that a person realizes her obligation to use the ordinary means of preserving bodily and emotional, as well as spiritual, health. This is not by any means the same as saying that self-preservation is the first law of life.

Moreover, when we say that preservation is the first law of nature, we are talking in a very natural way. In a sense, I think you could say correctly that in religious life, self-preservation is almost the last law, if it is a law at all. It should be almost assumed. We ought not, it seems to me, to be this preoccupied with ourselves.

Our Lord was referring to this, I think, when as a boy He asked Mary and Joseph, "Did you not know that I must be about My Father's business?" It was His work, He was saying, that was paramount. We should be so wrapped up in that work that as long as we are doing it reasonably and intelligently, the assumption would be that we are taking reasonable care of our health and we pay little more attention to it. Our health should not be a primary concern of ours. This in no way contradicts the duty of a religious who is in ill health to take whatever steps are required for the maintaining of her health. Nor of every religious to submit to periodic physical "check-ups" to reasonably safeguard her health.

In a very real sense, our health should be more the concern of our Superior than of ourselves. At any rate, I believe at least some of you are familiar with the findings of recent research on the health of Sisters. To summarize most briefly these findings, Sisters are notably healthier as a group than are either their married or single age mates in the world.

There is yet another fact of which you should be aware in this matter of the exercise of initiative and ambition. It is that every talent manifested in religious life comes at a price. I think you see to what I am referring. As soon as it becomes known that you can pin up a nice bulletin board display or happen to have a particular flair for doing something well, people begin to call on you to do it for them. Any talent which is revealed in religious life is somehow or other going to call forth requests for its employment by other people in religion.

It is possible to be used by people, even in religion. Here again, the possibility, I think, that you might be so "used" is perhaps more the concern of your Superiors than it is of yourself. The danger of such a thing happening is not, in itself, a terribly alarming one. The idea that hard work ever hurt anyone is the sheerest nonsense. True, you must get a reasonable amount of sleep and recreation, but the idea that long hours and hard work ever killed anyone is simply absurd. However, what can do damage is a person's emotional reaction to the work. This is quite another thing.

You yourselves, it seems safe to say, are witnesses that if a religious woman is loved and knows she is loved and is wanted and needed by those who really matter, long hours, serious concentration, and heavy chores ordinarily will not even begin to hurt her. In fact, Sisters, you might ask yourselves just what is wrong with occasionally "being used" by your fellow religious in the sense that they make frequent calls on your time. It is not too clear that this is hurting you in any way.

Besides, every religious who shows talent that can be used by other members of the community must learn to say "No" sometime or other. There must be, from time to time, a selection in the things that she does. There are just so many hours available to you for tasks and undertakings of various kinds. Accordingly, those things which appear to you to be best suited to your most effective operation, demand that you say "No" to some things and, what may be even harder, be willing to request others to help. I am reminded here of those words of Caryll Houselander,

> "Oh God,
> Send me where
> You want to be

Among those whom
You wish to be among
To do that
Which you wish to do
In my life."

There is another area about which something needs to be said here. We have been talking about initiative and ambition as the indispensable requirements for really effective work by the individual. This is true, also, of a community. A community, as a group, in order to be particularly effective must also be characterized by initiative and ambition. This is really not feasible where there is a division in the community, with resulting cleavage between the members, especially where it is between the Superior with some of her followers and another group whom she does not have "with her."

This reiterates, of course, something we said earlier about these divisions in community, and introduces a new facet. It is this. With the best of faith, a member of the community may be drawn into the position, especially by a younger member, of actually abetting and aiding such a division out of sympathy for the other member who has a grievance. Unless she is alert, this religious can allow herself to be used as an instrument in the driving of a wedge right down the center of the community.

It works this way. One person in the community has a complaint, let us say, against the Superior. She goes to another person who is very sympathetic and confides it to her. Let us say that Sister A, who has the complaint, goes to Sister B and tells Sister B that the Superior does not understand her, and in addition has been unfair to her, is inconsiderate toward her and, in fact, really does not care about her. Now the stage is set for this thing to happen. Sister B listens sympathetically because Sister A assures her there is no one else to whom she can talk.

Now we come to the point under consideration here. Sister B, with full sympathy, can respond with either of two sets of responses and there is a world of difference between the two, which at first glance appear somewhat similar. She can respond sympathetically by saying, "Yes, I certainly agree with you that Sister Superior has been unfair. Sister is *not* understanding and I have that same feeling that Sister really does not care for you. I feel for you in this." This pattern of response is "dynamite" in a religious community.

The other set of sympathetic replies, which appears to resemble the previous set, differs from it as night from day. In the second set Sister B says, "Sister, I understand; you feel that Sister Superior has been unfair to you. You also find that you cannot talk to her because you think she would not understand. It is your impression that she does not care about you, that she *really* does not care about you. I understand."

In the second group of responses she can be as sympathetic as in the first group but she avoids the devastating thing done in the first set—driving a wedge between the one in authority and the rest of the house. In the first set, as soon as she said, "I agree with you, Sister Superior is unfair. . . ," she committed herself. She had taken the side of Sister A against the Superior. You have, then and there, a divided house that could mushroom out until the effectiveness of the community would be lessened considerably because a house divided against itself cannot really function for God to the fullness of its potential. It is well for us to remind ourselves of the reality that, from time to time, there are individuals in religion capable of thus trapping a sympathetic person.

When you analyze it, you see that the initiative and ambition that must characterize the whole community is one that is actually the responsibility of *every one* of the members and, therefore, is a shared thing. If this type of wedge is permitted to be driven through the center of a house, you may well find some individuals in the house who still demonstrate initiative and ambition as individuals, but what of the house as a whole? Within that house you are going to have a faction fighting against any really significant community effort. This division of a community against itself is a form of violence. It is as if, in a living organism, one part were to fight against another part. What kind of a race could an individual run who would find a member of his body militating against another member?

This matter deserves the most serious consideration, because it is one that can slide in under the guise of charity, sympathy, and genuine sisterly love. The motivation for it can be the highest. That is why religious must be constantly vigilant against the insertion into the community of this kind of insidious thing. No matter how sympathetic you are to any individual's cause, you simply will not subscribe to anything unfair or unjust to one you love.

You are well aware that one of the worst things that can happen to a country is civil war. Where you have brother pitted against brother and sister against sister, it is a much more destructive thing than some other type of war. In something of a parallel, to permit a wedge to be driven through the center of the community on *any* score is not permissible.

Going back to our example, if Sister B were to feel in conscience that she should do more than merely listen to Sister A, she might undertake gently to point out to Sister A that a clear line must always be drawn between what one *knows* and what one *suspects*. She might make clear to Sister A that her feeling that the Superior is unfair to her is a real experience, whereas the establishment of that unfairness on the part of the Superior, as a fact, is quite another thing. She might even help, at the same time, to teach her the valuable lesson that loyalty to her Superior demands that she simply will not listen seriously even to her own judging of the Superior's motives. Sister B might attempt this even though she, herself, might be having her own difficulties with that Superior. To agree with another's judgment of unfairness is to commit one's self, and the justification for a loyalty which would refuse to pass judgment on the motivation of another person is so well founded in reality that it really needs no defense.

Candidly, to conclude that one really is in a position to be sure of the motives of another person, is "to play God." Add to this the fact that the particular individual about whom the judgment was made has a right to the loyalty of the one so judging, and you see, further, why this type of thing is untenable. However, a peril that flows directly from sympathy and even empathy for another person in the community can readily gain entrance into a religious house. The proper insurance against it is the constant reminder that to commit oneself to the position that a Superior or any other religious has failed in justice or charity or does not love the members of her community, is indefensible on any score.

Father Christoph: Yet every religious has a right to be heard, and there is no contradiction here. I do not think that it takes long for those in charge of religious to discover who have axes to grind or who are "one-tracked" in their thinking. As Father just mentioned, we reassert the fact that religious *must* feel, insofar as this can be arranged, that they may express themselves, that they may have licit outlet for their proper ambitions. Moreover, this type of self-expression is to be espoused and encouraged. Venturesome thinking and imaginative inquiry are assets—nay, more—necessities to a healthy religious community.

9 *Growing in Maturity*

Father Christoph: In line with our endeavor to keep these remarks highly practical, I would like to ask Father how early in religious life should initiative and ambition be both permitted and encouraged.

Father Evoy: From the very beginning. This would be from the postulancy on. No matter how inconsequential the opportunities to exercise initiative and ambition might appear, the over-all pattern would be to permit fitting opportunities as frequently as would be feasible within the framework of good government. Toward this end, for instance, the way a young religious performs certain tasks should not be spelled out in minutest detail where this can possibly be avoided.

Toward this same end, should this young religious venture to suggest a different way of doing something, she should be given to understand early that she will always receive a hearing. When does ambition, as it is distinct from initiative, begin in the religious life? "From the very beginning." In terms of our previous remarks, ambition as such can concern both those things which an individual person might do, and secondly, those which the religious family might do to scale hitherto unconquered heights.

It seems to me that this type of ambition might well start at the very beginning of religious life. From the first months of religious life, those in charge could encourage the young members in the community to be alerted to the talents that God has given them and also to try to foresee the most effective employments of these talents.

A Postulant Mistress can instill in the young religious the importance, in the future, of calling to the attention of her Superiors, with reasonable frequency, the talents that each judges herself to have. The young religious should also be encouraged periodically to manifest the interest she experiences with regard to various kinds of work. I see no reason why a prudent venturesomeness should not be cultivated in the younger religious from the very earliest period of her religious life.

She should discover that not only is she free to ask questions but that her reasonable inquiries actually meet with approval. She ought to be able to feel that it is desirable for her to raise points which are problematical. Presumably, these queries would center largely on potential means to advance the work of the community and other related things that she might creatively conjure up and try on for size. At the same time she would be given to understand that some of the things she proposes might get no more than a brief hearing because they would be judged to be worth no more. In this way, she could be exercised in the art of being creatively ambitious.

Father Christoph: Superiors should be alerted to spot the individual who is afraid to do anything on her own. This must be detected early, for if she has not had some opportunity to express initiative by the age of eighteen, nineteen, twenty or twenty-one, it is asking a little too much, I think, when she is placed in the classroom at the age of twenty-two or twenty-three, to suppose that she is going to be endowed with a tremendous amount of initiative to push things to their conclusion. The initiative and enthusiasm she brings with her to the novitiate must be exploited.

We are not surprised at the failure of some religious women in the classroom simply because they have never been encouraged to think for themselves, to plan for themselves, to act for themselves. So the earlier the individual is given an opportunity to express herself and her own initiative, the greater the possibility that she will, before she is in the classroom or hospital or office or whatever her work, give promise of doing something for the community. From the very beginning of religious life, therefore, the Subject should be encouraged to manifest her talents as she sees them. Meanwhile, the Superior, also should make her own personal investigations to check on what talents the Sister possesses.

In general, a greater effort, I think, can be made by religious Superiors in the preparation of their Subjects for the work of their institutes. The mind of the Superior should be, "How can we get full value from this individual?" Not, indeed, to exploit the individual—that is not the idea—but the generous young woman entering religious life wants to give her all, wants to do her best work. It would be a denegation of the ideals of the community if a Sister who has a clearcut liking and ability in biology should be prepared for teaching bookkeeping or something similar, with no consideration given to her interests and talents.

Father Evoy: That is why we insisted on the Subject's obligation to inform Superiors about these.

Father Christoph: If those in charge of the formation of Sisters were able to take them and develop the talents that they possess, it seems as obvious as one and one are two, that happier religious would result because they would have a sense of competency in doing their work. Is this not doing God's work in the best possible way? Does this not tend to spread an atmosphere of contentment in the community? From the very beginning of religious life Superiors should give young religious a clear idea of the world in which they are living, and this starts with the world of their own community.

A young Sister may wonder if it is not prudent for her to stifle her initiative and ambition so as not to be regarded as a little "upstart." Is she an "upstart"? Not necessarily. As a matter of fact, it is not prudent to suppress one's initiative. Here the supposition is that if you show that you have initiative, that you are ambitious, that you have drive, you will be considered an "upstart." I do not think this is generally true, because Superiors welcome new ideas and welcome some type of initiative on the part of individuals. They even bemoan the fact that too many religious seem not to care enough to suggest ideas.

So the ambitions of the individual should be expressed to those who can do something about it. Sister would be only a little "upstart" if the manner in which she acts betrays something of the upstart. I do not think it is prudent to hide one's ambitions for fear of a label. Young religious should be told at the very beginning that there is a very large element of human respect in religious that can prevent them from doing the things they can and ought to do.

Since we are human beings we are always thinking how Sister X, Sister Y and Sister Z, and not just Superiors, are going to judge us. We should be a little impervious to their judgments. Young religious should be told that they are not going to be judged badly, anyway.

Father Evoy: We *should* care what the Sisters think about us because we love them. So what they think about us; whether they care about us; how they feel about us *should* matter. But it should not be able to paralyze us so as to prevent our doing what our conscience tells us we should do. It would surprise me very much if occasionally, at least, a young religious were not brash, because I do not expect the wisdom of the ancients in her.

The young person in religion normally does not have the

wisdom of an older person and for this reason, if she expresses herself at all, she can be expected to voice some opinions that *need* to be corrected. A young person, at times, is going to be unrealistic; she is going to be imprudent. Still, by being able to express herself and then by being shown where her views are good and where they are wanting, she grows little by little to full stature as a religious woman.

We do not learn prudential judgment by some type of innate gift. We learn it by making our mistakes, correcting them, and going on. Sisters, do we not on occasion assume the opposite when a person fails in a job we give her, and we say in effect, "She will have to be dropped from the list. No more important jobs for her. It is more than clear that she cannot be trusted with a job"?

But, you see, if she has been allowed to make errors a number of times, the presumption is that when she is forty years of age she will not then be as likely to fail. If, however, she is never given a second chance, we can be almost sure that even if later on she has the almost unspeakable courage to undertake something, she is almost sure to fail, because she has been considered incapable over the years. She has known only failure. She has never experienced successful achievement.

On the other hand, the reasonable presumption is that if she had been able to make several mistakes and learned from them, she would now have reached a stage where she could do a number of things and do them with no more than the average number of mistakes. And we all make them. The only person who makes no mistakes whatever is the one who makes the biggest mistake of all—that of doing nothing. There is a realistic hope, I think, that if religious are dealt with thus patiently, most will develop some initiative and ambition.

Closely related to this consideration is the sense of personal propriety one takes in regard to the things of the community. I am not referring to a feeling of ownership in the sense of exclusive possessiveness; I am talking rather about the viewpoint that since this is "ours," the religious is personally interested in it.

An actual incident will serve well to exemplify this. When we were building our new Jesuit Faculty House at Gonzaga University, one of our Priests was looking through the building and walked up to the man in charge and said, "I don't know much about this, but I just took a quick look at the blueprints and I'm wondering whether they should be putting up this wall." The supervisor said, "Well, I think it should be here but maybe we had better go back again and look at those blueprints." After studying them a bit he said, "That wall shouldn't be there at all. Father, you have saved us a good deal of time and money. Thank you." What I am pointing out is the fact that he cared enough to check what was being done not to *his* room but to *our* building. You understand?

When I was speaking of cultivating and encouraging ambition, especially in the younger Sisters, I mentioned that they ought to be encouraged to be prudently venturesome. It strikes me that this might be spelled out clearly for them in some such way as this: They might be told, for example, "If someone came up to you as a religious and asked, 'What part of the ship of state do you want?' the religious would answer immediately, 'I want the steering mechanism—for Christ.' " As a religious, as an apostolic person, she would want that which would give the greatest amount of influence and impact on persons. This is the kind of adventurous thinking that should be fostered from the very beginning of religious life.

Father Christoph: Ambition in an individual is a consequence of her desire to achieve. A sense of achievement is part and parcel of our feeling of being someone. Everyone wants to have some sense of accomplishment—to do things—and ambition is the expression of this desire to achieve. We have mentioned that there is room in every religious community for initiative; that the end of a religious institution is not to stifle but to channel initiative. We ought to have ideas, but the counterpart of this is the receptivity of those who are "running the show" so to speak.

Far from stifling initiative, the religious community is an ideal place where initiative, within the framework of religious discipline, has perhaps a better opportunity to express itself than any other place. So many people who are not in religion are doing the things they are doing, earning their living the way they are earning their living, because that was the only job available at the time and they got "trapped." They are doomed to do that kind of work the rest of their lives.

Sometimes, even people with a certain amount of professional preparation find themselves hamstrung by circumstances. In religious communities we find this less true, in general, because the opportunities for the expression of practically every kind of ability can be found. You are artistic—there is an opportunity for you to manifest your artistry. You like gardening—you find an outlet. I do not care what it is—there is always an opportunity. We should not be loathe to express our interest or to do something about it. However, a word of caution is appropriate here.

I said that initiative must be expressed within the framework of religious discipline; that means within the framework of your constitutions and rules. Everyone who has an idea does not have a *good* idea. So if we are thwarted in our goal-seeking, it may be that our ambitions are irrelevant, or, if not irrelevant, impossible. If they are not impossible, they are not "smart" and I use the word in quotations; I mean not prudent. So there must be a prudent check on the run-away ambitions of individuals.

This can be seen as young religious grow up. Here is a young religious—she is twenty-four years of age and she is given charge of something. We will say we are going to put on a pageant. She gets all the permissions she needs; she has talent; she has ambition; she has know-how, and she has ideas. But is she expensive! She does nothing by halves. It is a community of thirty people and she has everyone working for her to make the thing a success. They are wearied. Do you know what that means? They are hanging on the ropes maybe a week before the pageant. It will take a month or more for the Sisters to recover from the activity. But it was tremendous. Everyone is talking about it. Not only the members of her community, but the members of other communities a couple of hundred miles around. It was terrific! Do not ask her to do anything like that again; or if you do, be sure that limits are put on her, because there was a certain amount of imprudence in her demands on others and maybe on the check book.

Father Evoy: Father, I think that you are not finding fault with the fact that she did a good job but with the imprudence displayed. When asked to put on a school pageant, she produced a professional pageant. She was asked to do something well in the C league and she wound up attempting, and carrying off well, something in the Double A league. Because this whole undertaking was quite disproportionate to the finances and the available manpower, its toll was just slightly short of crippling.

Father Christoph: I do not know what Father Evoy holds in this regard, but I have a suspicion that he agrees with me that we do not learn to be prudent. Prudence is both a natural and a supernatural gift. By definition, "Prudence is the virtue which inclines us to choose the best means for the ends proposed." I do not think that we develop prudence all of a sudden. We either have it or we do not have it. We either have so much of it, or we have more or less of it.

We do not increase in prudence, but the prudent individual becomes more prudent, objectively, in her judgments and her activities because of her experience. So I expect a prudent person at the age of twenty-two to make a lot more mistakes than someone with the same amount of prudence who is forty years of age, because the latter has more experience behind her. Actually, I do not think one really grows in prudence. At least, as far as natural prudence goes, this is my experience.

Father Evoy: You sort of asked me a question so I thought you might like me to answer it. I really do not know for sure whether an individual can actually learn prudence. My present position is that after a certain age, an individual who still has a notable absence of prudence does not seem to be able to acquire it. Now, that age is what? I would say, somewhat facetiously, at the end of adolescence, which should place it somewhere around forty-two.

Seriously, it is most difficult to tie this down to a definite year even though we are talking about an average. As far as men are concerned, my experience has been that if they reach their forties and are known particularly for lack of prudence, I have yet to see them acquire it later. Since men perhaps never quite catch up with women, maybe we can put the corresponding age in women around the late thirties. If they do not have it by then, perhaps they will never acquire it. There are individuals of all ages in religious life who do lack prudential judgment and "savoir faire" especially in the realm of social perceptiveness.

Let us face it. They are not prudent. They are not tactful. You hold your breath when one of these persons opens his mouth because you know very well where the shoelaces are going, since they are the last things in.

So often this type of person, despite all of the schooling and helps of other members of the community, does not seem to improve in any marked way. Nevertheless, in full recognition of the fact that occasionally we find an individual who, from the very beginning, is unbelievably imprudent, we still stress the importance of encouraging becoming ambition from the earliest days in the individual religious person.

It seems that in every individual there is some innate intellectual curiosity, some hunger to know. Accordingly, that which expresses itself in questions such as, "What can I do best?" and, "What can we do best?" is healthy. If you do encourage this from the earliest years, you should anticipate that, at times, the younger individuals, particularly, may be asking critically about things not excluding even the constitutions of the religious community. However, the hope is that they would learn that such criticism should not be done in a negatively critical fashion, but in a positively intellectual weighing of the intrinsic worth of these things.

Father Christoph: There is an intrinsic difficulty in trying to achieve this, particularly among the young religious. Without the experience of their elders and without an understanding of the actual ramifications of the institute, they may hold in question things that are really extremely important for which at this moment at least, there should be no serious questioning. There is the danger of the untrained, unqualified individual saying, "Well, we shouldn't be doing this." There has to be some type of limit on this kind of inquiry. That is where those who are training and those who are concerned about the preservation of the spirit of the institute have to make prudential judgments.

Father Evoy: Well, it is possible that occasionally the expression of this freedom to inquire would be in bad taste. We recognize the peril in this type of exercise of freedom in a religious community, and to avoid any such bad taste, we ought to teach young religious very early to express their opinions in terms of "It seems to me," rather than "This is so." Do you see? Such expression of intellectual humility is but a healthy recognition that they do not know all the facts and so are not certain of their position. At the same time the permissive atmosphere in which these expressions are welcomed has the additional beneficial effects of reinforcing in the young religious a wholesome sense of identification with the community and a consequent vigilant propriety regarding whatever belongs to the community.

Father Christoph: I would go along with Father Evoy and add this: very frequently the intense love of these individuals for their institute tends to prevent them from allowing a certain amount of freedom. They do not want anything changed. They are afraid that this is going to subvert the institute. They are more committed to the past than they are alert to the needs of

the times; more concerned about preserving the old than preserving the institute itself in a dynamic world; more handicapped by formalism than adaptive to new issues. Failure to
adapt has disintegrated and made obsolete more than one institute in the history of the Church.

Father Evoy: The whole context of our remarks that so many of
these characteristics hopefully are to be found at the beginnings
of religious life, focuses our attention on one consideration. It
almost trumpets forth the importance of putting the right person
in charge of religious in their early formation. The reason for
this, if I may be pardoned for using the expression, is that she is
there "first with the most." Indeed, you could do with a religious
female version of Superman to take charge of these young religious. It is of the greatest moment that you have in that position
a person well suited to it. She should be knowledgeable, secure, a
warm motherly person with a solid knowledge of the institute as
well as thoroughly informed in a number of other very important
areas of knowledge.

It is difficult to think of a more important position in the
community, barring none. The initial formation of a religious
person is so important that the one who is conducting it must
personally know her Subjects and have a picture of the entire
community which includes what its various members are doing,
and how they are going about it. She should be reasonably intelligent so as to be able to give the young religious an intelligent
presentation of what she is conveying to them.

It is clear that unless she is a person very secure in her own
right, she will not be able to permit them an "open end" atmosphere in which they are not only permitted but even encouraged
to ask, in good taste, the questions that they should ask from the
very beginning. If she were insecure she would not be sufficiently
free of her own emotional involvement to give them intellectually satisfying answers. For instance, were a question about some
custom or well-established procedure asked of a basically insecure

Mistress who was not sure why it was done in this particular way, she could not give them the only possible intellectually satisfying answer. She could not admit that she did not know. At no time should novices feel that the answers are being given by a person standing behind a defensive wall of fear.

Father Christoph: "Take it on faith."

Father Evoy: Yes. This is an excellent example of an answer from a very insecure person. "Take it on faith. This is the way we do it so just take it on faith." Well, obviously any intelligent person in that group is going to want to ask, "On whose faith? Did God reveal this? If not, who did?" Since the institute is in many ways a human creation operating under the blessing of the Church, the only intelligent approach is to look at it with an effort to see why and how this particular aspect in it is designed toward the objectives of the community.

Father Christoph: The religious can, in her thinking, become grooved in a rut—things are done this way because they have always been done this way. Has not this been held up to our admiration at times? I do not deny that this may be justified at times, but in an institute that has been in existence a hundred years or more there must be modification, adaptation, changes to meet the challenges of our time. Religious institutes at the time of their founding were up-to-date—meeting the problems of their age and place. The same founders, were they to come back to earth, would be the first to say, "Away with the old, now useless or pointless, and let us adapt our rules and constitutions to the needs of our times." Be as *dedicated* as the founders, but also as *modern.*

Father Evoy: It always reminds me of one of Father Martin D'Arcy's remarks. He tells that at a cocktail party he was approached by a woman who asked, "You're a Jesuit, aren't you,

Father?" And he answered, "Yes, I am." She continued, "I can
always tell a Jesuit. You're all turned out of the same mold."
Father D'Arcy replied, "Madame, I am pleased to be able to
inform you that some of us are moldier than others."

What he was saying, in effect, should be true of every religious
community. Its individuals, right or wrong, should characteristically think for themselves. There is no such permissible thing
as being turned out of a mold of any kind that takes away the
individuality of the person. This means that there should be no
stifling, no muffling in any individual of that person's own individuality.

Father Christoph: You still want to be Sister Particular and not
just Sister Anonymous. Traditonally, religious women have
tended to remain anonymous. Look at the authors of some of the
older books on religious life, etc., "By a religious of X community." Well, I see no particular value in that type of anonymity.
Part of the personal satisfaction—and we are entitled to a certain
amount of personal satisfaction—as a member of the community
is that I still am myself. I just do not want to be "like Father
Evoy" and Father Evoy does not want to be "like me."

Father Evoy: This reminds me that my experience has been that
whenever I have picked up a book and found that it was written
by, "a Sister of X community" I spontaneously sensed, somehow,
that the book would not be worth reading. This appears unquestionably to have been a prejudice of mine, but I think in a sense
it is also a confirmation of Father Christoph's point, inasmuch as
I experienced a slight revulsion when I encountered such uncalled-for anonymity.

It is interesting to note in this context that I have found it to
be really trying and highly annoying to identical twins when
certain people keep mixing them up. Each of them wants to be
known as himself. Complete anonymity seems to go against something built into a person. I do not like to hear people say to or of

a religious, "You are one of them." Whether the "one of them"
refers to the Jesuits or a particular community of Sisters, if this is
the full designation of the person's identity, I find it somewhat
disconcerting. I suspect that everyone of you has been introduced
sometime or other as, "This is one of the Sisters of such-and-such
a convent or community." This was the entire introduction. It
rankles in you. It is even more common when there are several
Sisters together, to hear, "These are some of the Sisters of so-and-
so; I want you to meet them." We spontaneously get a peculiarly
unpleasant feeling when this happens. When I am introduced to
someone else, I am satisfied only with being introduced as this
individual—myself. I am not just "one of these."

Without doubt, it is so extremely important that the Mistress
of postulants and novices instill the correct pattern into the
young religious. The projection of the Second Person of the
Blessed Trinity into the world of mankind through the Incarna-
tion is an act of love, and love characterized His life among men.
Accordingly, the adult attitudes toward religious life, toward our
state in life, should spring from love and not from fear. The
Mistress must be one who can teach that "We do these things
because we love. We don't do these things because we are afraid
that we will be punished if we do not do them."

Father Christoph: And I suggest that the Mistress be trusting, and
allow the Sisters more latitude, and presume that they are trustworthy. The spirit of surveillance is not the spirit of motherly or
fraternal solicitude. Even novices do not want to be spied on.
The Mistress is to see that her Subjects retire, get up on time, say
their prayers, go to the chapel when their confessor comes. This
is not spying or an attitude of distrust at all. This is a maternal
solicitude as a result of which she sees to it that the members of
her community have every opportunity to grow religiously in
religious life.

The line that we draw between surveillance and solicitude
may be a thin one. Perhaps what I am trying to say is that it is an

Maturity in the Religious Life

attitude. If you do not trust, you engender in the individuals the reaction: "If I have the name I might just as well play the game." We have said that grace builds on nature, but sometimes there is an awful lot of the natural in us. When Superiors do not have the largeness of heart to trust us, and especially when they make this explicit, we are liable to reciprocate with actions that are characterized just by natural motivation.

Father Evoy: Father, it would be difficult for me to attempt to recall how many religious women have told me, "When my religious Superior does not trust me, it kills something in me."

Father Christoph: There is the persistence of a pattern of behavior in religious communities of both men and women, I think, based on something that was true, maybe a couple of hundred years ago, but not true any longer. The tendency on the part of Superiors to give directions in minute fashion and to presume lack of intelligence and competency on the part of Subjects, is almost traditional in religious communities. Every morning you go and get your charges. You get your information on how to do this, that, and the other thing, and the pattern is repeated over and over again.

For the past fifty years, when you have been assigned to a new mission, you have gone to the Sister, whatever you call the treasurer, and to the Superior, and you received a detailed outline on procedure how to get to the new assignment. Your ticket is purchased for you. If you need a berth, the berth is purchased. You are given enough money. They know the price of the taxis from here to there and from there to your destination. Everything is put down in minute form for you so you cannot miss. You cannot miss, that is true, but you could not feel less adequate. This is so much like treating you as a child. There was a reason for this years ago. When your religious communities were started, or at least when they were flourishing before the nineteenth century, a very large number of religious women, especially, were uneducated. Remember, they did not have the educational role that they have now. Women did little academic teaching. If they taught, they taught the fine arts: painting, music, and yes, cookery, for that is a fine art today (so few people can do it). The cultivation of their intellectual abilities was neglected.

So they did not have enough understanding of the world. Many religious women could not read or write; hence all these directions had to be given. But times have changed. The individuals a hundred years ago were treated as persons, but as diminished persons. We are human beings with capacities and capabilities. We have given some evidence that we can use our capacities and they should be exploited.

I am not blaming Mistresses or Superiors for current practices, because it may even be in your rules to follow these patterns. I am just saying that there should be an accommodation made today to the fact that religious Superiors are now dealing with intelligent people. Let us have some evidence of this and allow room, within the framework of religious obedience, for as much freedom as is possible. In keeping with the philosophical axiom, "He who wishes the end, wishes the means," when a Superior gives an assignment, the Subject should be burdened, as much as possible, with the responsibility of carrying through that work without bothering the Mistress or Superior further.

So frequently I hear Subjects say that they cannot get to the Superior. There is a line-up every day waiting to see the Superior. Well, if the Superiors delegated more of these things and allowed for the reasonable use of the Subject's initiative, they would not have to be around so much; and they would be better able to fulfill their primary function as mothers of their communities. A mother of even young children allows for some initiative and for some responsibility. The Mother Superior of a convent ought to do that also, and as Father said, give responsibility commensurate to a woman of your age and experience out in the world. Religious life is not meant to make us a group of helpless, irresponsible, dependent children.

Father Evoy: Because the Mistress of postulants and novices is vigilant regarding anything which could aid the young religious to become a person of initiative and right ambition, there is another factor which she ought to consider seriously. These young people are social beings. Now, it is true that each of them presumably thinks repeatedly about many important things in her meditation and other prayers. But her significant thinking must also, in large part, be within a social context. A religious should be given frequent opportunities to communicate, because in all reality, there are many areas in which she cannot really think richly unless she is communicating with other persons.

Would you like a good example of that right here? Father and I could not do this without a live audience. Even though we are both provided with adequate notes covering the material we are treating, to sit down and write out or dictate onto a tape everything we are saying here would be simply unthinkable. Neither of us would have as much to say because each needs this social stimulation of our awareness that we are communicating to you. The fact that we say it is not nearly so important to our thinking as is the fact that you are really listening. Do you see?

Father Christoph: The personal relationship that has been characteristic of the religious' relationship to Almighty God has almost fenced her off from communicating with her fellow religious. Outside of the stylized and formalized recreation, certainly among religious women, there is very little opportunity to sit down and talk things over.

Frankly, at our ten o'clock coffee session in the morning at the University, I learn more about more things, for I have the people there who know what they are talking about. In mentioning something, even in their field, they stimulate me. They make me ask questions. They make me more competent. They make me more alert, and at times they drive me to books. This is something that, it seems to me, should be exploited. This is the aspect that, unfortunately, has been played down in religious life.

When we get together, it is in recreation or in silence or in prayers. The recreation is too formalized at times even to be recreating, so we need that freedom to talk to fellow religious as long as we are not gossiping.

Those in charge of religious, particularly at the beginning of their training, should reflect that the religious who finds that she is isolated constantly and must do practically all her thinking alone, and does not have a chance really to communicate with others, is going to be deprived of a richness which is there if only permitted and encouraged. Community living carries a certain amount of silence in the course of the day. Perhaps this is an area where we should re-evaluate and see if we should not consider some time where the individuals would get a chance in informal groups to talk over what they want to talk over.

In reviewing some of the aspects of personality of which Superiors of young religious, especially, should be mindful, there is one which has been implicit in what we have been saying, namely, the dimension of responsibility. This has reference to the capacity of an individual to accept responsibility, to understand and adequately execute orders. It means that a religious has to assume responsibility for her own attitudes. In religious life, on account of our training, responsibility for a longer or shorter period of time is removed from us to a great extent.

We can, therefore, go through life as very dependent individuals and move only when we are moved, do only what we are told to do, never being willing to show any initiative. We mentioned, when we were talking about initiative, that this matter would come up again when we talked about responsibility.

There are several facets of responsibility. The first is the need to be made responsible. Do you know what that means? We should be given opportunities to show how responsible we can be. We have to be given opportunities even to make mistakes. You know, God could have ordained that men would never make mistakes, but if God did that, if God ordained that men could not sin, then God would have had to make us unfree. But God wanted a free service, so He ordained an order in which we could fail Him. If God did that, I think that Superiors could at least try to take a page from God's actions and give the Subjects an opportunity to fail in order that they could show that they are responsible.

Father Evoy: I want to develop here a point made by both of us. As Father Christoph just said, we have to learn to be responsible for what we do. But this is the second step. The first step is that we have to be responsible for being we. Let us put that in the singular. I have to be responsible for being myself. I cannot take away responsibility which, as a person, I have for being I and give it to anyone else. Does not obedience take away that responsibility? No, Sister, it does not. Obedience presupposes my having assumed the responsibility for myself.

Perhaps an example here will clarify this. You walk into the office of your higher Superior and say, "Mother, I have thought about this for some time and have concluded that I could make a tremendous contribution to our work if I could take a trip around the world, and actually be right there in each of these countries to gain knowledge on the scene itself. Just think! Armed with actual experience of all these various cultural facets, I would return so enriched that I could give it forth the rest of my life, and there still would be a great deal left. The investment required to make this tremendous contribution to the work of our community would be no more than six thousand dollars and it would take less than a year." And Mother, when she catches her breath, says, "No."

All right. You come back in a week and say, "Mother, there's a tour through Europe this summer . . ." You present the request to her. Mother answers, "I can't see my way clear to grant you this permission; however, I will take it up with the consultors, but, frankly, I don't think they will favor it." So the counsellors apparently were opposed to it. Nonetheless, you are back next week and say, "Mother, down in California this coming fall they are having a meeting and I'd like . . ." She says, "All right. All right. You may attend it." You come back and announce to the community, "I'm going to San Francisco, and it is clearly God's Will for me since it is all under holy obedience."

Is it? Before you may walk in and ask Mother if you may have permission to go around the world, you have to square it first with yourself. Only after you can judge it right to ask for it may you take the request to your Superior. You have to square it with yourself first before you can permit yourself to ask Mother to allow you to go around the world, or to Europe, or to California. In a word, you have to give yourself permission to ask the permission from a Superior. In like manner, before you may go in to your Superior and say, "Sister, I received some money as a gift, and may I use it for this particular thing?" you have to clear it first of all with yourself. Note that you might just not be able to give yourself the green light for this. In this case you might even put it to your Superior in those terms. You could say, "Mother, I don't really know whether or not I am justified in asking for this permission, but since it is not clear that I am not justified in doing so, I would like to present it to you, as such." The point I am making is that you may not simply shrug off all responsibility for the permissions you ask and proceed to wear down the Superior until she gives you something. Is this notion of assuming the responsibility for what one seeks from a Superior new to you?

If you back away from all personal responsibility and put the whole burden on authority, you are saying in effect to your Superior, "Would you mind dealing with me as if I were some kind of a robot?" Your original dedication and commitment when you came into religious life was not made for you by someone else; it was voluntarily made by you. It came from you, and every subsequent action is made by and from you. You cannot make anyone else, in or out of authority, responsible for the proper area of your own being.

So before one talks about her responsibility for doing anything, no matter what it is, for taking on this responsibility or that one, she must first of all assume the responsibility for being she—the person she is—and answering for herself to God. This becomes so strikingly clear when we reflect that a religious cannot go up on the last day in the final judgment, and say to God, "Please, dear God, don't ask me about anything; talk to my Superiors; they are the ones responsible." She cannot, because we know that God would say to her, "I'll talk to your Superiors in due time. Now I want you to give an account of yourself."

Father Christoph: Father's emphasis on being responsible for yourself and for your actions means you have to make a judgment about whether or not this is the thing to do or say. Then you go to the Superior. Very true. Within the framework of reasonable religious discipline, and within the limits laid down in your constitutions, those who are in charge of you should give the widest latitude for self-expression and responsible actions. Superiors do not expect us to act like children. As a matter of fact, they are reasonably annoyed if we act like children. But sometimes Superiors do not allow for the widest expression or even for a wide expression of responsibility. This bothers me. It is more common in communities of women than of men.

Whenever I discuss this with religious women, I usually get the same answer; that it is the nature of women to be more concerned about detail, and so if a task is given to a Subject by a Superior, there is just the natural tendency for the Superior, in the case of a woman, to give more detailed instructions than a man would do. I have heard that hundreds of times, but I still marvel at the detailed instructions. I have tried to accept it in the context in which it is explained. Nevertheless, I think that, as much as possible, the Subjects should be made to feel that this is their project; that they should do it; and that they should be the responsible agents.

Father Evoy reminds me of an incident that I do not recall clearly, though I do have a vague recollection of it. He took my place at Gonzaga University when I went away to theology.

Among other things, he was to be coach of the debate team. In those days the debate team did not have a budget. Or if it did, it was for a very few dollars. Father asked me, "What do we do?" And I said, "Well, we get the national question; we prepare the students; and then there will be a number of tournaments to which we send students, and you go along." He said, "Well, how do you get the money?" I said, "You beg, borrow or steal it."

Father Evoy: And then he ran up the stairs.

Father Christoph: That was his instruction. This is more or less characteristic of our pattern of doing things, except the instruction to steal. Something is dumped in your lap and . . . yes?

Father Evoy: They are curious. All right. I admit it; I stole it.

Father Christoph: I cannot say I approve—but is it not nice to know that as a Superior you can sit back; that people will do what they are told to do, and finish the project without returning every five minutes to ask for more direction?

A religious, a man, came to me and said, "I find religious obedience unbearable." I asked, "Why?" He said, "Because there is always someone telling me the next move." The fact is that in his own community it is not the rule that every next move is told an individual. He is an over-dependent individual, and therefore, has to be told. But the thing that is screaming out for recognition in himself is this sense of responsibility which he has not taken. He is at present incapable of directing himself, and yet he is human enough to resent being directed at every turn— the ambivalent attitude which is found in every over-dependent individual.

Religious life is not intended to make us over-dependent. That is not the end, and if it happens, something is wrong with the training. We are supposed to be obedient. We are supposed to be responsible. We normally put at opposite poles independence and dependence. I should rather use these two at opposite poles: dependence and being responsible. We are not supposed to be independent, but we are supposed to be responsible. We are not expected to be dependent except insofar as obedience calls for it.

Father Evoy: Would you mind terribly if I used a horrifying example here? Recently, I read an article in which some scientists, including psychologists, are predicting that they will be able to control human beings completely by some type of short wave. It has been established now, through experiments on monkeys, that you can bury electrodes in the cerebrum, and you do not need any attached wires at all; you simply push a button and the individual monkey performs the actions you desire.

They predict that the day will come when, by such means, we can have a tremendous "human" labor force in this country. At that time, the one in charge will just push the right button and these human automatons will proceed to work industriously. He pushes another button and they all commence to eat. Another button sends them all back again to work. These scientists, with tongue in cheek, I hope, pointed out that you would not have to limit the work of these human robots to a forty or even fifty hour week. It would merely be a matter of leaving the "work button" on as long as needed. Then the button could be pressed which would send them directly to bed. After an electrically controlled night's sleep, the one in charge would simply start the process all over again. Does this not sound like one of those horror movies, after which the youngsters have nightmares? But these scientists appear to be in dead earnest about such predicted control of human beings.

This is a shocking thing. It is the type of thing that Karl Stern has been crying out against in pointing out repeatedly that the great danger of our day is the de-humanization of man. Horrifying as this example is, I think there is a possible danger of something psychologically paralleling this occurring in a religious community, without our fully appreciating it. I am merely pointing out the danger of something in religious life that would amount substantially to the same kind of thing. It would be produced not by means of electrodes and switches, but by means of what Father referred to earlier as prolonged and intense "brain washing" in a religious community.

This refers to the danger of becoming unduly concerned about conformity of behavior to the point that everyone in practically every way must conform, or else. This is the danger of not being enough concerned lest religious become passive, other-directed, and if I may coin the word, "non-selfed" beings. Let us put this in a positive context. We insist again that to the extent that religious are at their best they are individualized persons as God made them. While I am by no means sure of my interpretation, I think that when Gertrude Stein said, "A rose is a rose is a rose," she was saying two things. She was stating that every rose is different from every other rose. She was also declaring that every rose is indisputably like every other rose. We recognize a rose wherever it is. Yet we are aware that this rose is not that rose, nor are the two identical.

The application here is obvious. A religious is a religious is a religious. They are alike and they are different. Their alikeness must, among other things, be in terms of a reasonable conformity. But the greater danger by far is not that there might not be enough conformity; it is that there might be too much conformity. We feel that we can scarcely overstress the danger of producing a depersonalized passivity in individual persons so that each of them is psychologically turned out in the same image. Lack of conformity is not the great peril. It seems safe to say that the very nature of religious life keeps us vigilant against any notable lapses in conformity. There is, however, no comparable factor constantly alerting us to the ever-present danger of losing one's own individual personality.

Father Christoph: To accept responsibility—to be able to take a job and see it through without having someone "blocking" for you, clearing the way, removing every obstacle—this is the area of maturity. One of the problems in religious life is the failure of religious to become responsible because of the nature of religious life. You are in the novitiate or even in the juniorate. What responsibility have you except to have your body in a certain place at a certain time? Everything is done for you. What responsibility have you about the meals unless you happen to be working in the kitchen? Then you have only the responsibility of a specific task. The maturing factors of human life that are characterized by assuming more and more responsibilities, are not found in the beginning of religious life. There is a perpetuation of a pre-adolescent pattern of living. You ask for every permission; you do everything when you are told to do it, and the way you are told to do it. You do not even ordinarily make any suggestions in the novitiate. Not that you could not, but it just does not occur to you to make a suggestion because you are bewildered by the newness of religious life. So Mistresses of novices, especially, must recognize that the individual who is denied the exercise of a sense of responsibility may grow up never to develop it, to care about having it, or even to want it.

There is a kind of security in not having any responsibility. It is so easy to let someone else take it. It is so easy to do something and then say, "Well, it is not my fault. I did what I was told." But this is not mature. As we grow older, we should be willing and ready to assume responsibility. On the other hand, suddenly to throw a large responsibility at an individual who, up to this time, has never had one, and then be irate with her for her failure, does not make good sense, either. We do not develop responsibility overnight. It is just like presuming that a girl is a child today and an adult tomorrow.

On the one hand, we should not shirk responsibility. Superiors should make us a little more responsible, teach us the hard facts of life; so that we become dependable individuals within the sphere of our own activities, whatever they may be. To acquire and to develop a sense of responsibility, is obviously another dimension of maturity.

Father Evoy: I would like to make one little comment here. Father, when you said that there are many people, who by thirty or thirty-five years of age do not want responsibility, I think that strictly speaking a distinction should be made. They very definitely would like to have it, even though they would not be willing to shoulder it. If they could somehow or other delete from it everything burdensome and obligating, they would love to have it. The key blocking fact here seems to be fear. This type of religious would like to have and even to be able to hold this responsibility if she were able, but since she feels clearly not up to it, she could not dream of carrying any real responsibility much as she would like to.

Father Christoph: If the individual had a reasonably well-developed critical faculty, she would want to be responsible and to have responsibility. Father, you are correct. She is afraid, and there is a lot of difference between not wanting and being afraid. She is afraid of responsibility.

Father Evoy: That is a good point. An individual can, in a real sense, be kept a child to the point where she no longer views this shirking of responsibility as unbecoming to a mature person. She looks at it, not as would an adult, nor from a mature perspective, but more from the point of view of a youngster. To exemplify this, by a preposterous example, were either Father or I suddenly to break into tears here and the one who broke into tears did not consider it in any way inappropriate, there would be something greatly wrong with his ability to evaluate himself critically.

Now the fact that an individual religious might feel that she were wholly fulfilling her sense of responsibility by some minor thing like setting the table, says a good deal about her self-critical ability and its failure to develop. This is why we have emphasized that Mistresses of postulants and novices be alerted to tendencies in the young religious to retreat from appropriate responsibilities.

Father Christoph: Can you understand how such an individual could find a refuge in religious life? She is a religious. She does not have to be responsible. But the natural in her wants some kind of expression, wants achievement, wants accomplishment, and so she settles for what? Practically nothing. Remember that for her, setting the table is something, and it brings out two points that we are trying to show you; first, that an adult can have a very poorly developed self-critical faculty, as a result of which she puts the emphasis on the wrong things and makes much of nothing. I am reminded of a priest, a religious, whose greatest achievement in the area of responsibility was his ability to take a car into town and bring it home unscratched. Every facet of his life was dictated by rule and by the directions of Superiors. There was no room for exercising his own judgment, and so he settled for this satisfaction. What a commentary on the sense of responsibility! What a commentary on his self-critical faculty!

Secondly, it shows the intrinsic urge which is in every one of us to be something in our own right; to be able to say, "I did this. I have accomplished this. I am responsible for this." Even within the framework of religious obedience, there are all kinds of areas where responsibility should be delegated and accepted by the Subjects and in which they should make a good account of themselves.

Father Evoy: A Mistress of novices assumes that those under her are individual persons. She appreciates fully that, in the last analysis, they must be responsible for themselves. Hence as far as is consonant with the present stage of training, she trusts them not only to be themselves but also to exercise some ingenuity in the way they carry out their assigned tasks. Mistresses of novices, especially, should remind themselves, from time to time, that those under their guidance are being prepared specifically to be leaders in the present day world. If these future leaders have not, in their preparation, been given the opportunities to assume a reasonable amount of responsibility, later on their tendency will be to manifest this deficiency in their relationships with others. Thus we expect that in the future those under their charge will also be deprived of the responsibilities they should have, because these leaders were "trained away from" such giving of responsibility. It is tantamount to saying that they have actually been trained to be non-leaders, in a religious community whose goal is to prepare leaders in the modern world for Christ.

Father Christoph: I want to go back to a point that Father Evoy made a bit earlier because I think it needs further elaboration. I refer to the fact that we justify anything by going to the Superior and having the Superior approve of it. We throw the responsibility from our own shoulders to those of our Superior. Superiors are large—I do not mean physically, though they may be that also —Superiors are usually gracious and generous. Superiors are, at times, also a little afraid. They want to make their Subjects happy; they do not want to bear down too hard, for they also have a responsibility under God. If they think the refusal of an outrageous or outlandish petition or request is going to be received very ungraciously and very unreligiously by one of their Subjects, they are liable to feel compelled to grant this petition or this request. The Subject goes away blindly feeling that she has the blessing of obedience upon her actions. In reality, she has extorted this permission from her Superior.

It is a kind of blackmail. This is the point that Father Evoy was making: you have to square your request with your conscience first, assure yourself that it is a reasonable and justifiable request, and then you take it to the Superior and attempt to get her blessing on the project. But you do not absolve yourself of the primary responsibility. First, you check it out, then you bring it to the Superior. This is the way obedience works. It pertains to the essence of obedience, that through devious means we do not twist our Superior's will to our own will. You cannot, you may not, absolve yourself of your personal responsibility.

It would make government easier if we thought out our problems, if we knelt *before* Almighty God and made the decision *before* Almighty God *before* we bothered Superiors about it. Note we are now very much in the real order. We cannot divest ourselves of our responsibility for ourselves. We are human beings. We are persons and we have personal responsibility. Superiors should presume that they are dealing with mature religious. This is the presumption. The presumption must always yield to the fact; so if Sister X proves that she is not a responsible individual by her actions, then her Superior must be a little more careful about giving Sister responsibility. But until that occurs, the presumption is that each one is a responsible individual.

I want to repeat something we said before, because I think religious are sometimes kept in a state of perpetual adolescence by Superiors and by the Superior's interpretation of the rule. To keep you adolescent is not intrinsic to a religious constitution, nor is it the duty of Superiors to keep you that way. What do I mean by a state of perpetual adolescence? Superiors are afraid to let you make decisions. They treat you like children. Do you remember when you were about fifteen years of age? At one time, your mother or father said, "Who do you think you are? You're just a child." And maybe less than an hour after, "Why I'm surprised. You're a young lady." That is the way Superiors sometimes treat young (or even older) religious women. They treat them like children and they can grow into a pattern of acceptance in which they do not make the decisions they should. They do not assume the responsibility that is theirs, and very frequently, because of the need for power and the insecurity and inadequacy of Superiors, the Subjects are treated like puppets. Like the centurion in the Gospel, the Superior orders, "I say to one, go and she goeth, and to another, come and she cometh," without any regard for the fact that maybe there is room here for the expression of individual initiative.

Of course, this keeps religious immature. However, all of a sudden, responsibility is thrust on their shoulders, and they are unequipped and unprepared for this responsibility. There should be, it seems to me, a growing evidence on the part of Superiors that religious are women and able to shoulder responsibilities. As I say, it is not the mind of the Church that religious should be perpetual adolescents. But the way some religious are ordered about, one may quite rightly conclude that they are; and so we may be responsible for their immaturity.

Father Evoy: Sisters, the Jesuits in this country, during their first seven years in religious life, do not ordinarily mature much psychologically. During that time we do not have any serious responsibility of any kind. We have no weighty decisions to make, no serious dependence of others on us. We are carried along year after year until we arrive at what we call "regency." The term "regency" refers to our teaching experience before ordination. At the end of our first seven years, we walk into a classroom, and it is ours.

We are ordinarily given one or more student activities in addition to our classes; and for the most part, no one tells us how to conduct things or what to do. These are ours also. We are not instructed in great detail about anything. Three years later, the somewhat immature individual who walked into that classroom has notably matured. This exemplifies the point that Father is making. In the religious life of women, to the extent that the individual is given little or no opportunity for making any serious decision of her own or for doing any important thinking of her own, she is kept in the state not unlike that of a Jesuit's first seven years.

This lack of opportunity to mature may be permitted to slip even into the classroom if, in it, a religious woman would not be permitted to change the location of her desk or replace the ejaculation written across the board or do any thing of moment without specific permission from her Superior. Or if in the hospital a religious might not be permitted to make even this or that small change without permission. Such absence of responsibility may creep into any field of work in which a religious woman may not be given any notable amount of responsibility. The point Father and I are laboring is that Superiors, from the very inception of religious life, should make a special point of looking for opportunities to give each member of the community a chance to exercise her native ingenuity.

Father Christoph: It would appear that some Superiors feel that a postulant, novice or young religious has nothing important to say. Probably it is true that their statements or suggestions are not world shaking, nor will they determine the course of the community for the next thousand years; but there is a relative importance. Young religious should be given an opportunity to show their capacity to assume responsibilities, so that when responsible offices or duties are thrust upon them they are not completely dumbfounded. We grow into responsibilities as we grow in responsibility. Unless some responsibilities are parcelled out, the Superior is going to be burdened with details—making dental appointments and such trivialities.

Father Evoy: Otherwise, it can be disastrous. This pattern of having someone do her thinking and deciding for her can produce in a religious a passivity which in my judgment is one of the most devastating things that can befall a human being. Father Christoph indicated that the individual, thus victimized, finally gets to the point where, at thirty or forty years of age, someone says to her, "Here, Sister, this is your responsibility," and she simply cannot face it. She has had no preparation. She has not one bit of confidence in herself. She has never had the opportunity to develop any, and strictly speaking, it is unfair to ask her now to shoulder heavy responsibility, when all during these years she has been preserved hothouse-like from any such need to do her own thinking as well as her own choosing. These two talents of hers, her intellect and will, have never really been given the chance to mature. If other persons have prevented her developing them, they can leave her somewhat destroyed. This is why we have to be alerted time and again, lest in religious something may be going on even undetected, which is, in reality, a devastating type of brainwashing. It will wash out of individuals much that is properly human, and leave them animated caricatures strolling about in religious garb, rather than living.

I would dread it were I to have to answer for the fact that this had been done to even one individual under my care. It is my experience that, for the most part, when this is done by Superiors, it is done with no malice whatever. It is done with good will, although with a lack of understanding and a lack of appreciation of what is really transpiring. It can be, nonetheless, devastating.

Father Christoph: Unfortunately, in some places, it is tradition that these things are done. They do not have to be done, and the sooner these things are changed, I think the more efficient and effective religious people will be.

We have been saying that this should begin even in the novitiate. The atmosphere which should exist in the novitiate, and in all areas where instructions are given, should be one in which an individual should be permitted to ask questions and to have explanations of what is being told her. I think that it is almost habitually true that the young novices and postulants are in a sense—now, I am careful how I put this—cowed into a kind of submission in which they are afraid to open their mouths out of fear they may seem to challenge or contradict what is being told them; or that they may seem to be non-conformists, when actually they are looking for clarification. Or it is quite possible that a statement is made which does not seem to square with something that was said on a previous occasion. But to call this to the attention of the Mistress is sometimes construed as impertinence.

This ability to carry on a frank discussion is very necessary to insure the type of conformity that we want to have. This conformity is not something that is impressed on the individual, but rather it comes from the individual's willingness to accept it and appreciate what is commanded. I think we have a new aspect in the training of religious and in the experience of a number of people today who are dealing with the younger religious. I think you are already familiar with the term "dialogue obedience." This seems to be a name that is given now to a kind of discussion that goes on when a command is given. I certainly do not approve of dialogue obedience, but where it is possible, a reasonable explanation should be offered for a given command. The command should be intelligent and intelligible.

On the other hand, I think that it is wiser not to give a reason if it is not a good one, because a poor reason promotes a lot of questions in the mind of a religious. Frankly, I would rather be told to do something and be given no reason, than to be given a reason which challenges my credulity. Reasons should be given, if possible. Individuals should have the opportunity, and should be encouraged to discuss, encouraged to speak their minds, encouraged to ask questions. The clearer our ideas, and the clearer the objectives, the easier it is for us to conform and cooperate. We should not make things as difficult as possible in religious life. However, the relationship of a Superior to an inferior is not one of peers. I am afraid that some modern ideas of obedience give the impression that the Subjects can challenge any command on the basis of an assumed equality.

Recently, I had occasion to discuss something with the dean of one of our universities, and he was completely upset by the inability of religious graduate students to fill out a card or do the ordinary routine work of registering for a class. The presumption that they were registered in the graduate school when they were not, coming to school without anticipating whether the courses they were to take were being offered—he gave me a whole rundown on the apparent defects in the preparation of religious men and women for graduate studies. I said, "Well, don't blame the religious. When you went through your studies, did you ever fill out a card? No. You just went to class and someone else filled out the card." So if this has been true of these young religious, put the blame where it belongs—uncalled-for dependence.

These are little areas of responsibility and of independence that should be literally forced upon the Subject, so that when she is expected to do things at the age of thirty or thirty-five, she does not collapse from fear. This is what we mean by perpetuating completely needless adolescent traits in individuals. Once again, religious obedience is not servility. Religious obedience does not demand or even want a type of subservience in which there is no room for self-expression. There is a becoming type of independence that each individual, even as a religious, should exercise.

If the constitutions and the rules and the Superiors operate as they should, and if Subjects do their part, you do not have to change the nature of religious observance. You have to change some of the current interpretations of religious obedience. May I add a word of caution. When we discuss these things we are always worried about the imprudent. I suppose, like the poor, the imprudent we will always have with us. The fear of the Superiors that the imprudent will be a burden to the community and say the wrong things or do the wrong things is a real possibility. This is the nature of imprudence.

One of the ways to clear the field of the imprudent is to discover at an early age what a Sister can do and what she cannot do. We test the spirit in the novitiate. Why do we not test the degree of prudence and the sense of responsibility? We think that with experience, our judgments take on new dimensions. You will note from your own experience that Sister X, who was imprudent at the age of twenty, is still imprudent at the age of sixty.

Now, there is prudence of speech and prudence of action. Some people are always putting both feet in their mouths. They are saying the wrong things to the wrong people at the wrong time. All right. We have to keep them in the background. Every community has its share of such, you know. There is prudence in action. There is prudence in dealing with other individuals, with fellow religious, with externs, with Priests. But we are not going to prove ourselves prudent unless we have the opportunity. The presumption is not that we are *imprudent;* the presumption is that we are *prudent.* So everyone should be given an opportunity to show to what extent she is responsible.

Father Evoy: Since I am to be responsible for myself, I should be trusted to be so responsible. If I am visiting with a man, with parents or with students, I should be trusted from the word "go" to conduct myself on the basis that I am responsible for myself. This may sound strange to you, and yet when we reflect on it, it is not strange at all. I think the reason why so many religious are afraid to talk to externs is because they have never been given the opportunity to be responsible for themselves in this way. It is possible for individuals to be imprudent, but if I am dealing with another person in a reasonably public place, there is no reason in the world why I should not be trusted completely by others; and why, therefore, I should not endeavor to trust myself.

In other words, instead of following the first inclination to duck an encounter with someone, I walk over to him, telling myself, "Somehow or other I am going to go through this." If I can do that with reasonable success as a novice and as a junior professed, I can do it later on as a professed. And I can become in this way responsible for myself. This is tremendously important because, as we mentioned, God does not want to be served in religion by vitalized automatons. He wants to be served by people who freely judge and decide for themselves.

10 *Intellectual Maturity*

Father Evoy: In treating intellectual maturity, we are immediately reminded of interesting statements made by two recent Holy Fathers. First of all, Pius XII remarked, "Whoever aims at sanctifying himself and his neighbor, must be equipped with solid learning." He was talking particularly about religious. John XXIII in his *Mater et Magistra* had a number of relevant things to say, but rather than give any specific statement of his, we simply note that he emphasized the importance of these three aspects: observe, judge, and act. These he enumerated as the characteristics of a mature person, and especially a mature religious. These remarks afford us an excellent introduction to the area of intellectual maturity.

We are reminded by them that, as religious, we should be critical, in the best sense of the word, of all things, not excluding even the human aspects of the Church. After all, the Church herself in the Second Vatican Council has given us the lead in this. Even in our religious life much of the Divine, so to speak, is immersed in the human. It is the mark of mature wisdom to recognize the human and therefore the fallible, in need of evaluation, as distinct from the Divine, which needs no such evaluation. Our concern is not with how God is doing, rather our concern should be, in fact *must* be, with how we are doing to enable God to operate more effectively within the framework of His Divine Economy.

Father Christoph: There should be a certain boldness in our intellectual interests. The Church gives us much freedom along those lines. This should be the green light for religious to recognize the fact that the secular may be used in a much more apostolic way. So we should become proficient in the areas in which we try to lead others. Again, to paraphrase Cardinal Suenens, our effectiveness is going to correlate with our knowledge of the world in which we live and the people with whom we deal. So if we are going to be teachers, there has to be an opportunity for us to obtain the learning that we need.

The pattern in the past, for the most part, has been to take too much on faith. This inhibits intellectual curiosity. It inhibits the inquisitive mind. We are apparently afraid of finding something that contradicts an uncritically accepted but almost infallibly regarded position or attitude.

Father Evoy: Our apostolic zeal must be founded on truth and the penetration of that truth. To this end, we start in the novitiate to teach the religious that the real world is imperfect. We point out where and how and why it is imperfect. We give religious standards to the young, but we keep these standards always related to the world as it is. We continually demonstrate that human systems are imperfect; that our religious community is imperfect; that the Church in some of its human aspects is imperfect; that we as individuals and as religious are imperfect.

We show this, not in any carping way, but rather in a constructive way. If we are deficient we want to be the first ones to know about it, regardless of where that deficiency is. To that end, each Sister should be given a scale of values which would serve her as a yardstick. Over against that scale should be pictured for her things as they *really* are in the world. Deeply in each religious should be instilled the necessity of constantly checking against that yardstick the various specific means being used in the community. It is a matter of evaluating and re-evaluating, in a day-to-day pursuit, the effectiveness of these means. In addition, it should be made clear to the religious that our knowledge of the world is not something that is complete at any time. Accordingly, the necessity of knowing the world as it really is demands that we keep abreast of the world's needs peculiar to our times. Only thus is it possible to devise means that will be admirably suited to the objectives we have in view. It takes courage and even daring to face up to the fact that there is no merely human aspect of our lives, no matter what or where it is, which can be exempted from our evaluation and re-evaluation. In religious communities, particularly, one has to risk feeling guilty in daring to regard critically procedures and even standards that have been sanctioned over the years.

Father Christoph: Historically, a number of religious institutes have completely disappeared simply because the objectives for which they were established were either achieved or no longer existed. Consequently, a group of religious without a purpose then existed. From the history of America we can trace the activity of the Polio Foundation and also the Tuberculosis League. When these organizations found that the principal ends for which they were organized ceased to have much cogency, they said, "Why give up this organization? We have a tremendously vital group here; interested, capable, with know-how and experience. Let us change our objectives so that we fit into the community and fulfill a need just as important, just as interesting as the ones for which we were established." In the same way, religious institutes have to re-evaluate the goals for which they are striving in terms of the needs of the times.

If this be true, then it seems to me the only way it will be achieved is by periodic re-evaluations. I am not saying this should be done every three or every six years. But if there is a reason to suspect that a particular work is time-consuming and that is about all, and there are better works to be done, then I think that this should be seriously discussed. And Superiors should not feel that this is a threat to the traditions or to the institute itself.

Father Evoy: Nevertheless, this approach constitutes for many of us something of a challenge, and a very serious challenge. We can easily take the over-all attitude of a readiness to evaluate all things human in terms of their worth. But when we contemplate taking this into the sacrosanct area of the constitutions and rules of our religious community and dare to ask, "Should these, also, be re-examined in terms of their relevance to present day life?" we react with something like shock.

It helps to reflect here, I think, that the founders of our religious communities want us to re-evaluate the constitutions and rules to see to what extent they are still a fitting instrumentality to the end originally contemplated.

Father Christoph: Apparently the reason for the establishment of this specific institute was the fittingness of this particular work for the time and place.

Father Evoy: It would not at all be a matter of judging whether the substance of the constitutions and rules should go, but whether or not there should be modifications in specific aspects of them which would make them better suited to the needs of our day.

An example might help here. Many religious communities have gradually grown into large financial institutions. Hospitals and schools have become undertakings worth hundreds of thousands of dollars. The day when a person was placed in charge of a large organization with no preparation whatever is gone, we hope. Not only must religious educate and train Sisters in various academic and professional fields, but they simply must recognize the need, in this day, to train administrators. Such training must, it seems, include on-the-job experience. We should take a page from the practice of present day enterprise, which selects potential managerial material and puts them through a training program appropriate to their specific type of undertaking. They train them to be supervisors, managers, and executives. The organization's continuity under the best available leadership is thereby guaranteed.

Father Christoph: The Church is setting the pace and perhaps, as Cardinal Suenens remarks, religious communities ought to try to catch up with the Church.

Many religious communities in America are European imports, or at least the models for their constitutions are of European origin. Two of the recent Holy Fathers, Pius XII and John XXIII, have indicated that there is need of modernization in some of the rules, in some of the traditional patterns of behavior and dress. Apropos of this, the idea that the ruling body of an institute has some kind of divine intuition relative to what is good for the community and what the community should do, has no foundation in fact. The concern and interest that an individual has for her community is evidenced by the ideas that she will conjure up and talk over with others and desire to bring to the attention of Superiors.

Subjects have a duty, because of their love, interest, and concern for the well-being of their institute, to make suggestions; and those who are in charge—the Superiors, the local Superiors and the Superiors General—should listen. They need not necessarily do anything about what is said, but they should welcome the ideas of the members of the community—the ideas of both the older and younger members. No religious community should be a gerontocracy—a group ruled by "oldsters." The "oldsters" have no particular monopoly on ideas. As a matter of fact, the older members of the community tend to be conservative, and because of their attitude they may tend not to welcome new ideas.

They are afraid of giving up traditions. They are especially concerned about losing the original spirit, particularly the spirit of the foundresses.

The spirit of most founders and foundresses of religious communities was in tune with the needs of their day. If the needs change, usually there is enough flexibility in the constitutions of an institute to provide for such changes. But the point I really want to make is that there should not be rejection of ideas from members of the community other than the governing group.

We have evidence of high morale when members of an institute feel concerned about some aspect of the community and feel free to make representations to Superiors. Those in authority should encourage the concern of each individual for the welfare of the institute. Everything human suffers from human limitations, and religious institutions are human. As adults we ought to be permitted to criticize and make suggestions. We should be permitted to make these judgments out loud without being afraid we are going to be labeled disturbers of the peace—a threat to the unity of the community or even a threat to the community itself because we may be innovators.

One of the ways in which we make progress is to look at things as they are and evaluate our efforts in terms of the present needs, conditions, and the like. Every so often we should do this to reorientate ourselves, sometimes to get back on the right track to our goals. We should not be afraid to make known our feelings in this regard. We may have some good ideas, and Superiors should not feel that suggestions like these are threats to the stability of the community.

Father Evoy: What would you think of an individual who could not face self-criticism?

Father Christoph: It suggests the presence of a tremendous amount of anxiety and insecurity within her.

Father Evoy: What would you think of a community that could not face self-criticism?

Father Christoph: It is the same thing, only on a group basis. The re-evaluation of ends and means that should periodically be faced by a religious community is frequently ignored. A community may be doing the same old thing in the same old way when there is no longer any need for doing it; or at least for doing it in the same old way. I can understand why Superiors cannot allow every new idea, every new wrinkle, every new apostolic work to be embraced by the institute. You cannot do all the good that can be done in the world. Every once in a while religious institutes have reassessed themselves in terms of their apostolate. Cardinal Suenens, in his book, emphasizes this when he says that religious women need never think for one moment that their apostolate can be taken over by lay institutes, but that perhaps they should be engaged in different kinds of work.

What institutes of priests, brothers, and religious women have to do is reassess the situation and adopt and adapt themselves—adopt the things that are necessary so that they can adapt to the things of the day. If you have ideas that do not conform to the institute, I do not think it is such a wise thing to propose them casually. But at congregations or chapters of the institute there is no reason why things cannot be proposed—suggestions for changes made. But we cannot just take on new works. We cannot spread ourselves so thin that we kill the members and destroy the morale. So perhaps, in view of the changing world conditions, we should eliminate some of the activities that have absorbed so much of our manpower in the past. And sometimes the limitations of the institute ought to be re-examined.

You can see, also, how some things are not contrary to the institute and may yet be beyond the institute at the present moment. One may become very ambitious about a certain project. Let us say I become very interested in the apostolate of the alcoholic. So I want the Jesuits to set up a house and give me—no, just myself for the work. Father Rector says, "This is fine. It isn't exactly the kind of work the University is doing but you may use the work as a sort of laboratory. So we will permit you to do it." I do it. Then a few months later I say, "I need twenty thousand dollars." We do not have that kind of money, so I beg it under the name of the University. The Rector says, "Well, we could use that money elsewhere in our educational program. We may have to have a meeting to determine whether this is a practical objective." Eventually, I get the twenty thousand dollars. A year later I ask him for five other men. I involve the University and the whole Province. If this is important and manpower is limited, maybe some traditional activities should be eliminated.

My own ambition is driving me. My initiative is urging me to go beyond what we are doing. I get carried away by the love of God, the zeal for souls, but my contemplated undertaking is not exactly what our institute is doing. This happens often in communities of religious women. A project is picked up and then the community is saddled *"per omnia saecula saeculorum."* The institute does not have the equipment, does not have the individuals prepared for this particular type of work, and it becomes a burden. You cannot leave it because of public sentiment, because of what it would do to public relations; and it becomes a perpetual burden and drain on the personnel and financial resources of the community.

When we are thwarted in our ambitions because of the limitations of the institute, all I can say is, "Well, these are the interests of the institute and this is the work." So we do not have a program in our community to take care of the deaf, dumb, and blind. What of it? There are all kinds of activities within the framework of your institute in which you may become interested. Direct your initiative along those lines.

Father Evoy: I would like to make a little stronger case for doing something new. I would prefer to have Father Christoph risk involving the community in something rather than think that he is in his room "sitting on his hands." We should recall that there is a corrective for all these potential involvements and the corrective is *obedience*. Let us say a religious Subject addresses her Superior, "Sister, it just occurred to me that there is the grandest opportunity of getting a Sister aboard every flight of X Air Line. You see, the passengers on these long flights have time on their hands and tend to get bored. With a Sister present, these passengers would have both the time and the occasion to talk about religion. So it would be a wonderful apostolate, I think, for a Sister to be on each flight, particularly on the longer transoceanic ones."

On the face of it, this may sound consummately immature and imprudent. But the point I would like to make is that the only way something gets started is to have someone propose it. A Superior can always say, "I don't think so," or "Sister, I do not think this is prudent." From the very first appearance of such a proposal the corrective of obedience is there. The Superior may reject it or experiment a little with it. She may say, "Go ahead. Start on a shoestring and don't let this thing grow too fast." All right. So Sister begins.

Admittedly, I am taking a rather extreme example. So let us say Sister initiates the work according to the directives given her. Later on she may say, "Sister Superior, we need ten more people for this work, and incidentally, we need some literature and other things. It will amount to three thousand dollars." The important thing is that her Superior can still say "Yes" or "No." The person who has started this thing has only to keep herself under obedience and she has all the safeguards she needs. Moreover, it is well to recognize that an ambitious religious is likely to make some suggestions that will not always be worthwhile. But in obedience we have the checks for the mistakes and for the imprudences.

Father Christoph: Every institute was founded for a specific purpose, to fulfill a specific need. This justified its existence. But take the case where the traditional ways of doing things may no

longer be justified. This is again where Cardinal Suenens is a
little displeased with religious men and women because, he said,
they should accommodate themselves to the current ways of
doing things, even sometimes to the current ways of thinking. In
general, they should meet the apostolic needs of the day. When
necessary, they should change the traditions. Let us be specific.

It was unthinkable a few years ago for a Sister to go out on the
street unaccompanied by another Sister. Well, it becomes rather
expensive to send two Sisters wherever one Sister is supposed to
be going. For a time, a transitional period, men and women may
be a little surprised to see a Sister walking down the street by
herself, but they will get used to it. We should not think it any
stranger than for a woman to walk down a respectable street by
herself. There should not be the feeling that the Sister cannot be
trusted, and I do not believe that was the thought in the mind of
the person who made these prescriptions. You see, this is the
traditional way of acting—the biblical two-some. At times you
have to break away from tradition. Tradition can lead to a
deadly type of conformity. Religious communities have withered
on the vine simply because no one in the group was able to break
through the "crust of custom."

But sometimes tradition does not crack and there can be
deadly conformity. "We've always done it this way." As though
the way you did it fifteen or twenty years ago was the only way.
We have to make room for new ideas. There is no necessity to
adopt all new ideas, but we should examine them. As I mentioned, too many religious communities are run by a gerontocracy. This is in the interests of preserving the "genuine spirit of
the institute." But loyalty to purpose and ideals is not the exclusive prerogative of the aged. Youth, too, may have this loyalty.
But the pattern of control by the ancient persists—and the reasons? Sometimes, the prescriptions of canon law are a factor; you
have to be thirty-five years of age for some positions. You know, it
is strange how we correlate intelligence with age; prudence with
age. Yet, there is no necessary positive correlation. An individual

who is twenty-five years old may have more prudence than one who is seventy years of age. There should be more freedom in choosing leaders who have prudence regardless of their age.

Father Evoy: Father, do you not think that much of the unadaptability that we find so frequently in religious life is something of an accretion from over the years? If twenty years ago anyone had come to ask for the use of a tape recorder or film projector for a given class, those in charge would think, "What is the matter—can't she teach?" In some ways we may still be geared to days gone by and still be living according to the patterns of that period. Much of the picture has changed. We must never forget that we are living and laboring in an age which has situations and circumstances proper to it. We are charging tuition or fees for our services and, thereby representing ourselves as professional people.

Sisters, I think that at times, people outside would be surprised at the dearth of becoming professionality present in certain of our organizational procedures. They simply would not believe it.

Father Christoph: Cardinal Suenens says that there is still a place for religious women and the religious vows. The religious state is defined in Canon Law as "a permanent mode of living in common by which the faithful, besides obeying the commandments, also observe the evangelical counsels embodied in the vows of obedience, chastity, and poverty." This is the essence of religious life. The kind of work done is not specified; but there are traditional things that Sisters have done. We have to be big enough to recognize that some of those things are not of the essence of religious life. Many of these observances were formulated at a time when religious men and women, for a great part, were uneducated. Someone literally had to lead them around. Today this is not so, but these traditions die hard. A tradition that is maintained ought to justify itself. If there is no reason for the tradition, then eliminate it. We can start new traditions, if necessary. To keep the old because it is old is ridiculous. Society by its very nature is dynamic. Times change; attitudes change.

For instance, going to bed at nine or ten o'clock (whatever the hour designated for retiring) is not of the essence of religious life any more than getting up at five o'clock in the morning is. If a change is called for, be ready to make and accept it. There must be more latitude given to Sisters on the basis of the new work that they are going to do. Once a Sister was not to go out after dark, but now it becomes a necessity sometimes in the interests of education, to do so. A part of the wisdom of understanding religious life is to be able to distinguish the accidental from the essential. We have to distinguish, also, the "status quo" from the eternal.

We are in religious life to save our souls, and so we are living our lives according to the constitutions of this or that institute. Now that is the eternal. The "status quo" is the present situation in which we find ourselves, and this may call for adaptation. I am sure that your Mother Foundress, if she were here, would be amazed, in one sense of the word, at what you are doing. Holding to the traditional because it is traditional may be the sign of a small mind. Traditions may justify themselves, and when they can no longer justify themselves, they should be discarded. In keeping with the pattern of modern living, there must be changes, and we must not think that we are less religious because we fit into those changes.

We must, as I said, distinguish between the "status quo" and the eternal, and we have to re-evaluate, every once in a while, the world in which we live. The readiness to undergo self-analysis is something that is not easily acquired. We always like to think that we are doing a pretty good job, and we are sometimes afraid that if we examine ourselves too closely, we will find that we are mediocre. Rather than face this, we shun self-analysis.

It is fortunate, in a way, that the accrediting associations require self-evaluation. This gives us an opportunity to look at ourselves. If we were not under the gun and pressure of these organizations, we would not be willing to re-examine ourselves; not only because expense and time are involved, but also because it is so nice to think we are "pretty good." So let us not look too closely lest we find we are not as good as we think. We have, therefore, some things that are pressed upon us which we cannot ignore, e.g., accrediting agencies. We belong to them, but we are "Johnnies-come-lately," in a sense. We have a commitment to excellence in education. That means that it is no longer sufficient to have the initials of your religious community after your name as though that in itself qualifies you to teach. These initials do not make you a better professional person. Let us face the fact that it is necessary for us to join, with a certain amount of enthusiasm, these accrediting organizations with all their professional demands. We participate in meetings. We prepare individuals of the community to represent us adequately.

These things cost money, but as mature women you must accept these additional burdens. You are either going to have to accept these ever-increasing expenditures and secular associations or you are going to wither away from inanition. I say this seriously because the economic demands on our schools—grade schools through college—are so tremendous that we sometimes wonder how we will survive. But if we are going to survive it will be because we recognize the importance of being in the forefront intellectually and academically.

Hence we take our place in these organizations. We are active members because we represent the Church, Catholic education, Christian nursing, etc., and our own communities. This becomes a necessity not only for public relations, but because the urgency of the times requires that we have the proficiency, the preparation, and share the wisdom, knowledge and experience of others. Knowledge begets power and we do not wield the power that we should as educators, because sometimes we do not have the knowledge; and an unbecoming modesty keeps us from standing up and being counted. We ought to count a lot more than we do.

Father Evoy: As Father Christoph just pointed out, there was a time when all that was required was that the letters representing your community be placed after your name. This is no longer true. Today, I trust, you would shudder if someone were to recommend assigning Sisters to teach religion before they had an adequate preparation in college theology. It would be unthinkable unless they knew at least as much as a girl graduate from a Catholic college who has taken, say a minimum of six courses in college theology. This question did not even have to be raised in days gone by because a Sister taught only the catechism and, somehow or other, it was taken for granted that, in view of her training, she would know what the catechism meant.

Today we find this hard to believe. Let us suppose that a particular religious teacher is using the catechism in her classes. When we examine it closely we see that the catechism is very much like a survey text in any course. It is one of the more difficult books to teach, because it covers just about everything in its field. If she is teaching it correctly, the catechism teacher leaves herself vulnerable to questions on any and every aspect of the matter being covered. You recognize immediately that today it would be unfair to the community and to the religious herself to appoint a Sister to teach something for which she was not equipped. The example I have just used is a very practical one. Sisters, all too often we still have an individual religious teaching religion to the children before she is trained in theology.

It is so easy to become enslaved by traditions of an unhealthy nature. I am referring to that which was fitting in another age, but not in this one. On the other hand, we are scarcely surprised at the difficulty experienced by the newer generation in understanding, appreciating, and properly evaluating some of the better traditions. It is quite possible for the younger religious to suffer from myopic vision, due to which they can be wanting in understanding, appreciation, and sympathy toward the worthwhile in the old ways.

For instance, the young religious taken up with formal education may find themselves unable to understand and respect religious who are preoccupied with the various domestic works in the community. These latter religious strike them as not doing anything really important. On the other hand, the people who have been in religion for years find themselves with quite the opposite problem. Their inclination is to say, "We did not do these things when we were young religious, therefore they are alien to our institute." They find it difficult to grasp and evaluate correctly some of the new things being done and the newer ways of doing them. For example, they may be unable to understand the need for leisure, for free time, and for the unusual freedom of operation required by the young Sisters in advanced studies.

Indeed it is a form of violence to self for certain individuals who have been in the community for years to accept these innovations as proper or right. It is so terribly difficult for them to grasp the point that the reason they did not do these things earlier was because they were not suited to that age, but are fitting to this one. It would not be suitable, here and now, to operate completely as they did in that particular age. When you spell all this out in terms of maturity, it becomes apparent that maturity in the younger groups demands that they endeavor to appreciate what is worthwhile in the traditional; whereas maturity in the older Sisters requires that they strive to separate what was proper to their time from what is essential to their religious communities.

Father Christoph: Religious women, even in active communities, sometimes boast that they have little contact with the world. And this is not *per se* necessarily virtuous.

Father Evoy: In the present day, badly-needed contact with the world does not come by just talking with people. It is true that talking with people is helpful; for as long as you are dealing with people and trying to understand them, you are in real contact with them. A good deal of our needed knowledge of the world is derived also from the ordinary media of communication. These certainly would include a newspaper and a news magazine. At times, even subscribing to these poses a real problem for a given community. If the solution to this little financial problem is worked out by deciding to borrow magazines, etc., I hope I am stressing the obvious, when I suggest that such borrowing should be done from another religious house and not from externs. For instance, to be a bit more specific, here are questions confronting the Superior of a religious community that is poor: What can we afford? To get along with insufficient heat or to go with insufficient food, or to survive without enough proper reading material in terms of periodicals and newspapers? Right off hand I do not know the answer because *all* of these are necessary.

Father Christoph: May I suggest an answer. We once had a Superior whose concern was books and he told us, "You know, if you miss a couple of meals, you most probably won't starve to death. But if you miss a couple of issues of a magazine maybe you won't be able to get them." He suggested that one of the last areas of retrenchment should be in the field of buying books. If you are in school, the field of current literature is a necessity to function adequately. In this area, again, there is need to be mature about books and magazines.

Father Evoy: For instance, many communities do not subscribe to, let us say, magazine A, because they do not consider it proper reading matter for religious; but there might be a special issue of this magazine, on the assassination of President Kennedy, for example, which fifty years from now may be a classic. Magazine B, which is regarded as undesirable in general, puts one out on this same occasion. This issue should also be in all the libraries because it is a picture study of the assassination of the President of the United States. These particular copies of magazine A and magazine B *should* be in our community. This is not subscribing to the over-all principle that these two magazines should at *all* times be in our communities. It is only *if* and *when* they put out something worthwhile that this would be so.

Keeping ourselves mature intellectually requires a vigilance. For instance, if, as a religious, I say with regard to this particular magazine, "We don't read it because it is slanted in its reporting of the news," this statement is more mature if it is a judgment I, as a religious, have made from my own examination of the magazine. It is notably less mature if I am saying it simply because a Superior or someone else said it. So what we are talking about here is not simply the necessity of providing the opportunities for religious to keep themselves informed by making reading materials such as books, magazines, journals, etc., available to them. It is more than that. It is saying to the religious, especially the young religious, "Not only may you do this, but you are *encouraged* to keep yourself informed on the things that are very important."

The informed religious knows the things that are important— the big things going on in the world, as well as some of the small things going on in her own little area of activity. She needs to know the things that are happening in her community and her department, but she may not confine herself to these, except at the cost of keeping herself immature. If she chooses this, she should know that she is a less capable member of the community, because in religious life we cannot use an immature person as well as we can a mature person.

The evaluation and re-evaluation within the context of life as it is really lived, especially in the United States by religious women, is of the utmost importance.

In some religious communities I know, the members are occupied with a multitude of things that seem to be important. Besides their teaching they do all their own housekeeping, their cooking, and the rest of it. This leaves no free time. This type of situation needs to be re-examined. In such a situation, granting at least for the time being that there will be no change in the multiplicity of tasks to be done by the members of the community, there is posed a problem of some consequence. It is that when some work of greater value to the community comes along, something must give; otherwise, this important new work must be jettisoned on the preposterous basis that there is no time for things of greater moment.

There are certain opportunities for cultural enrichment and intellectual enrichment to which religious should subscribe as far as possible. It is clear to you, I believe, that they should be given every encouragement to thus better themselves for Christ. To be more precise about this, there are some cultural events, such as plays, concerts, and lectures, live or on TV or radio which are really worthwhile. There is a problem here for religious women because these things take place frequently at night, and were a religious to attend she would be kept up beyond her ordinary bedtime. To take advantage of the opportunity to attend these would be impossible if a religious had to do every required thing in the course of her long day, and still get her full measure of needed sleep. Normally, for religious women, each day is crowded, as you very well know.

Glance for a moment at the normal day of a religious. She gets up at the accustomed time in the morning and performs her spiritual exercises, which include morning prayer, meditation, Holy Mass, etc. She goes right through the day, until, somewhat exhausted, she retires to her night's rest. If any member of the community were on occasion to take advantage of something culturally beneficial, what would give way in this tight schedule of spiritual, academic, and domestic duties? Must it be her sleep that is curtailed? If she had to stay up at night and nevertheless get up at the accustomed time in the morning, the time would have to be deducted from her required sleep. But Sisters, is this being realistic? Are we not arguing with one of the realities of life when we contemplate taking away sleep time from religious women, since this time is already cut down to a minimum?

If she is not to be robbed of necessary sleep, what then must give way when there is something additional which the religious should be permitted and also encouraged to attend? This is where a religious Superior must have real vision. She must possess the type of intellectual appraisal which sees these and other things, whether religious exercises or cultural events, as so many means to the end of this person's religious vocation. From this vantage point the Superior would see with clarity that the Sister taking in this particular culturally enriching event must eliminate something else beside her sleep.

After carefully studying the entire situation, the Superior might decide, for instance, that the only thing that could be eliminated on this particular day would be the time spent on Sister's meditation. By way of an individual action, there seems to be no reason whatever why a Superior would not judge that on the day following this cultural event, a waiver be given to Sister on her meditation. She would be told that she was not to make it that day since something judged by her Superior to be actually more important occurred the previous evening and took up the time normally allotted to her meditation. It goes without saying that this would be only an occasional thing.

Father Christoph: A mature religious would not take advantage of such a situation. As a matter of fact, if a religious recognized or realized that for her, meditation is absolutely imperative for an efficient and spiritually effective job, she would find time during the day to make her meditation. Here is where the early training of cultivating the initiative of a Sister would prove itself.

Father Evoy: She might be able to, Father, as you say, but it should be made unmistakably clear to her that she would be free of any obligation to do so.

Father Christoph: Yes, she would be free of the obligation to do so, but then she would be so mature in her attitude, she would have been exercised in initiative enough, to know what she could and what she should do.

Father Evoy: Meditation is another means to an end and there is nothing about a particular meditation that is so sacred that it would be unthinkable to contemplate waiving it in view of something else very important. The something we are talking about could occur conceivably once or twice a month, because in my judgment at least, this is about as often as we find things worthwhile enough to be really enriching to the person and to the community. In this type of situation, to excuse Sister from the obligation of morning meditation and permit her to sleep during the time ordinarily given to meditation is a very prudent and reasonable thing. This whole consideration serves nicely to point up that it is of some moment for a Superior to be intelligent. Obviously, this is not to be understood in the sense that she is to be academically superior, but in the sense that she is of a practical bent of mind, enabling her to see things as means to an end; that she possesses the wisdom to occasionally replace one of these means in the life of a Subject with another more important means.

Father Christoph: She has a hierarchy of values presumably shared by the members of the community. Sisters, you may be shocked at what we say, since traditionally so much emphasis is placed upon the morning meditation. Let us face it. The morning meditation can descend to empty formalism. When it is put in proper perspective it gives a tremendous vitality to our daily work. But again, this proper perspective postulates a hierarchy of values; and on this particular occasion, this event would be regarded as more important than this specific meditation. We are not downgrading meditation or saying that it is unimportant. We are saying that in a specific instance we can conceive of something that is even of more value than this one meditation.

Father Evoy: It is quite conceivable that a religious might, also under and with the blessing of authority, occasionally omit her meditation or some other spiritual exercise in view of very important work that she would be doing. Such work might be in conjunction with an unusual press in her regular line of duties. Such a justifiable omission might easily be linked to charity in consideration of time given to another person.

Father Christoph: There is a fear that discipline will break down and the whole institution will be destroyed by innovation. Frankly, I would rather use the word renovation here, than innovation. We are concerned with a renewal of spirit which would call for the elimination of empty traditions and shallow customs that have little utility today.

Father Evoy: Yes. We are aware that this might threaten some older members of the community. But we must ask ourselves, "Is the old good because it is old?" On the other hand, with equal diligence, we must ask ourselves the question, "Is the new good just because it is new?" Do we subscribe to change for the sake of change? Does just the fact that something is new, in itself lend it a validity? So it can be extremely difficult, at times, to choose one's way along the happy mean between the two extremes of canonization of the old because it is old, and the rejection of the old because it is old.

Intellectual maturity demands that we constantly re-examine these traditional patterns in terms of their potential for the fulfillment of our end. We do so with the full realization that every one of these customs which has come down through tradition, was at least originally regarded as a means to the over-all goal of the community. This traditional heritage includes meditation, and oh, so many things! To take the view that these are only various means, and to have the courage to act in keeping with that vision is certainly a mark of maturity in a Superior, and also in a religious Subject. On the other hand, this type of perspective

270 Maturity in the Religious Life

demands among other things, the frank recognition that after all, change can be made something of a tin god; and that there is a fascination, especially for the young, in the new, the novel, and the unusual. The tendency to espouse change for the sake of change may be found in religious life, also; because in religion we happen to have a good many young people.

In the older members, intellectual maturity postulates an unclouded frank recognition that they are inclined to cling to the way things always have been done. Their tendency is to hold fast to the old, regardless. They may not even suspect that their security is linked with the old ways. At the same time, human nature being what it is, we should in no sense be surprised that the young religious are inclined to advocate change. We are well enough aware of the fact that revolution in any country has at its head the youth. Since it is a revolt against the going order, youth is in it. In a national rebellion the odds are that the college youth and the other young people of the nation are going to be involved, because they have no commitment to the established order.

Father Christoph: They have no involvement, no vested interests in the going concern and the "status quo." They also see the limitations of certain elements of the "status quo" more realistically than we do. We tend to become conservative after following a pattern for any length of time. This tends to keep us doing a thing in a certain way. It makes us blind even to the possibility of doing it in another way. We tend to see and regard it as, "Well, this is the way it has to be—this is the only way." It never occurs to us to discover if there is another way. On the other hand, youth sees some of the foibles of age, some of the limitations of traditional patterns. Because of its enthusiasm and its lack of commitment to the going social order and the community as it stands, youth is brash enough to suggest change. Somewhere between these two extremes, as Father Evoy said, we will find a mean that is specially acceptable and helpful to the community.

I am not particularly impressed when I hear of a community adhering to a tradition established four or five hundred years ago.

Father Evoy: Merely for the sake of custom?

Father Christoph: Yes. While we are re-evaluating things we should check the obstacle courses in our community life. How are these obstacle courses structured? By making it impossible for an individual to do anything without having every next move checked and counter-checked by half a dozen individuals. The other day a Sister and I were discussing the span of authority. From what she and others have said, I am sure that many of your communities have beautiful charts of—what do you call it?— "the chain of command" or something like that? What are they good for? According to your chart, you have Sister Superior at the top, and then different ones below her with various groups under their charge, so that an individual religious would only have to go to one person for direction.

Is it not frustrating when told to do something to be faced with the necessity of obtaining keys from ten different people? Does it not discourage you and crush your morale, when after having a project approved, you then have to clear every day with four or five people? This is what happens at times. For example, you are going to give a play. You have a multi-purpose room, which is used as a lunch room, for basketball, sometimes, and at other times for practice of one type or another. Should there not be just one in charge? I am not telling you how to run your institutions; I am merely saying that you should not have to go to half a dozen people to clear something. Sister X is in charge of the gym. I do not care how many people use it—they go to her and clear with her when they want to use it—and there is no problem.

If all have equal right to the gym and no one is in charge of it, then the Sisters have to run to the Superior. Sister Superior is then making decisions that decrease her efficiency tremendously because she has more important things to do than to determine who is going to use the gym at eight or nine o'clock in the morning. She should have more time for her community. She should be able to take care of individual needs. See how initiative is stifled?

Father Evoy: This obstacle course which Father Christoph was talking about has been allowed in some instances to grow to the point where it is almost unbelievable what it has done to the effectiveness of certain individuals. Let me exemplify. To begin with, you have to go to the Superior to get permission for a movie projector, for example; then you have to go to this other person —if you can find her—to get it. When you have found her, she asks you, "When do you need it, Sister?" You say, "I will need it at two o'clock." Sister says, "At two o'clock? Yes, I think I can arrange that. I will be in my office for a few minutes at one-fifteen; you may pick it up then." This kind of thing goes on and on to the point where, after a while, you either give up completely or you spend more time just seeing the thing through than it is worth.

Sisters, this kind of bottle-necking *should not be.* It is a tremendous deterrent to anyone's even trying to do anything. More often than we like to admit, it has been allowed to flourish like a rank weed in religious communities, even though, of its very nature, it is a destructive type of thing. It is something that has been allowed to come about, I think, largely by default. While women are capable of a greatness of soul, perhaps beyond that of men, they are also capable of a pettiness unknown to men. Perhaps only a woman could let so many things get in another person's way that the latter would find it just about impossible to get something done! The situation in some communities has become so inconceivably cluttered up that it is most discouraging for anyone to so much as try to do anything.

Father Christoph: There is another aspect to this, Father, which I think is a common defect among religious. What is the care of no one is likewise the concern of no one. We have to be realistic. People must have keys; people have to have control of things and know where they are; but there should not be any greater difficulty in securing the facilities to do your job than there is in the business world, or in any other organization. There is only one organization, I think, that has more red tape than religious communities, and that is the government. But the government deals with a different type of person. It dare not allow too much leeway, so everything is blueprinted and one may not deviate. This is not true in religious communities. The supposition is that we are always dealing with intelligent, interested, and conscientious people. But, at times, we are treated like children in religious life.

These things are not our concern, so we may become very careless about the things given for our use. To exemplify: we have little need for money. When we are given money, we do not know its value, and we are careless where we put it and what we do with it. I was remarking about this to a Sister the other day and I mentioned, "I can't recall the last time I counted my change." Now, I should. I am not naive. I know that people are not completely honest, and yet I do not want to suspect anyone of wanting to cheat. But it is good business to count. As it is, if someone does cheat me, I just go back and get more money from the procurator. That is an attitude we cultivate, and it is an unhealthy attitude. Again, this is not my tape recorder so I do not care about it. So it is out in the rain, and I wonder who left it there, and on I walk. This is detachment from responsibility because it is not my own. We should take a healthy proprietary interest in things that belong to the community.

We are vowed to care but sometimes we do not. Our vow of poverty means that we care, but in the practical order we do not. Perhaps that is why we have red tape, and that is why we have to have seven keys to get something. Nevertheless, I do think that most of this is explainable in terms of the person possessing the keys having the attitude, "I have the key. You have to come to *me*. This is *my* domain." There is some of that. It also suggests the lack of delegation or the failure to share authority. Superiors should examine their consciences in respect to some of these things. They can make Subjects happier and increase their personal morale which cannot but enhance the social morale of the community.

You have to have leisure. At one time, if a Priest or Brother or Sister had leisure, Superiors put a broom or a pick or a dishcloth in one's hand. The reason for this was the mistaken idea that the apostolate was achieved through a kind of physical activity, a kind of commotion. I can recall some years ago when one of the younger Fathers said to me, "I don't understand this preoccupation with doing things." He said, "We are supposed to be learned men; we are supposed to be scholars, and we are supposed to be efficient teachers. Why can't Superiors let me alone and just let me study? Why do I have to go out and preach a sermon on Sunday, and do this or that?" He was trying to make the point that if we are going to be good in any line, in the things we are designed to do, we have to have leisure.

Before we are anything else we are religious women, and as good religious women we need a certain amount of time for spiritual growth. I say you cannot grow on a couple of ideas you received in the novitiate, because you may not have gotten them straight anyway. They have to grow on you; you have to mull over them, and you cannot think of all the good ideas and good thoughts possible. Why can I not use the writings of others who have thought these things and who are willing to share them with me? But I need leisure to do this. This is one thing I find woefully missing in the patterning of the lives of Sisters.

Father Evoy: This area of intellectual maturity, Sisters, consists principally in keeping yourselves really informed, and in striving to comprehend the meaning of what you receive intellectually.

This is so very important. Since this suggests it, let me return for a moment to another area. It is also very important, for the rest of your lives, to remain critical in the best sense of the word. By the term "critical" I mean evaluative. Sisters, you should go on evaluating and re-evaluating everything in your religious life. As we mentioned earlier, your religious community itself is a means to an end. Every means to an end must be assessed and reassessed with a readiness to correct or change anything that is deficient.

These critical examinations are not going to be conducted effectively unless you are aware of where you are going, and what you ought to do to get there. So far as your regulations, methods, systems, or almost anything goes, you should strive to be both individually and community-wise critical, and should remain thus critical. You should be your own most severe critics and your own continuous critics; so that when and where pruning would be necessary, you would recognize it first, and get busy at it. To do so often takes not only genuine intellectual vision, but courage as well; because to the extent that you do "lop off" or change that which needs to be so treated, you are going to run counter to persons' feelings. Perhaps the extent of the correction needed is so great that only a beginning can be made here. It may take courage to do even that.

But you should constantly re-evaluate any customary way of doing things where it is not clear why a given thing should continue to exist. There are many things that are thus to be re-examined. To take but an example or two. The practice in many religious communities across this country is that any Sister going to a physician may not be with the doctor alone, even for a physical checkup. Her Sister companion must be present also in the examining room. You certainly should take a long, hard look at this sort of thing; and regardless of its historical explanation, ask whether or not this should be permitted to continue. Again, as Father Christoph mentioned, the custom that a religious should never leave the convent without a Sister companion is one which cuts severely into the over-all effectiveness of the community, because of the tremendous waste of the Sister companion's time. Should not this custom be modified in certain situations? Clearly there are times when a Sister should not be out alone. But are there not times and circumstances in which she should not have to inconveniently take some other person along in order to go out of the convent?

Many individuals today are looking at the late President Kennedy in terms of his badge of courage. Regardless of their differences with his policies, they admit that once he had the vision to see what he thought needed to be done, he was willing to move in and begin. He certainly did not get very far. They point out that even he was well aware of that, for he said, "We won't finish this in a thousand days or during the lifetime of this administration—but we can begin." There is a parallel to this, I think, in religious life. We can at least begin. It is rather interesting that in the Second Vatican Council the Church has led the way in this area. She has frankly pointed out that changes are needed in many places. She has undertaken to begin these changes. These renovations have reference even to the Mass, the Divine Office, and the Sacraments; in fact to almost anything that is found to be in need of modification. The Church is saying that this is worth doing and she is beginning.

Now Sisters, I think we are safe in stating that there are well-known churchmen who have been very, very badly hurt by some of these changes, just as there have been others who wanted even greater changes. The over-all position of the Ecclesiastics who, aware of both of these more extreme positions, still went ahead, was one that required real courage. In your religious community there should be a similar courageous vigilance that occasions your examining and re-examining not only some things but everything, in terms of its suitability to the specific apostolic end of your community.

You should be repeatedly asking yourselves, "How apt to our end is this particular thing, here and now?" To take one practical application very close to home in terms of the speakers here,

Father Christoph and Father Evoy should periodically ask themselves, among other things, "Should we continue to run Gonzaga University? Why?" Unless we do this and are satisfied that we can answer it in the affirmative, with a wholly satisfying reply, we are here showing a lack of maturity.

Father Christoph: One aspect of this intellectual curiosity is intellectual perfection. This demands leisure and we must recognize the fact that religious women should have more freedom to pursue their own intellectual and spiritual perfection. As a matter of fact, there is a close relationship between the spiritual and intellectual development; but this business of having a full day of teaching, five days a week, and then having so many chores to do on Saturday, and Church work on Sunday, deprives the individual of the leisure necessary for either intellectual or spiritual development.

We are talking about intellectual development. We are no match for people living in the secular world who can find an hour a day or maybe two hours a day or maybe a weekend to study. Our occupations are so numerous and so demanding that at the end of the week we are lucky if we can find fifteen minutes to write a necessary letter.

Father Evoy: There is a danger here that we might not only present people in religious life with the opportunity of escaping into activity but almost be encouraging them to do so. They can be so busy about so many things that they do not have time to think about the genuinely important things. I am afraid that we do not give enough attention to the importance of knowing what is important.

It is true that you do a certain amount, at least so we hope, of thinking about things of considerable moment during your meditation and other prayers; but there is need of another aspect of your thinking. Your leisure should be able to provide you with the opportunity, at least, for a "gab session." You should be able to communicate, because there are many areas in which you cannot think richly and productively unless you are communicating with other persons.

The traditional concept of the religious' relationship to Almighty God has almost fenced her off from communicating with her fellow religious. Outside of the stylized and formalized recreation found in religious communities of women, there is very little opportunity for them to sit down as normal people and talk things over. This is an aspect that I think, unfortunately, has been played down in religious life. When we get together in recreation or in silence our attitudes are stereotyped. The recreation is too formalized at times to be even interesting or recreating, so we need freedom to talk.

If an individual is isolated constantly and must do all her thinking alone with no chance to communicate with others, she is going to be deprived of a richness which would be hers for the taking could she but communicate with others. In community living we have a certain amount of silence in the course of the day. Perhaps this is an area we should re-evaluate to see if we should not at least consider having some periods where the individuals can gather in groups and feel free to discuss what they think really needs to be discussed, or whatever they want to discuss.

Father Christoph: I already mentioned the ten o'clock coffee. There was a time when we went to coffee and never sat down; and we drank our coffee in silence. Now, as far as I know, this custom has disappeared. Here you are. You come out of two classes in the morning, at least I do, at ten o'clock. I am a little tired, but I am stimulated sometimes by what I have heard in class or what I have said. I may have said something brilliant and I want to share it with my companions. If I have to stand up and just eat in silence, it breeds this attitude: "You are in the world, and I am in the world. Don't interrupt me. Don't disturb me; I am communicating with God." But I am not. I am just dying to say something—something worthwhile.

Father Evoy: Father is pointing up the need we have to re-evaluate the pattern of so much silence connected with eating in religious communities. Sisters, whether I eat by myself in a restaurant or in a convent dining room, I ordinarily finish my meal in less than ten minutes. I am afraid I must admit on reflection that I have a tendency either to bolt my food when I am eating alone, or else let my food get cold while I become wrapped up in some good reading. Eating is a social activity. It always has been and it always should be among non-savages.

In religious life we have assumed that religious should eat either in silence or along with community reading, outside of the times it is "free" or "Deo gratias." There are times when individuals do not particularly feel like talking. But perhaps again you ought to re-evaluate some of these customs in terms of present day needs. Should you not actually have more conversation at meals and less spiritual reading? Refectory spiritual reading is something that you so often either do your best not to hear or else just tolerate. If, however, it happens to be a book or an article that you are interested in, you must strain to hear it.

Father Christoph: And be annoyed because you find it too difficult to hear between the clattering of dishes and the like, or because you have a poor reader. It is always a problem. Now in this same context, and, I think, also in need of re-evaluation, is another stereotyped pattern that very often exists in religious life. You come down to the table and sit across from *her* every day. Frankly, you are up to here with her, you see. I mean, here and now, as far as any inclination to communicate with her goes, you really have nothing to say to her. It is almost like bringing the old prayer wheel into social communication. The best you can do is force the "small talk." You actually have nothing to say to her. You have a number of things to say to several individuals over there. But they are over there, and she is here confronting you. Should this pattern not be re-examined? Must you always sit opposite the same individual?

This is one of the reasons, Father, why it makes it easier to have reading at table, because one dries up awfully fast. If I had to sit opposite you every day, I would not be talking to you. I would not have anything to say, and one needs the stimulation of a new face, a new idea, a new interest. There are some individuals with whom you cannot talk, and some with whom you can talk much better than with others. Now, it is true, this type of thing is not entirely free from dangers. You could have the equivalent of cliques grow out of this freedom to talk to anyone you chose, and to sit with anyone you chose. But here again, as mature people, this is part of the responsibility each of you must carry for being yourself in the full sense of the word.

When concerned about the productivity of leisure we ought to take that into consideration. At table, were my eating conducted in leisurely fashion for at least one meal a day, given a nice conversationalist, I would learn something and she would learn something; and I would be improved. I would be exploiting my leisure and enjoying it.

Father Evoy: In terms of intellectual maturity, we notice one thing in community life that is all too common: we find individuals who are not adequately informed on current events. I mean that they are not up on the more significant things that are going on at the present time. I am referring to the big national and international events. These happenings pertain both to the Church and to the secular world. A withdrawal of interest in and knowledge of so many of these events is possible in religious life, because only too often a religious may, with no notable amount of opposition, retreat into the little bailiwick in which she teaches this particular thing or performs that particular function; and the rest of the world ceases really to matter to her in any notable way. Whatever her motivation, her attitude seems to be that she could not really care less.

The mature religious has a certain broadness of interest primarily flowing from the very fact that she is a member of an apostolic community. To be apostolic implies that one is intensely interested in and concerned about people. When we talked earlier about our sensitivity to people and our interest in people, we certainly implied that the significant happenings and events that take place in the world of people must be of great concern to us. We should at all times be interested in the major occurrences of the entire world. Accordingly, news that concerns major happenings any place in the world should catch and hold our interest.

Father Christoph: To be ignorant of current events, of major issues that face the people is not to be regarded as a sign of desirable detachment from the world and of holy other-worldliness. There are some religious who judge themselves to be God's chosen ones because they are completely detached from this world. They think that interest in the affairs of the world denotes a secular attitude which is, in some way or other, undesirable in a religious. The golden mean is forgotten.

Father Evoy: Father is indicating something of the view that religious life might be regarded as a hide-away from the world instead of what, in reality, it is: the powerhouse from which an individual, refreshed, moves out into the world. Again, this is an area where you need to re-evaluate. You are from the very beginning to be on guard against ever being corralled into your own little section of the world which becomes so small that it can hardly be called real. To be interested in people: what they are doing, what they are thinking, what they are feeling, what they are experiencing; these things should be important to you, because by reason of your vocation you are vitally interested in people.

As religious, you are not saving souls. You are saving persons. You are saving people. You are instruments in saving *people*, not souls. People have experiences; they have feelings, views, and they do things. It is almost embarrassing to have to recognize that while we have so often and so vigorously inveighed against regarding Sisters as children, and against their being treated as children, they themselves sometimes lend a basis to such an attitude. I think that some religious and particularly religious women, quite unwittingly give some grounds for the view that they are not fully in the real world; because they do withdraw themselves, in large part, from that world. Withdrawal is always an actual danger. It is a danger especially in religious life because religious life constitutes a society within society. If the religious society becomes an over-all sealing entity in its own right, in which an individual takes refuge from the larger society, then it is distorted.

This is a danger against which young religious particularly should be warned. I remember very well a remark made to me by a highly intelligent woman when she was particularly irked. She said, "You Jesuits belong to *the* Society. You know, for years I naively thought you belonged to society." I can recall mentally picking myself up off the floor from the impact of the remark, because I had to recognize that, at least in some instances, it was not wholly false. So young religious, especially, should be told that they have a real obligation to keep themselves as well informed as they can about the more important things going on in the life of people.

Father Christoph: This does not mean that we have to read everything that is available: every new magazine, book, and the like. But it does mean that when we get together, we should be able to talk about these things, and we can talk about them only if the information is available and the opportunities for discussion is permitted.

Father Evoy: The fact, for instance, that our Holy Father went over to the Near East, and that it is the first time in history this has happened, would obviously be of interest to religious. Should it not also be of interest to you that there are thousands upon thousands of elderly persons who constitute a national problem in the matter of medical care? So the Congressional bills and the over-all picture of what is being done in terms of things like "Medicare," should be of interest to you. This is by no means to say that there is need for you to be authorities on these things. What you should have is an educated, interested person's grasp of these things. If I may be permitted the term, a gentlewoman's knowledge of such events is quite fitting and proper to you.

Father Christoph: I think that this knowledge would also make religious more acceptable to the people, because we are always accused of not being aware of what is going on in the world; of not being in tune with reality. We do make demands upon people without realizing the limitations of income, the circumstances of family living, and the like. This is an accusation that I constantly hear directed at religious, particularly Sisters. They are not aware of all the demands that are made on individuals, as far as time and money are concerned. So if we had, as Father says, a gentlewoman's knowledge of these things, I think the effectiveness of religious women would be tremendously improved.

This raises the question, too, of the way we deal with tradesmen, cab drivers, yes, even Priests. The brash manner in which we make demands on cab drivers, red-caps, and the like; and the almost insulting tips offered them, suggest that we know neither the value of their work nor the value of money. Apropos of this, sometimes stipends are offered to lecturers which would indicate, if they represent the value the offerer put on the work, that what the lecturer had to offer was very little. A mature woman would inquire from others what size tip or what size stipend to offer.

Again, at the risk of seeming to paraphrase Cardinal Suenens, the fear that the lay institutes will take over the work of the religious communities of women is unfounded. Religious women have something to offer that the lay institute does not have, for it is the collective representation, the idealization of the collective efforts (which is not always noticeable to the naked eye in the case of the lay institute) that still make the religious important. But Cardinal Suenens says also that unless religious women become aware of the problems of the day, and go out to face these problems, and help people meet these problems, their work is not only going to be handicapped, but it will have to be taken over by lay institutes by reason of the religious communities defaulting in their objectives. He inveighs very much against the apostolate to the children, only. He talks about the apostolate of the parents, the apostolate of the alumnae, the apostolate of the public in general—areas not being reached by religious women, simply because they are not prepared to meet them; and again, because the institutes of religious women in general forbid this type of relationship with others.

The religious of the future will have to make some type of adjustment so that the effectiveness of their work will be realized in these areas. This means that they will have to be intellectually alert. They must have leisure to exploit their own learning; to expand their own horizons. They must have time for lectures, "gab fests," and the like, which so often give tremendous insights to an individual.

Father Evoy: Add to these the culturally enriching things on TV, radio, and live performances. Certain of these are often difficult to fit in, but you should begin thinking, as I indicated earlier, that this is part of your cultural diet. If you lose touch with people, you lose much. First of all, you lose sympathy.

The magnitude of the danger of losing touch with people is seen in this: if you love them you should try to know and to understand them. Really to know them, you must know them in the world in which they live. Unless you know them this way, you do not appreciate the problems confronting seculars. If you try to love them at a well-withdrawn distance, you will find you are unable to feel for people, in the many areas in which you *should* feel for them. They have all kinds of problems, you see. The plain fact of the matter is that you are not apostolic, really, if you are withdrawing yourselves too far away from them. Frankly, as apostolic religious, you are just not mature if you withdraw from people to live in your own little religious castles quite apart. The peril, especially for a religious, is that she can come to regard this little castle as a fortress well secured behind the moat of religious detachment, with the drawbridge of her cloister drawn up securely. This keeps out the world. The only ones she need confront are the persons who, somehow or other, occasionally gain entrance, if indeed, there happen to be any at all who cross the moat. Moreover, if she happens to be working in a place where there is no contact whatever with people from the outside, she can become as isolated, for all practical purposes, as if she were living in her own private sanctuary.

In our discussion of how important it is that a religious keep herself informed on knowledge requisite to her being a more effective instrument, we might carry our exploration further. I think that among other things, in this context we should mention the need to re-evaluate the time at which young religious receive certain academic courses. I am referring to the period in their training when these subjects are given them. At least you should consider whether it might not be well to give certain studies earlier than they are given today; such classes on grace, the sacraments, the Mass, Scripture, . . .

Father Christoph: Canon law and moral theology.

Father Evoy: These things are vital. It seems to me that many religious have been permitted in the past to remain largely ignorant of the obligations and the rights that are theirs from canon law. Ignorance in moral theology has, I feel, led to false consciences; while incorrect notions of dogmatic and ascetical theology have led to a kind of sentimental piety that in the long run will not stand up under the pressures of life. Then, of course, what happens? These erroneous notions are fed to other people, not only within, but outside the community as well. Your objective should be a community well-instructed and well-informed in terms of the things we have been talking about here. Religious should have an adequate knowledge of whatever things are in keeping with their vocation. This is certainly in line with maturity. This also brings me to a related matter. I refer to the important and interesting bearing of maturity on one's attitude toward poverty.

Father Christoph: First of all, I think it is almost axiomatic that religious do not know the value of a dollar. This is because of the fact that the average religious has so little control over funds. Religious enter religious life as adolescents—for the most part— and very frequently they have not had much actual experience in the handling of money. Consequently, they are being taught some of the principles of poverty in the early years of their religious life when everything is given to them, and controlled for them; and they can be completely out of focus with the realities of the economic world in which we live. The evidences of this are the penuriousness of some Superiors and the liberality of others.

When some individuals are given money, they think it is going out of style tomorrow, so they spend it very freely. This is one of the consequences of their not having had to earn it when they were younger, perhaps, or their not appreciating the value of money. The others who are penurious have an exaggerated idea of the value of a dollar. It seems to me that they think, as Superiors, that the basis on which to approve of a Superior lies in the way she can economize. Throughout their training period, religious ought to be given an opportunity to understand the role of money in life. I think it would not be a bad idea, occasionally, to inform the young religious of what it costs to maintain them; of the expenses that are connected with the house, so that they at least get an idea of liabilities and assets; the outgo and the income. Normally, since it is not the business of the young religious to be concerned, they are not told. But I am thinking in terms of preparing the young religious to be responsible for money. Let them know a few little things. It does not hurt. One of the reasons why we are reluctant to tell certain things about the community finances is that many religious never learn when not to speak. Domestic affairs are supposed to be kept domestic, within the household. To inform the Sisters is a calculated risk. But if religious have some appreciation of the cost of living, and how the community manages to make a go of it, maybe they would appreciate the role of money. It should not be presented as though needy things should be denied them.

There is a happy mean between liberality and penuriousness; not frugality, but penuriousness; and this is going to be achieved only by allowing young religious to handle money. It is axiomatic that the more you dole out funds by the penny to religious, who are to spend the money in specific ways; the more you specify what they are to spend and how they are to spend it; the more you find that religious men and women tend to spend all the money they get. It is a challenge to the ingenuity of the individual to see what he can get away with. In those communities where religious Superiors are generous with the Subjects, just from the standpoint of human psychology, the dividends are tremendous. "This Superior trusts me, therefore I am going to bring back all I can." Again, I think that this is borne out by the experiences of religious Superiors who have been extremely minute in giving directions to Subjects relative to the expenditure of money. But poverty has even larger overtones than this. We take the vow of poverty but if we are not given a solid foundation on the implications of the vow, we can transfer our need for possessions to some other thing. After all, poverty contradicts a natural drive in man to possess. If we do not adequately satisfy for that natural drive, individuals are going to possess in some way. Every community has its hoarders. In the hoarder the drive to possess is not adequately satisfied by something that sublimates it.

Father Evoy: Let us keep this very practical. I think, by and large, cab drivers are notably reluctant to pick up a group of Sisters. Do you know why? Because the cab driver's livelihood comes largely from his tips, and I suspect he would not make a living if he transported Sisters exclusively. This inadequate tipping is common to women, but more especially to Sisters. I think religious women are particularly prone to this sort of thing by virtue of their faulty conception of poverty.

There are few other areas where a lack of maturity is as manifest as in that of operations concerned with poverty. This, as Father said, is centered about the correct uses of money. A prominent person in this country maintains that religious communities waste thousands of dollars each year because of poor business procedures. He asserts, moreover, that not only are there communities in large numbers that do not closely follow their budget, but also many that do not even have a budget. This is shocking to businessmen of our day. Unfortunately, you have seen in certain Sisters evidences of incorrect views on the use of money. Some seem to feel that they may not spend a cent for something as reasonable as a newspaper, even on a long trip. Sisters have gone without meals on long journeys because they could not reconcile with their conception of poverty the expenditure of money for food. The regrettable aspect here, it seems to me, is not that these Sisters missed a meal, but that they felt they *had* to in order to be good religious.

Of course, the solution to this type of problem is certainly not to be found in the detailed instructions given by one in authority to the traveling Sister, who is informed just exactly what, where, and how she is to spend every penny in the course of her trip.

It is seen immediately that this is once again the old "treat her as if she were a child" attitude. It is of the same objectionable cloth in fact, as final instructions to departing Sisters who have been in religion for years, in which a Superior tells them, "Now you are to omit none of your spiritual exercises while you are away." How many a Sister has reacted to such over-solicitous instructions with the strong feeling that she would like (just to show that Superior) to determine *not* to make all her spiritual exercises.

I think, Sisters, that religious women often appear penurious or stingy in the tips they give while traveling, simply because they are not properly informed in these matters. They do not know any better. They have never been told that there are certain times when tipping is called for; moreoever when tipping is a "must." It should not be taken for granted that they have correct ideas about this custom. A person might give evidence of such unfortunate ignorance by giving the wrong tip, by giving either far too much or too little. One can appear very immature if one does not know how to tip.

Today, for the most part, a reasonable tip is somewhere around fifteen percent. Most people go along with that. It should not be assumed that Sisters are aware of that; nor even that most women in the world are. As I mentioned earlier, Sisters came by unsuitable habits of tipping honestly, because their mothers and sisters in the world are also inclined that way. They tend to hold a tip down to a bare ten percent, if not less than that. Let us take an example. A woman gets out of a cab. The bill is $1.20 and she gives the cab driver a dime. This, perhaps, no man could do, but it is carried out by her with no awareness whatever of impropriety or unbecomingness.

Another aspect in this area of the relationship of poverty to maturity is somewhat embarrassing to mention. Sisters can quite unknowingly impose on lay people. I am referring now to one manifestation of their lack of appreciation and comprehension of what money is; what it means; and its worth. There are people who feel like ducking when they see a Sister coming. They love the Sisters, but they say, "They will wring you dry. They will take your car for any and every occasion. They will use your gas and oil with no thought of the inconvenience to you. They are about as responsible in these matters as adolescent youngsters are. As the adolescent brings the car home with the tank nearly empty, so, also, do the Sisters."

It happens to be a fact that Sisters are not always fully adult in their whole view of this type of thing, just because poverty can be misunderstood so very badly. Under the guise of poverty, a religious can feel that she may not in conscience spend a dollar of her own money, but she can let you spend any amount on her without even giving it a second thought. She can request the use of your car just when you need it for your family affairs. She can thus impose without even realizing that she is doing so. There are so many aspects of immaturity that can hide themselves under the cloak of alleged poverty.

Most unfortuntately, at times it would appear that the worth of a person in the community is calculated largely in monetary terms, of her savings or earnings. More surprising still, she can be told openly by Superiors and others that she is one of the more valuable members of the community because she is worth more in terms of money to the community. In a sense, this is a natural temptation to religious because they are also professional people, and as professionals, money is part and parcel of their whole activity. While we shall exemplify but a few of them, it should be kept in mind that the kinds of immaturity that can conceal themselves beneath the cloak of poverty are very numerous.

In religious communities these days people are sent away for graduate work and for degrees. Eventually they return. For some years now they have been living with, dealing with, talking with professional people, and, in general, functioning in a professional manner. They come back only to find that what masks itself as religious poverty bottle-necks them so badly and so unreasonably that they are tempted to quit. In order to obtain permission to travel or to buy necessary things they must weather the looks and the remarks of individuals whose own unsound views of holy poverty would forbid this or prevent that.

Understand that I am not talking about the individual who, degree held on high, returned astride a white charger, almost fully resigned henceforth to tolerate the community. Not at all. I am talking about the conscientious, intelligent individual who came back only to discover that after numerous futile attempts to operate efficiently, she is finally tempted to give up. She finds that she has to go to one person for a permission, and to another person for a key. She cannot square such loss of her valuable time as is required to find these individuals in order to obtain a particular thing.

All of this horrible inefficiency masquerades under the garb of poverty. To add to her frustration, she may be reminded, time and again, quite unintelligibly, that poverty calls for this kind of inefficiency. She happens to be intelligent enough to see that poverty itself is a means to an end; and so she perceives at once that whenever poverty in an individual instance is advanced as the alleged reason for blocking the effective work of the community, or the efficacious efforts of any of its members toward the community's end, then there is a need to take a long, hard look at what is being justified under poverty.

It can be simply maddening. I so well understand how a religious could be so frustrated that she could hardly endure it. Being blocked repeatedly by various forms of immaturities that insist on concealing themselves under the vow or virtue of poverty can try one's soul. Sisters, very frankly, this can be so terribly frustrating because it can be, at times, an encounter with well-intentioned stupidity. When one is informed that a desired pattern of activity is opposed to poverty, and is told as the final proof of that statement, "We have never done it this way," it is more than a little hard to swallow.

There is an area where the use of money can be a most important sign of a Superior's attitude toward a religious. I am referring to the handling of money by the Superior in her relationship to those who are hospitalized. It is likely that this is in large part the case because the religious, by reason of her vow, has no money of her own. The thing I am indicating is the Superior's solicitude that the sick Sister should have, at all times, money to buy newspapers or other miscellaneous things; and, moreover, that she be given to understand by the Superior that she is not to hesitate to use the money for such things. This, in itself a small thing, so often becomes the unmistakable evidence to the sick Sister that her Superior really does care. Moreover, the sick person treated thus favorably by her Superior, feels that she is being dealt with as a responsible adult, which is most satisfying to her.

Again, it does not seem to penetrate the thinking of some people that you have never had occasion to send people away for study and professional training before; and that this is, indeed, a different day and age. What has been defended in the name of holy poverty would make intelligent people blush. We would be less than honest were we not to point out that at times poverty has been misinterpreted in perfectly good faith to block, to slow up, to defeat, and to discourage the most praiseworthy undertakings of religious. A few more large areas in which immaturity can hide behind alleged poverty would be clothes, travel, and food.

Father Christoph: I think that an important point with respect to travel is the need for a change of attitude toward certain modes of traveling. First of all, traveling used to be done by train. I think the Sisters are entitled to privacy—even more privacy than the individual extern. Hence there is no particular value in sitting up all night in a train.

Father Evoy: A religious about to take a roomette on a long train trip said, "A religious is entitled to take her cloister with her."

Father Christoph: Yes. Then with respect to the modes of traveling, there is the value of a person's time and convenience. I think that it is a little ridiculous, at times, to expect individuals to spend twelve, thirteen or fourteen hours on a little three hundred mile trip. Do they not have anything else to do? Is there not something more demanding? Could they not use their time more suitably? Do they have to wait for five hours in this town, for instance, for another train? If there is no money, you cannot expect anything more efficient. Most people are quite willing to accept that; but what is so difficult for the even half-intelligent religious is to see where (at least according to them), money is being wasted, and then something like this, that is not only a convenience, but even perhaps a necessity, is ignored on the basis that it is going to cost a dollar or two more. Most religious are willing to "make do" when there is not any money.

Father Evoy: I think I am sympathetic toward the fact that in a given situation there simply might not be enough money. Perhaps the fact that there is a lack of the money needed by an active religious community to pursue its work with efficiency might also say something about maturity in relation to poverty in that community. A Superior who finds herself thrust into a situation where the standard of living might be sub-human because of the shortage of funds, may be baffled as to how to solve the problem. What she does know is that she will not permit her daughters to endure this kind of living. She will be like a tigress, not resting until she finds a solution. Never will she let her daughters be treated in this manner. If this means she must fight the pastor, the parents' club, or a good part of the town, she will do it. If necessary, she will approach even the Bishop and her higher Superiors to request that the place which cannot provide her Sisters with a decent livelihood be discontinued.

Father Christoph: Let me emphasize that in another way. The demands that are sometimes made on children—twenty-five cents for this, fifty cents for this, and a dollar for this—when there are so many ordinary demands that parish schools must meet, seems unjustified. These collections can amount to a considerable sum if a family has two or three children in school. Someone gets the idea that we need a new statue of the patron of our school. It is going to be marble, and will cost six or seven hundred dollars. Get the money from the children! There seems to be no realization that such things are needless impositions which irritate people, because they prove that Sisters have no concept of the cost of living.

This is in the same category as the pattern already hinted at of the Sister who wants to make a particular trip and asks her Superior for permission. Her Superior says, "Yes, but I can't give you any money. You will have to borrow a car; and since we do not have the money for gas, you will have to borrow the gas, also." There seems to be little appreciation of the fact that if they really do not have the money, it is questionable if the trip should be made. Maturity would dictate that in this situation they should consider how necessary the trip really is. If it is important, they should endeavor to work out some acceptable way of getting the money necessary for it. Simply to impose on others is not a mature pattern of handling any problem. A fully mature person never imposes on other persons. Some religious want to be poor provided they do not have to suffer poverty. One way to avoid suffering from poverty is to impose on friends.

Father Evoy: Well, I think that every one of you here knows at least one religious who in a peculiar way is very observant of poverty. She will own nothing of her own. She will simply use yours until it is gone. No matter what it is, she will use it to the last bit of its usability. For her, this wears the mask of holy poverty. Father Christoph earlier implied the incredible immaturity implicit in the action of a Sister who sends the children home to plague their parents for something. Sisters, we know that modern advertising, without qualms of conscience, uses the television and radio effectively to influence the child to put pressure on the parent in order to sell their product. As a result, many a parent in a supermarket has a very difficult child on her hands if she insists on purchasing brand A, which the child does not want, rather than brand B, upon which the child is insisting. This commercial pressurizing of children is brutal.

You are not under the obligation of judging the morality of what these people do. You are concerned about the morality and ethics of what you, the religious, do. You do not have to know very much about the psychology of a child to realize that sending a child home to cry herself to sleep, because she has to have the money for this or that or the other particular thing, is about as unkind and unfair a way to hit parents as one can imagine. Many of you are in a position where you can literally aim children at their parents and make life just miserable for everyone concerned. Do you fully realize what you are doing? Do you know what it does to a mother and father to have their little child in tears, pleading with them, "Sister says we have to have this," when the parents honestly cannot afford it?

Here again, under the trappings of religious poverty, is one more area in which there can be a lack of the delicate sensitivity that you should have at all times toward other people. It does throw light on what was said earlier: how difficult it is to be considerate of other people and really to feel for them unless, and until, you know them. I should like, for a moment, to point out another area outside of poverty which is part and parcel of the same lack of delicate sensitivity toward people. I am referring to something which often is done in perfectly good faith by religious, and yet which in and of itself is devastating in terms of its effects on a child.

It is this business of the "stand ups." How many adults appreciate the nightmarish experience of the child who is told to stand up in class for something that in the eyes of that child is a matter of public humiliation and shame? The later uncontrollable sobbing of a child at home bears frightening witness to the crushing impact of these "stand ups." How many adults really comprehend sympathetically the child's experience in response to such demands of the teacher as the following? "All those who did not receive Communion with their parents on Sunday at the chil-

dren's Mass, stand up." "All those whose parents did not attend
the parish mission, stand up." "All those who missed attending
Sunday Mass during the summer, stand up."

The unspeakably mortifying nature of this type of experience
is usually not even suspected by the Sister, because of her lack of
sufficient perceptiveness of the child's feelings in this area. Often
enough, the child's mother could tell her something about the
unsuspected damage done, however. Of course, this "stand up"
can be employed in the context of poverty also, as for instance
when a teacher says, "All those who have not yet brought their
money for such and such, stand up." Sisters, if we did nothing
better here than bring you a full awareness of how disastrous,
how shattering this type of experience can be to a child, it would
be worth every moment of our time.

Father Christoph: Still another aspect of poverty which should
be carefully evaluated is the matter of wearing apparel. You are
professional people, and you are expected to look nice and to
smell sweet and to present the ordinary appearance of urbanity.
So therefore you should re-evaluate this pattern of mending, of
patching patches, and having, obviously under the guise of poverty, habits that should have been discarded a long time ago.

Father Evoy: A good thing can become an enslaving thing.

Father Christoph: That is right.

Father Evoy: And it can become, for the person who is insecure,
the touchstone of that individual's security.

Father Christoph: Sanctity. Perfection.

Father Evoy: How true. As long as you are wearing the oldest
religious habit in the whole community you have tangible evi-

dence of the fact that you are one of the most observant members of this religious community . . .

Father Christoph: . . . leading a life of perfection according to our rule.

Father Evoy: This also has the unhealthy aspect of stressing, unduly, preoccupation with oneself. I think it is well to remind yourselves right here that you should expect strong resistance to even a suggestion that individuals change in these areas. Where one's security is closely tied up with one or the other of these patterns of "overdone" poverty, there is the experience of threat to one's person involved. The reaction might therefore be almost unbelievably disproportionate to the apparent importance of the change which is being sought.

Father Christoph: There are so many things toward which we must have mature attitudes: the house we live in, the food we eat, the work that we do. We can be petty and immature about many of these things—pettiness and immaturity go together.

We are going to spend a few minutes speaking about the attitudes that we should have as educators. Even if you are not educators, your attitude toward learning as an instrument in the apostolate of hospital work, child training, or whatever it may be, is important. Pope Pius XI at a private audience granted to the Mother General of the Ursulines, said, "For priests and nuns, there are not only seven sacraments, there are eight. They need the sacrament of knowledge. Without the acquisition of sufficient knowledge and culture a spiritual life has no basis on which to rest." He was not speaking only of your own spiritual life. The sacrament of knowledge—is that not startling? First of all, he was obviously using the word sacrament in an analogical sense or in a sense used early in the Church. Knowledge is a holy thing. To that extent it is sacramental.

You need knowledge to be a good religious. You need competency in the things with which you are concerned so that you can work efficiently and effectively. There is a maturity of knowledge required for a religious so she can be an efficient and effective person as a *religious*. Thank heavens for the spiritual opportunities that are granted—the opportunities that are yours today— to get a sound, theologically and morally correct idea of religious life.

When Father Evoy and I were in Detroit some time ago, a Superior said boastfully, in a very nice way, at the close of a meeting, "And we will be there at the next session of the Ecumenical Council." She was speaking of the possibility of women participants, or at least observers, at the Ecumenical Council. That is because men are no longer the sole proprietors of knowledge. With adequate knowledge of all phases of religious life, you can be better religious, because you will have a clearer understanding of your rights as well as your obligations. Perhaps I should not speak so much about rights. Rather let us talk about duties. If you know your duties, you will know your rights; the obligations of your state; the nature of sin; where virtue leaves off and where vice begins, or vice versa. These things enhance your own spiritual life, for the process of becoming spiritually greater is a continuous process.

Father Evoy: There are many aspects of this intellectual maturity about which we are talking. You will recall that for a child in the world, things tend to be black and white, especially in judging others on the score of their moral imputability. Take, for example, a child whose father has a problem with alcoholism. Because his father fails to maintain his sobriety, he is bad, no good, and that is all there is to it. The child may even love intensely this father who to him is regrettably so wicked. He never stops to wonder why his daddy is trying to irrigate his sorrows. The child simply never asks himself that question.

Perhaps ten years later he will discover that his church-going, pious, most exasperating mother would tempt many a man to turn to drink. Then he may understand in part why his father had the problem that he had, and he can begin to feel for his father. Thereafter, he will not feel it necessary to whitewash his father or conceal the form of the problem that he had. He will at this later period understand his father's problem, at least to the extent that there was some provocation for such weakness. This growth in understanding exemplifies what we learn about maturity in the matter of judging others morally. In capsule form, as we grow more mature, we find that we become more and more reluctant to pass moral judgment on anyone.

One striking piece of evidence, incidentally, bearing on this very point is furnished by the habitual "gripers" in religious life. The one characteristic which these chronic complainers invariably manifest is an immaturity which borders on the childish. The very substance of their complaints is grounded on judging almost with the certainty of omniscience the *motives* of other people. It is childish thus to play God and even more so to fail to recognize that one is so doing.

Sisters, as you become more mature, you see in a particular individual what *appears* to be evidences of hatred, vindictiveness, and many other things. Now, you do not know what this particular individual is going through. Could it not very well be that she is carrying a cross that would crush you? Under the circumstances, to withdraw from her would have to be squared with the possibility that what she did to cause such a reaction in you was perhaps the only thing that she could do. How immature it would be to categorize her in smug fashion as one of the less charitable members of the community; or worse, as not being a good religious. You know, at times, one begins to wonder if that Last Judgment is really going to be needed. Has not most of the judging already been quite well taken care of here?

This area of intellectual maturity in a religious starts with her own recognition that she is not in possession of all the facts needed to make a judgment of the moral responsibility for a pattern of behavior in another individual. The strongest position that she may take, really, in terms of the fragmentary knowledge available, is to maintain, at least to herself, that this unbecoming behavior *appears* to be morally imputable to this person. It looks, therefore, as if the individual could be morally responsible but she is not certain, and since this is her Sister, she will not hear anything ill spoken of the one she loves, even by herself. Accordingly, she will do her best to give her Sister the benefit of the doubt. This is simply a form of maturity.

Father Christoph: There are a lot of little things, accidentals, in religious life which, I think, should undergo a certain amount of reconsideration and re-evaluation. You know there was a time when we could not have fountain pens in the Society of Jesus. There was a time when only a few of ours had watches. Now everyone has a watch; everyone has a fountain pen; and those who need it have a typewriter, because it expedites our work. I can type three times as fast as I can write by hand, and what is more, I can read it. I do not think we are going to be better religious by having a transistor radio in our possession, but I do think that there are certain things that religious do not have which would make them more efficient without giving scandal to the laity.

These things are common in all religious communities; for example, not being able to use the telephone without clearing it with the Superior or with the next one in charge. (I think that once upon a time this was an extraordinary means of communication.) Or letter writing. All kinds of permissions are required to write letters; and we wonder about the utility of all these permissions in our day and age. These are traditional ways of behaving, and I am not suggesting that the Mothers General get together and change things overnight. I am just saying that these customs should be given another look. We should re-evaluate them to see if they are as important or as necessary as we think they are. Customs are not necessarily wrong nor are they necessarily good or useful today.

Let us take a look at them. They should serve a purpose. Up to twenty years ago we wore our birettas to the dining room. You would think that we were in a Jewish synagogue. Why did we wear them? No one knew the reason. A rule said that we should wear them. Then, if in the reading, the Holy Name of Jesus was mentioned, we all had to reach up with our greasy fingers and doff our birettas. If the Superior came in late or left early, we had to doff our birettas, and honest to goodness, if you saw our birettas, you would well understand why they were dog-eared and greasy. As a matter of fact, we no longer have to wear them at Mass, which is a realistic attitude of the Holy See. Historically, the basis of wearing the biretta was to cover a bald head, because the refectories were cold. But now, thank heavens, we have warm refectories. What was once customary is no longer serving its purpose.

Father Evoy: Today I think one might defend the position that long-distance phone calls for the majority of religious would be an unusual thing; whereas local calls and ordinary letter writing would not be. Yet, if one must get permission for each and every call or letter, does this not imply that these are still regarded as extraordinary? If so, why? This is the type of thing in regard to which one must keep asking oneself—Why? Why birettas? Why this? If they have always done it, good. But why? Remember, there was a day, not too long ago, when you operated on the basis that every one of your girls who went out on the street, even with a date, had to have a chaperone with her. This is no longer true.

In the matter of phone calls made with permission, a Sister often finds that whatever she says on the phone might just as well be shouted through a megaphone to everyone in the community. The public placement of the community phone eliminates privacy. But the other members of the community have *no right* to invade this area of a Sister's personal privacy. There is here, experientially, something of a violation of one's person. Where there is no other phone should not the wisdom of continuing such an arrangement be questioned? When there is another phone in the Superior's room, it would make the world of difference were it made clear to the members of the community that they were free to use it for a phone call whenever such a call called for privacy.

You fit yourself to the needs of the day. You adapt to the current situation. Accordingly, I think right here is the place for us to return for a look at silence as viewed in terms of intellectual maturity.

Father Christoph: What is the purpose of silence? Isn't it the remote preparation for prayer? It enables us to maintain a spirit of recollection. Now, to the extent to which silence rather than conversation would interfere with recollection, it would have to be eliminated. First of all, you have the silence of places and the silence of time. The silence of places—in the chapel we speak only when it is absolutely necessary; and in many refectories, outside of the time when you have Deo Gratias, or "free" at table, there is silence. Then there is the silence of time. This is usually during the private prayers, examination of conscience, meditation. It means that when all of your day's work is done, you are ready to retire, and you do not want anything to distract you from your morning meditation.

Silence for the sake of silence is devastating, because activity is part of life, and you cannot have activity without a bit of wing fluttering. We have in our own community, I think, *theoretically* as much silence as any other religious community; *practically* we have more because of our work. So if I am called to the parlor at ten or eleven o'clock at night, I am talking to someone, and this is legitimate. If I have to see someone at ten or eleven o'clock at night in his room, I go to his room. The presumption is that we are not just exchanging pleasantries and the jokes that we heard during the day. The supposition is that out of the time appointed, there may be something important to say.

I would suggest that instead of dashing to your rooms, or

spending an hour in the common room correcting papers and reviewing study guides for the next day's classes, that right after the day's work it would be a good idea to have a little relaxation where you could vent your spleen if necessary, talk about the events of the day, and have a good laugh before you got back to your books. This is something that was not envisioned when religious institutes decided on much of this silence.

What was envisioned? There was a lot of freedom with respect to your teaching, with regard to the direction that you received from other individuals. But, as I never get tired of saying, today the lot of a teacher is not a very happy one. You have your principal breathing down your neck, and she is awfully close. You have the Province Prefect of Studies right behind her. You have different accrediting groups making many demands upon you, and the rigid pattern which educational endeavors take on today. These create tensions which require more than just occasional breaks from the common order, or we are going to go berserk, and that includes Father Christoph. I think we should take another look at some of the strictures that are made on our so-called "breaking of silence."

Father Evoy: Again, it is a matter of suiting the pattern of behavior to the need of the times. Sisters, there was a time in this country and in Europe when after evening recreation the whole day was over, and the great silence started. This was sensible because the Superior did not want the Sisters just chatting away all evening, and they really had little else to do. Ours is another age. Sisters, many a night after ten o'clock, Father and I are in the parlor with someone. Going to one's room in silence in the evening is a luxury that not every religious can afford today.

Let us be very specific about this. You may find that one of the girls comes to see you in the evening. It may have taken her about seven weeks to muster the courage to face you alone. She has very carefully chosen this time when she can assume that you are not going to be otherwise interrupted. She is determined to

confide in you *as she has never confided in anyone else*. But this is
great silence. Could you turn around and walk out on her now?
It would be more kind to her to hit her with a club. I said even a
child knows that hurt feelings take far longer to heal than a
broken arm.

Let us pursue the example further. This is an actual instance.
A Sister went to her office to finish up some work after great
silence had already begun. An older girl knocked, entered the
office, eyes downcast, went over and put her head on the desk and
started to sob. Finally, she managed to get out, "Can you still
really accept me after you know I am a slut?" What if Sister had
said, "Look, dear, I am not permitted to speak to you now. Will
you come back tomorrow and see me when I may talk to you?"

There is in the moral theology of the Church a term called
epikeia. The presumption is that you have heard of it. As applied to our example here, the Sister judged that this particular
time of talking to the girl, which on the face of it appeared to
run counter to the rule, was a reasonable exception to the rule
according to the mind of the Church.

Father Christoph: May I give the real definition of *epikeia*?
Epikeia is the interpretation of the mind of a lawgiver. You can
never use *epikeia* when it comes to the moral law, because God
envisioned every exception, or any possibility for any opportunity for an exception, when He made the law. No human lawgiver can do that, and so every human law admits of *epikeia*.
The prudent individual is the one who determines whether or
not this particular situation calls for *epikeia*. So great silence is a
rule. *Epikeia* says this: If the lawgiver were here, she would say
to you, "For heaven's sake, Sister, use your head, open your
mouth and talk."

Father Evoy: This is a fine example of a religious doing her own
thinking and deciding. She must do her own thinking also in
reconciling the regulatory in her life with her personal private

life. There is a certain area of personal privacy to which an individual is entitled, even in religion.

Even though this is a sensitive area and a delicate one to introduce, because it so readily lends itself to misinterpretation, it must be stated and stated clearly that maturity demands of a religious that she know the licit boundaries of her rule and constitutions. These latter are man-made things which have the blessings of the Church, but because they are man-made they share some of the shortcomings which are part and parcel of being human. For instance, no set of rules has ever been written that foresaw every conceivable situation that could arise in religious life. The underlying assumption in every rule and constitution that has ever been written is that nothing is contained therein that would violate human dignity.

Accordingly, no rule or regulation could ever require a religious to contravene the Natural or Positive Divine Law. It is the responsibility of each and every person in religious life to judge, in a given situation, whether the observance of a religious regulation might do just that. There are times when an individual might have to make this judgment without help from anyone else. The regulation which would forbid a Sister to run while out in public would obviously not apply where saving a person's life required that she run. A fellow religious discovered to be suddenly and extremely ill could constitute an exemption from the great silence. A most grave and moral problem might demand, by way of an exception, that a religious would phone or write without permission of the Superior, when such permission would necessitate an unwarranted revelation; or be morally impossible for the Subject because of the very unusual nature of the situation. In a word, religious regulations can never force a person to do the illicit or the impossible. It goes almost without saying that a religious, where possible, would seek the advice of a confessor or other Priest in order to avoid self-deception in such an important matter.

Unfortunately, there are areas where one's personal privacy

might be invaded by a Superior or others in a most hurtful manner, because of misinterpretations of regulations. This need for privacy, even for privacy to study, cries out in some religious houses. Many Sisters across the United States are permitted to study in their rooms only with special permission.

Father Christoph: That is something that ought to be re-examined. I could never study in the presence of very many individuals; and if the room were very large and I were sitting right next to another, it would be difficult. However, there is such a thing as social facilitation. Social facilitation means the improvement in efficiency, the improvement of workmanship, as a result of just working in the presence of someone else. I am not saying that this business of studying together is not a good idea. Maybe it is, and maybe it is not. In my own personal experience, I would find it extremely difficult. I have to have plenty of privacy when I work or study or write or pray.

Father Evoy: Remember what we said about assuming responsibility for one's self? In a situation such as this, you try to be as honest as you can with yourself and ask yourself, "Would I be more effective in my study if I were alone?" If you judge that you would be better alone, then approach the Superior, whom you expect will believe that you are being honest, and ask her permission to study alone. If the permission is refused, then go back under obedience and study with the group. But you may return later to repeat your request to study by yourself should you find that you really cannot study with this group. You still keep it under obedience.

Father Christoph: We bring our lectures to a close. The task of everyone is to grow into maturity. This requires the cultivation of adult attitudes towards life, towards God, your neighbor, things. It demands the cultivation of sufficient frustration tolerance to face life without too much anxiety, to plan with vision, to act with prudence, to give with love, to suffer without bitterness, to strive without too great a sense of urgency; but especially to understand yourself and others. She is surely mature who, among other things, has the courage "to change the things that should be changed; to accept the things that cannot be changed"; and who has "the wisdom to know the difference."

11 *Concluding Remarks*

If men may speak of a labor of love, the present volume is certainly that. Many a time in these pages the authors have with candor said things that were not complimentary. They have said them because they cared. Unfortunately, when things are right they do not call for comment as do those things which are askew. The authors hope that they have not been presumptuous in simply taking it for granted that their readers would somehow sense their almost unbounded respect and admiration for the religious life, and for the very, very many wonderful persons whom they have had the good fortune to come to know in religion. Nor would they want their readers incorrectly to conclude that every community is characterized by the shortcomings pointed out in these pages.

Because the printed page is in continuous need of interpretation, there is the ever-present danger that it can be incorrectly interpreted. Unfortunately, the present volume can claim no exception to such a peril. If, as a result of what the authors have written here, Sisters appear to be very human, indeed all too human, perhaps this is all to the good. Too long have many people seemed to overlook the facts that Sisters are human beings and women, as well as religious. The feeling that the "taking of the veil" somehow changes these basic facts, is one that tends to do religious a terrible disservice. Whatever would indicate that they are no longer fully human and really women is dehumanizing and depersonalizing. Accordingly, it is scarcely mature to react with surprise to the awareness that these dedicated religious should remain human beings and women, and hence retain in some measure their human faults. Religious are flesh and blood just as much as any woman living outside the convent. To assume that they would be bereft of all human foibles would be preposterous. Their real acceptance of each other, and of those outside the convent, as well as their being accepted by others not in religion, must all take cognizance of the fact that Sisters are wholly human. Acceptance on any lesser grounds would fall notably short of reality, and hence necessarily be both superficial and transitory. People need to be reminded, it seems, that Sisters are real people, and even Sisters must be reminded that Sisters are real people.

As has been pointed out in the course of these pages, it is persons, rather than things, who enter into the very uniqueness of another person. A person becomes herself by incorporating within herself the ideals, values, and attitudes of other persons. A religious develops her own person to its fullest capacity, that she may, in turn, reach out to others. In so doing she will be calmly vigilant lest in her zeal and enthusiasm for the apostolate, she allow imprudence to betray her into assuming competency in fields in which she is not yet qualified. It is our hope that she will take advantage of every opportunity to approach the completely Christian answers to current problems. To step, inadequately prepared, into apostolic fields would be ultimately harmful rather than beneficial to those whom she wishes to help.

The authors, regardless of the impact of this work, remain in the debt of hundreds upon hundreds of religious who have given so generously of themselves in order to enable them to be more effective in helping a greater number to grow in maturity for themselves and for Him. Both priest-authors feel that they themselves have been enriched by their associations with these religious. If by means of these printed words they succeed in communicating to even one religious the knowledge requisite to become her best self and assume her rightful place in the apostolate, the authors will regard the present work as amply rewarded.